PLATO

Protagoras

Translated with Notes

by

C. C. W. TAYLOR

**FELLOW OF CORPUS CHRISTI COLLEGE
OXFORD**

Revised Edition

CLARENDON PRESS · OXFORD

*This book has been printed digitally and produced in a standard specification
in order to ensure its continuing availability*

1004068101 T

OXFORD
UNIVERSITY PRESS

Great Clarendon Street, Oxford OX2 6DP

Oxford University Press is a department of the University of Oxford.
It furthers the University's objective of excellence in research, scholarship,
and education by publishing worldwide in

Oxford New York

Auckland Bangkok Buenos Aires Cape Town Chennai
Dar es Salaam Delhi Hong Kong Istanbul Karachi Kolkata
Kuala Lumpur Madrid Melbourne Mexico City Mumbai Nairobi
São Paulo Shanghai Singapore Taipei Tokyo Toronto

Oxford is a registered trade mark of Oxford University Press
in the UK and in certain other countries

Published in the United States
by Oxford University Press Inc., New York

ISBN 0-19-823934-3

WARD SHORT LOAN COLLECTION
CLARENDON TEXT SIXTUS

General Editor: M. J. WOODS

PREFACE TO THE FIRST EDITION

The aim of this volume is defined by that of the series of which it is part, namely to provide students of philosophy with an accurate rendering and critical elucidation of the dialogue. While the main interest of the commentary is philosophical, the nature of the dialogue has necessitated the inclusion of more literary and historical matter than in some other volumes of the series.

The text translated is the Oxford Classical Text; any departures from it are mentioned in the commentary. The numbers and letters printed in the margin of the translation correspond as closely as differences of Greek and English word order permit to those of the Oxford Classical Text. Line references in the commentary (e.g. '309a 2') refer to the Greek text. No knowledge of Greek is assumed.

Books are normally referred to by author's name alone, with fuller reference in any case of ambiguity. Articles are referred to by author's name followed by the abbreviated title (see 'Abbreviations') of the periodical in which the article first appeared and the last two figures of the year of publication (e.g. 'Adkins *JHS* 73' = 'Adkins *Journal of Hellenic Studies* 1973'). Full references to all books and articles cited are given in the Select Bibliography. The Bibliography is restricted to items which I have judged likely to be useful to the reader for whom the volume is intended; those who require a fuller bibliography should consult, for years up to 1957, the relevant sections of the bibliography of Plato by Professor Cherniss in *Lustrum* iv (1959) and v (1960),[1] and for subsequent years the annual volumes of *L'Année Philologique*.

It is with pleasure that I acknowledge my indebtedness above all to the editor of the series, Mr. M. J. Woods, who not only invited me to contribute to the series, but has helped me through every stage of the work. He has read two complete drafts and suggested many improvements in content and presentation. I am also particularly indebted to Dr. T. J. Saunders and Mr. E. L. Bowie for

---

[1] Updated to 1975 by L. Bresson vol. xx (1977) and to 1980 by L. Bresson and H. Ioannidi vol. xxv (1983) (corrigenda in vol. xxvi (1984)).

v

PREFACE TO THE FIRST EDITION

their advice on specific points. Those many colleagues who have helped the work by criticism of my views on Plato in various discussions over the years will, I hope, be content with a general acknowledgement. I am most grateful to Mrs. E. Hinkes for her helpfulness and accuracy in typing the final draft.

Finally, I dedicate the book to my wife and children.

Corpus Christi College,   C.C.W.T.
Oxford
January 1975

PREFACE TO THE REVISED EDITION

In this edition the following changes have been made.

(i) An Introduction has been added.

(ii) Typographical and other errors in the original edition have been corrected.

(iii) The Bibliography has been extended to 1990, and additional references have been incorporated in the notes and in the Additional Notes.

(iv) A number of changes have been made in the translation, chiefly in the direction of greater uniformity in the rendering of key terms. The desirability of certain changes has been pointed out by various critics, to whom I acknowledge my indebtedness, in particular to Michael Stokes, whose *Plato's Socratic Conversations* has been a constant stimulus to greater accuracy. Those changes which I have judged to be of minor importance, which are the majority, have not been indicated individually; where I have judged the change to be significant for the argument, I have mentioned and explained it in the Additional Notes.

(v) The original notes are substantially unaltered, subject to the changes specified in (i) and (ii) above. The Additional Notes, as well as explaining substantial changes in the translation, incorporate a small amount of new material and, in a few cases, supersede passages in the original with which I am now dissatisfied. The existence of an Additional Note is signalled by a marginal asterisk at the appropriate point in the Translation or Commentary.

July 1990

CONTENTS

INTRODUCTION

The appearance of the revised edition gives me the opportunity to provide a general introduction to the dialogue, a feature the lack of which is, I now recognize, a defect of the original edition. It also enables me to comment on some general issues relevant to the presuppositions of my approach which have been raised by other authors since the publication of the first edition. Such detailed replies to critics as I have judged useful are confined to the Notes.

Like the *Meno* (whose thematic links with the *Protagoras* are rightly emphasized by Kahn *OSAP* 88) the *Protagoras* is concerned with the nature and acquisition of human excellence and with the credentials of those who purport to teach it. The *Meno* begins with the question 'Is excellence acquired from teaching, or otherwise?' and shifts immediately to the question (claimed by Socrates to be epistemologically prior) 'What is excellence?'. When that question is given the provisional answer that excellence is knowledge, it is then necessary to identify those who are able to impart that knowledge, and the claims of two classes of persons are briefly considered and rejected, on the one hand sophists and on the other well-brought up citizens, the custodians of the traditional values of the *polis*. The *Protagoras* treats the same themes in a different order. Socrates' young friend Hippocrates is far from the uncertainty which prompts the opening question of the *Meno*; he is certain that Protagoras is able to impart excellence, and his only anxiety is that Socrates should introduce him to the sophist. Socrates' first task is therefore to convince him that he (i.e. Hippocrates) has no clear idea of what it is that the sophist has to teach. They agree to find out from the man himself, and after an elaborate passage of scene-setting and introduction Socrates introduces Hippocrates to Protagoras as someone who wants to become eminent in public life and asks what he will learn from the sophist. In his reply Protagoras in effect identifies the two sources of instruction in excellence which were distinguished, and rejected, in the *Meno*. Human excellence is identified with the primary social virtues of justice and soundness of mind (*sōphrosunē*), which, as the foundation of communal life, are not the prerogatives of an élite (as Hippocrates' request had suggested), but shared by all civilized people, and transmitted from one generation to another by the educational tradition of the community. So far from presenting himself as a rival to that tradition, as in the *Meno*, the sophist represents his own activity as continuous with it, distinguished only by being (on unspecified grounds) better at achieving the aim common to the two. But his account of his activity leaves a number of questions unresolved, in particular the question of the relation of the specific virtues such as justice, soundness of mind and courage to one another and to excellence as a whole. Moreover, Protagoras has left the role of the intellect in the acquisition of excellence quite obscure; on the one hand his pretensions as a sophist appear to commit him to offering a specialized intellectual formation aimed at the production of an élite qualified to take on leading roles in the community, and in line with that expectation he claims (330a) that wisdom is the most important part of excellence. On the other hand his actual defence of his activity presents it as the education, not of the statesman, but of the decent, law-abiding citizen, in which the cultivation of the intellect is secondary to immersion in the moral tradition of the community.

The rest of the dialogue is devoted to the resolution of these problems. Protagoras clarifies his position on the relation of the virtues to one another and to overall excellence by asserting that the virtues are distinct constituents of total excellence, distinct in the sense that the possession of any one is logically and causally independent of the possession of any of the others. Socrates mounts a series of arguments designed to overthrow that position in favour of the view that the names of the virtues are all names of the same thing, viz. excellence, a thesis which I interpret as the thesis that 'justice', 'holiness', etc. are non-synonymous designations of a single state of the person, possession of which is causally necessary and sufficient for living well. (For the justification of that interpretation see the relevant Notes.) The initial arguments neither depend on nor issue in any account of what that state is; instead Socrates takes in turn pairs of virtues which Protagoras holds to be distinct (as defined above), viz. justice and holiness, wisdom and soundness of mind, wisdom and justice, and attempts to prove from premisses accepted by Protagoras (e.g. that justice is just and holiness holy, that wisdom and soundness of mind are both opposite to folly) that the distinctness thesis must be abandoned and the identity thesis accepted.

The discussion breaks down before any conclusion is reached, and there is a lengthy discussion of whether and if so how it is to be resumed. It is eventually continued via the exposition, first by Protagoras and then by Socrates, of a poem by Simonides, whom Protagoras has claimed as one of the forerunners of the tradition of sophistic education. The principal point of this episode is to exhibit the unreliability of interpretations of literary texts; since the author is not available for questioning, speculation as to his meaning cannot arrive at definitive answers. Hence any interpretation goes, even one which has Simonides maintain the characteristically Socratic theses that doing badly is nothing other than being deprived of knowledge (345b) and that no one acts wrongly of his own free will (345d–e). It follows, therefore, that a method of education such as that of Protagoras, which accorded a central role to interpretation of this kind (338e–339a), must forfeit its claim to reliability in the acquisition of knowledge.

The main discussion is now resumed, Protagoras maintaining the distinctness of courage from the other virtues, while Socrates attempts to prove the identity of courage with wisdom. When this argument too proves inconclusive the discussion changes tack. Socrates introduces the thesis that pleasure is the good (for the interpretation of this thesis see Notes) and argues from it to a substantive account of courage, viz. that courage is knowledge of what is fearful and what is not, which Protagoras reluctantly accepts. Summing up the course of the discussion, Socrates describes himself as 'trying to show that all things are knowledge, justice, soundness of mind, even courage' (361b); i.e. the goal of the argument (which Socrates acknowledges himself not to have reached) is a specification of that state of the person necessary and sufficient for living well, of which the names of the specific virtues are non-synonymous designations (see above). This turns out to be knowledge, as envisaged in the *Meno*, though the *Protagoras* goes further in the direction of specifying the content of the knowledge (sc. as knowledge of what is good and bad), which the *Meno* leaves unspecified.

This account of the thematic unity underlying the rich episodic diversity of the dialogue clearly rests on certain presuppositions which are, like all presuppositions, contestable. One such presupposition is that Socrates is represented in the dialogue as maintaining, and arguing for, the thesis of the unity of virtue (leaving aside for the moment the question of how that thesis is to be interpreted), in opposition to Protagoras' thesis of the distinctness of the individual virtues. As I read the dialogue, Socrates' role is not *restricted* to trying to convince Protagoras that, given premisses which he (i.e. Protagoras) accepts, he (i.e. Protagoras) is obliged to abandon distinctness in favour of unity. Socrates is, of course, represented as trying to do that, but also as trying to show Protagoras that the unity thesis is true, and the distinctness thesis false. He says as much, in the passage quoted just above; literally, the words are not those of Socrates, but of the personified argument, imagined as reproaching Socrates for inconsistency, but I imagine that no one would deny, on the strength of that, that Plato, in writing these words, intended them to express Socrates' (and therefore Plato's) understanding of what the argument was supposed (by Socrates, and therefore by Plato) to establish. It would hardly be necessary to labour what is thus obvious, had not Michael Stokes expended so much energy and ingenuity on the attempt to present Socrates' arguments as largely *ad hominem*, and in passing criticized me, together with others, for excessive readiness to interpret Socratic utterances as assertions or as rhetorical questions instead of as genuine questions designed to elicit the views of the interlocutor. On this specific point, it seems to me that the question of whether a given sentence of Plato's text is to be read as an assertion, as a rhetorical question (i.e. as a question having the conversational force of an assertion), or as a genuine question can be answered only by attention to its context, and that there can be no prior assumptions of probability one way or the other. On the general question of how far Socrates is to be construed as arguing *ad hominem*, it is fair to say that it is unclear just how radical Stokes intends his principle of interpretation to be. He suggests (pp. 28–9) that the *whole* point of the early dialogues (his italics) may have been to show that certain types of person typically used ways of thought and expression which laid them open either to direct self-contradiction or to the adoption of Socratic views as the only way to preserve consistency. But the second alternative assumes that the reader knows what those Socratic views are, something which he can know only from the dialogues themselves. (Stokes does not canvass the hypothesis that the reader is assumed to have independent knowledge of Socrates' views, and is surely right not to do so.) So it must be at least part of the point of the early dialogues to inform the reader of what Socratic views Socrates' interlocutors find themselves obliged to accept. And since Socrates' views are not, in general, stated by Plato independently of argument, we must therefore expect to find in the early dialogues some passages where Socrates argues for certain views. The only question is where those passages are to be found. There I rest my case. If I am wrong in my belief that Socrates argues in the *Protagoras* for the thesis of the unity of virtue, that must be argued by showing that a purely *ad hominem* reading gives a better interpretation of the relevant texts, not by appeal to the principle that *ad hominem* interpretations have greater prior plausibility.

That principle might be defended on two independent, though related grounds. These are

(i) Socrates notoriously maintained that he knew nothing, and eschewed claims to teach. Argument *ad hominem* is consistent with that fundamentally agnostic stance, whereas argument in favour of his own views is inconsistent with it.

(ii) Plato denied in general that written texts were a vehicle for the communication of knowledge (see above), and specifically that his own philosophy was contained in any treatise (*Ep.* vii, 341c; I assume that whether or not the letter is genuine the position stated here is Platonic). The dialogues, therefore, are not treatises, and we should not look to them for statements of or arguments in favour of Plato's philosophical beliefs. This creates a presumption in favour of *ad hominem* interpretations.

Argument (i) supports the conclusion that the dialogues contain no

assertions or arguments in support of *Socrates'* beliefs, whereas
argument (ii) supports the corresponding conclusion with respect to
Plato's. Neither argument is sound. Socrates denied that he had any
knowledge, and therefore that he taught, i.e. that he purported to
impart knowledge. He never claimed that he had no beliefs, or dis-
avowed the practices of supporting his beliefs by argument and of
using argument to persuade others that his beliefs were true. There is
therefore no inconsistency between Socratic agnosticism and the
occurrence in the dialogues of arguments in support of Socratic
beliefs (which even the strongest advocates of *ad hominem* interpretation admit to occur sometimes).

Argument (ii) raises large issues, which can be considered only
very briefly. I take it as self-evident that the dialogues are not
treatises, i.e. systematic expositions of the doctrines held by their
author. I believe that I have never claimed that they are, and, more
importantly, I believe that the method of interpretation which I
employ in this volume does not assume that they are. In employing
that method I sometimes assume, and sometimes argue, that Plato's
dramatic characters, including Socrates, are represented as maintaining views (see above), and sometimes assume, and sometimes argue,
that a view ascribed to Socrates was held by Plato at the time of
writing (for discussion see Gosling and Taylor ch. 3), Neither these
assumptions nor these arguments commit me to the plainly false
belief that the dialogues are treatises, nor do other aspects of the
method employed, e.g. the facts (for which I make no apology) that
a large portion of the commentary consists of elucidation of the
concepts and analysis and critique of the arguments used in the
dialogue.

I freely acknowledge that consideration of the dramatic structure
of the dialogue does not bulk large in the commentary, and that I do
not there explicitly address the questions (*a*) why Plato wrote the
Protagoras, (*b*) why the dialogue has the particular dramatic form
that is has, (*c*) why Plato did not write philosophical treatises and
(*d*) why, given his views on the written word (see above), Plato
wrote dialogues. It is not clear to me that a commentary on a single
dialogue requires consideration of the general questions (*c*) and (*d*).
For what it is worth, I record my dogmatic opinion that Plato did

not write philosophical treatises because he believed, for the reasons given above, that the treatise was incapable of imparting that reasoned grasp of truth which is the goal of philosophy, and that he wrote dialogues at least partly to stimulate the reader to undertake for himself the critical examination of theses which he believed to be necessary for the attainment of that goal. I hope that, even in default of explicit answers to questions (a) and (b), my views emerge sufficiently from the commentary, supplemented by the summary of the dialogue given above. In brief, I think that Plato had a number of aims in writing the *Protagoras*, including the following.

(i) To explore the nature of human excellence, and in so doing to stimulate the reader towards an adequate theory of its nature. As part of that undertaking I believe that Plato employed arguments whose main purpose was critical, together with a constructive argument offered as a serious attempt to recommend the thesis that the names of the specific virtues all designate the same state of the agent, viz. the agent's knowledge of what is good and bad. It must be emphasized that there is no incompatibility between the practice of offering *in* a written work what the author takes to be a sound argument and the belief that philosophical understanding cannot be imparted *by* a written work, but must be achieved by the reader via a process of critical enquiry.

(ii) To aid the reader to an adequate understanding of how excellence is to be acquired. That undertaking involved the critique of inadequate models of education, in particular traditional moral education and the education offered by the sophists; it is very plausible that the latter critique was also relevant to disputes over educational method current at the time of writing (see Kahn *Methexis* 88).

(iii) To provide examples of good and bad arguments and types of argument.

(iv) To entertain (cf. *Phaedr.* 276d).

Specifically with regard to question (b), I have nothing to add to what appears in the commentary and in this introduction. Were I to work on the dialogue *de novo* I might well decide that fuller consideration of that question could usefully supplement the type of question to which the actual work is principally devoted. I have, however, to say that the work of commentators who have especially emphasized that question (e.g. Stokes and Coby) has not convinced me that that enquiry should supercede what I have attempted, nor even that it should be the principal concern of a commentator. I must leave it to the reader to judge whether in saying so I express sound judgement, or am guilty of personal arrogance or methodological complacency.

The preceding remarks have been concerned with the general question of the extent to which Socrates is represented in the dialogue as maintaining and arguing for *any* views. The specific question of whether he is represented as arguing in his own person for the hedonistic thesis from which he derives the conclusion that courage is knowledge continues to excite lively controversy, which shows no sign of issuing in consensus (see Additional Note on 360a2–3). I wish to comment on a single contribution to this debate, Charles Kahn's argument that the *Protagoras* was written after the *Gorgias* (Kahn *OSAP* 88). He maintains, rightly in my view, that acceptance of the priority of the *Gorgias* makes it much more difficult, though not impossible, to read Socrates' espousal of hedonism in the *Protagoras* as sincere. Consequently that interpretation of Socrates' position, which I uphold in this volume, is, to say the least, considerably shaken if the case for the priority of the *Gorgias* is accepted. While the case which Kahn presents is undeniably a strong one, I remain unconvinced. The crucial objection to his thesis is the one which he acknowledges (p. 89) as 'the most difficult to deal with', viz. that whereas the *Protagoras* contains no account of the nature of the soul, and assumes that all desire is uniformly directed towards the good, the *Gorgias* contains a complex psychology, similar to that of the *Republic*, which recognizes the presence in the soul of good-independent desires. Kahn's response to this difficulty is to suggest that Plato, having discovered this psychology virtually at the outset of his philosophical career, deliberately suppressed it in favour of the Socratic intellectualism which is assumed not merely in the *Protagoras* but also in the *Laches* and *Charmides*, which he also dates later than the *Gorgias*; he acknowledges that he is unable to offer any explanation for this procedure. I find this suggestion much less plausible than the alternative explanation that the psychology of the *Gorgias* is a development from the simpler psychology of the *Laches, Charmides*, and *Protagoras*. Of course, if other evidence made the early dating of the *Gorgias* overwhelmingly likely, one might be prepared to swallow this unexplained anomaly, but Kahn's positive arguments seem to me insufficient. He places greatest weight on thematic connections, which link the *Protagoras, Laches, Charmides*, and *Euthyphro* with the *Meno* (relatively late), and on the other hand connect the *Gorgias* with the *Apology* and *Crito* (early). I acknowledge the thematic connections (see above, and cf. Gosling and Taylor 3.2.10, pp. 65–7), but doubt whether they support the thesis of the priority of the *Gorgias*. For the dialogue which has the strongest thematic connections with the latter is surely the *Republic*, which develops the psychology of the *Gorgias*, bases on that psychology an account of the virtues which is close to that of the latter, and, like it, appeals to that account to show that justice is advantageous to the agent. We might also recall the resemblances between the positions of Callicles and Thrasymachus, of which it may not unreasonably be suggested that the former is the more coherent and philosophically sophisticated. If so, the hypothesis that the *Gorgias* is later than *Rep.* I (thought by some to have been originally a separate dialogue) is not altogether without plausibility. (I make no stronger claim than that.) To the extent, therefore, that thematic connections provide evidence for the relative chronology of the dialogues, they point, in my opinion, towards the traditional relative dating of the *Gorgias* and *Protagoras*.

In any case, it is prudent to sound a note of caution regarding the use of thematic connections to establish chronological conclusions. It is obviously possible for an author to return to a theme after a considerable interval, and we have strong evidence that Plato did this in writing the *Laws* long after the *Republic*. Hence the fact that the *Gorgias* can be considered a philosophical sequel to the *Apology* and *Crito* in virtue of its frequent references to the trial of Socrates is *comparatively* weak evidence in favour of its having been written soon after those works, as Kahn acknowledges (p. 75, n. 13). He also acknowledges that the *Republic* is a sequel to the *Gorgias*, yet argues for a wide temporal gap between the two; one might also mention *ad hominem* the reference to the trial of Socrates in the Anytus episode in the *Meno* (89e–95a), which he dates to the late 380s. I do not wish to suggest that thematic considerations have no evidential force in questions of relative chronology; a cluster of thematic connections between a group of dialogues is *some* evidence that those dialogues were composed near to one another in time. I am, however, suggesting that the evidence of thematic connections needs to be handled with caution, and specifically that the connections cited by Kahn do not bear the weight which he wishes to put on them.

I should be lacking in candour if I failed to point out that the most recent stylometric study of Plato, that by Ledger, supports Kahn's thesis on the relative dating of the *Gorgias* and *Protagoras*. Brandwood, on the other hand, maintains (pp. xvi–xviii) that it is reasonably certain that the group of dialogues to which he assigns the *Protagoras* is as a whole earlier than that to which he assigns the *Gorgias*, 'although one or two works may be included in the wrong group'. Ledger is comparatively tentative in stating his conclusions, and acknowledges that conclusions about relative dating reached by stylometric methods depend on the choice of variables, allowing different scholars to reach incompatible results (pp. 225–6). Until such time as stylometric investigation converges on an agreed order of composition for the dialogues it seems legitimate and indeed prudent for the inexpert to suspend judgement.

TRANSLATION

PROTAGORAS

Friend. Hello, Socrates; what have you been doing? No need to **309a**
ask; you've been chasing around after that handsome young fellow
Alcibiades. Certainly when I saw him just recently he struck me as
still a fine-looking man, but a man all the same, Socrates (just
between ourselves), with his beard already coming. 5
Socrates. Well, what of it? Aren't you an admirer of Homer?
He says that the most delightful age is that at which a young man **b**
gets his first beard, just the age Alcibiades is now, in fact.
Friend. Well, how are things at the moment? Have you been
with him? How is the young fellow disposed towards you?
Soc. Very well, it seems to me, not least today. For he took my 5
part and said a lot of things on my behalf, and in fact I've only just
left him. But I've something remarkable to tell you; though he was
there, I didn't take much notice of him, and on a number of occas-
ions I forgot about him altogether.
Friend. How on earth could such a thing have happened to the **c**
two of you? You surely haven't met someone even finer-looking, in
this city at least.
Soc. Yes, far finer-looking.
Friend. What? A citizen or a foreigner? 5
Soc. A foreigner.
Friend. Where from?
Soc. Abdera.
Friend. And this foreigner struck you as such a fine-looking man
that he was even finer than the son of Cleinias? 10
Soc. Well surely, my dear fellow, what is wisest is always finer?
Friend. Oh, you mean that you've just met some wise man,
Socrates?
Soc. The wisest man alive, I believe, if you agree that that **d**
description fits Protagoras.
Friend. What's that you say? Is Protagoras in the city?
Soc. He's been here for two days now.
Friend. And you've just come from talking to him? 5

1

310a   *Soc.* Yes indeed. I said a lot to him and he to me.

      Friend. Well, if there's nothing else you have to do, why don't you tell us about your conversation? Sit down here, and let the slave there get up and make room for you.

5   *Soc.* Certainly. I shall be glad if you'll listen.

      Friend. And we shall be grateful to you, if you'll tell us.

      Soc. That's a favour on either side. Well, listen then.

      Last night, just before daybreak, Hippocrates, the son of Apollodorus and brother of Phason, began knocking very loudly on the door

b with his stick, and when someone opened it he came straight in in a great hurry, calling out loudly, 'Socrates, are you awake or asleep?'

5 I recognized his voice and said, 'It's Hippocrates; no bad news, I hope?' 'Nothing but good news,' he said. 'Splendid,' I said; 'What is it, then? What brings you here so early?' He came and stood beside me; 'Protagoras has come,' he said. 'He came the day before yesterday,' I said; 'have you only just heard?' 'Yes, indeed,' he said; 'yesterday evening.'

c   As he said this he felt for the bed and sat down at my feet. 'Yes, it was yesterday evening, when I got back very late from Oinoe. My slave Satyrus ran away; I was going to tell you that I was going

5 after him, but something else put it out of my head. When I got back, and we had had supper and were just going to bed, it was then that my brother told me that Protagoras had come. Late as it was, I immediately got up to come and tell you, but then I realized that

d it was far too late at night; but as soon as I had had a sleep and got rid of my tiredness, I got up straight away and came over here, as you see.'

      I knew him to be a spirited and excitable character, so I said, 'What's all this to you? Protagoras hasn't done you any injury, has he?'

5   He laughed. 'By heavens, he has, Socrates. He is the only man who is wise, but he doesn't make me wise too.'

      'Oh yes, he will,' I said; 'If you give him money and use a little persuasion, he'll make you wise as well.'

e   'I wish to God', he said, 'that that was all there was to it. I'd use every penny of my own, and of my friends too. But it's just

that that I've come to you about now, so that you can put in a word
for me with him. First of all, I'm too young, and then I've never
seen Protagoras nor heard him speak; for I was still a child when he
came here before. But you know, Socrates, everybody speaks highly   5
of the man, and says that he's a wonderfully clever speaker. Why
don't we go to him, so as to catch him at home? He's staying, so I've 311a
heard, with Callias the son of Hipponicus. Do let's go.'
     'Don't let's go there yet,' I said; 'it's still early. Let's go out into
the courtyard here, and take a turn to pass the time till it gets light,   5
and then let's go. Protagoras spends most of the time indoors, so
you needn't worry, we'll probably find him in.'
     Then we got up, went out into the courtyard and strolled about.
In order to test Hippocrates I began to examine him and ask him   b
questions. 'Tell me, Hippocrates,' I said. 'You are now planning to
go to Protagoras and give him money in payment for services to
yourself. What sort of man is it that you're going to, and what sort
of man are you going to become as a result? Suppose you had been   5
thinking of going to your namesake Hippocrates of Cos, of the
medical guild, and giving him money in payment for services to
yourself. If someone had then asked, "Tell me, for what service
are you paying Hippocrates?" what would you have answered?'   c
     'I should have said for his services as a doctor.'
     'And what would you hope to become as a result?'
     'A doctor.'
     'And suppose you had been thinking of going to Polycleitus of
Argos or Pheidias of Athens and giving them money in payment for
services to yourself. If someone had then asked you, "What is the   5
service for which you are going to pay this money to Polycleitus and
Pheidias?" what would you have answered?'
     'I should have said for their services as sculptors.'
     'And what would you hope to become yourself?'
     'A sculptor, obviously.'
     'Well now,' I said, 'you and I are prepared at this moment to go to d
Protagoras and pay him money for services to you, if our own
resources are sufficient to persuade him, and, if not, to spend our
friends' money as well. If somebody saw how desperately eager we   5
are in this matter and asked us what service we were going to pay

e   Protagoras for, what should we reply? What other name do we hear applied to Protagoras? I mean, the way Pheidias is called a sculptor and Homer is called a poet, is there any name of that sort which we hear applied to Protagoras?'

'Well, a sophist is what they call him, anyhow, Socrates,' he said.

5   'So it's for his services as a sophist that we're going to pay him?'

'Certainly.'

312a   'Well now, suppose someone asked you, "And what do you yourself hope to become as a result of your association with Protagoras?" '

He blushed—day was already beginning to break, so that I could see him—and replied, 'If it's like what we said before, then obviously I should be hoping to become a sophist.'

5   'But, for heaven's sake,' I said, 'wouldn't you be ashamed to present yourself to the world as a sophist?'

'Of course I should, Socrates, if I'm to be quite frank.'

b   'But then perhaps that isn't the sort of study you expect to have with Protagoras, but rather the sort you had with the reading-master and the music teacher and the trainer. You didn't learn any of those things in a technical way, with a view to becoming a professional yourself, but simply for their educational value, as an amateur and a gentleman should.'

5   'Exactly,' he said. 'I think that study with Protagoras is rather of that sort.'

'Do you realize, then, what you are going to do,' I said, 'or don't you?'

'What do you mean?'

c   'I mean that you are going to entrust your soul to the care of a man who is, as you agree, a sophist. But I should be surprised if you even know what a sophist is. And yet if you don't know that, you don't even know what it is that you're handing your soul over to, nor even whether it's something good or something bad.'

'Well, at least I think I know,' he said.

5   'Tell me, then, what do you think a sophist is?'

'Well, I think', he said, 'a sophist is, as the name implies, one who is knowledgeable in learned matters.'

'Surely', I said, 'you can say the same about painters and

4

carpenters, that they are knowledgeable in learned matters. But if   d
someone asked us which learned matters painters are knowledgeable about, we should say that they are knowledgeable about the
making of pictures, and so in the other cases. Now if we were asked
which learned matters the sophist is knowledgeable about, what
should we say? What craft is he master of?'   5

'What answer should we give, Socrates, except to say that he is
master of the craft of making people clever speakers?'

'Perhaps that would be true,' I said, 'but it's not enough; our
answer invites the further question: "What is it that the sophist
makes you a clever speaker about?" I mean, the music teacher no   e
doubt makes you a clever speaker about what he teaches you,
namely music. Isn't that so?'

'Yes.'

'Well then, what is it that the sophist makes you a clever speaker
about?'

'Obviously, about what he knows.'

'Presumably. What then is this knowledge which the sophist   5
himself possesses and which he imparts to his pupil?'

'Really,' he said, 'I find I've no more to say.'

Then I said, 'Well, do you realize the danger that you are going 313a
to expose yourself to in taking a chance like this? If you had to
entrust your physical health to someone, for good or ill, you would
weigh up the matter very carefully, and call on your friends and   5
relations for advice and take a long time to decide. But now in a
matter which concerns something which you value more highly than
your body, I mean your soul, on whose condition your whole fate
depends for good or ill, you haven't sought the advice of your father
or your brother or of any of us who are your friends as to whether   b
or not to entrust your soul to this stranger who has just arrived.
No, you heard of his arrival yesterday evening, so you tell me, and
come along at daybreak without any thought or advice on whether
you ought to entrust yourself to him or not, prepared to spend your   5
own money and your friends' as well, since you've already decided,
apparently, that you must at all costs become a pupil of Protagoras,
whom you neither know, as you admit, nor have you ever spoken   c
to him. You call him a sophist, and it turns out that you don't even

5

know what a sophist is; and yet that's the man to whom you're going to entrust yourself.'

When I had finished he said, 'It seems so, Socrates, from what you say.'

5   'Well now, Hippocrates, the sophist happens to be a sort of merchant or pedlar of goods for the nourishment of the soul; at least he seems to me something of that sort.'

'What sort of thing nourishes the soul, Socrates?'

'Learning, surely,' I said. 'And we have to make sure that the
d   sophist doesn't take us in by his praise of his goods, as merchants and pedlars of ordinary food do. For they don't know whether the stuff they are hawking around is good or bad for you, but they say that everything in their stock is good. Their customers don't know
5   either, unless one of them happens to be a trainer or a doctor. In the same way these people who make their living by hawking learning from city to city and selling to whoever wants to buy say that everything in their stock is good, but perhaps even some of them, my dear fellow, might not know whether 'what they are selling is
e   good or bad for the soul. It's the same for their customers, unless one of them happens to be a doctor of the soul. So if you happen to know which of their wares is good and which is bad, it's safe for
5   you to buy learning from Protagoras or anyone else; but if not, then
314a watch out, my friend. Don't take chances in a matter of such importance. For you know, there's much more risk in buying learning than in buying food. If you buy food or drink from a pedlar or a
5   merchant you can carry it away in another container, and before you actually eat or drink it you can set it down at home and call in an expert and take his advice on what you ought to eat or drink and what you ought not, and how much, and when you ought to
b   take it. So there is no great risk in buying. But you can't carry learning away in a jar; you have to put down the price and take the learning into your soul right away. By the time you go away you have already assimilated it, and got the harm or the benefit. So let's
5   consider this along with our elders; for we are still too young to settle such an important matter. But now, let's go and listen to Protagoras as we set out to do, and afterwards let's consult some
c   others. For Protagoras isn't there alone; Hippias of Elis is there too,

and I think Prodicus of Ceos as well, and many other wise men.'

We agreed on that, and went off. When we got to the doorway, we
stood there talking about some subject which had come up on the   5
way. As we didn't want to break off the discussion, but preferred to
reach a conclusion and then go in, we stood in the doorway talking
until we reached agreement. I think that the porter, a eunuch, must
have overheard us, and perhaps he was annoyed at the throngs of   d
people that the number of sophists was bringing to the house. At
any rate, when we knocked at the door, he opened it and saw us.
'Ah, sophists,' he said; 'he's busy,' and at the same time he slammed
the door with both hands as hard as he could. We began knocking   5
again, and he kept the door closed and said, 'Didn't you hear? He's
busy.' 'My dear sir,' I said, 'we haven't come to see Callias, nor are we
sophists. Don't worry. We've come to see Protagoras. Just tell them   e
we've come.' So eventually, with great reluctance, the fellow opened
the door to us.
     When we came in we found Protagoras walking in the colonnade,
and ranged on one side of him were Callias the son of Hipponicus   5
and his half-brother Paralus the son of Pericles and Charmides the   315a
son of Glaucon, and on the other Pericles' other son Xanthippus
and Philippides the son of Philomelus and Antimoerus of Mende,
who has the highest reputation of any of Protagoras' pupils and is   5
studying with him professionally, with a view to becoming a
sophist. Those who were following them listening to the conversation
seemed mostly to be foreigners—Protagoras collects them from
every city he passes through, charming them with his voice like
Orpheus, and they follow the sound of his voice quite spellbound—
but there were some Athenians in the procession too. I was   b
absolutely delighted by this procession, to see how careful they
were that nobody ever got in Protagoras' way, but whenever he   5
and his companions turned round, those followers of his turned
smartly outwards in formation to left and right, wheeled round and
so every time formed up in perfect order behind him.
     'And after him I recognized', as Homer says, Hippias of Elis,   c
sitting in a chair in the opposite colonnade. Around him were
sitting on benches Eryximachus the son of Acumenus and Phaedrus

7

from Myrrinus and Andron the son of Androtion and a number of
5   foreigners, fellow citizens of Hippias and others. They seemed to
be asking Hippias questions on science and astronomy, and he was
sitting in his chair giving a detailed decision on every question.

d   'And then I saw Tantalus too', for Prodicus of Ceos was also in
town. He was in a room which Hipponicus previously used as a
store-room, but now because of the number of visitors Callias had
cleared it out too and turned it into a guest-room. Prodicus was still in
5   bed, wrapped up in a great many sheepskins and blankets, as far as
I could see. On the beds next to his sat Pausanias from Cerameis, and
e   with him a young lad, a fine boy in my opinion, and certainly very
fine-looking. I think I heard that his name was Agathon, and I
shouldn't be surprised if Pausanias were in love with him. There was
that lad, and the two Adeimantuses, the son of Cepis and the son
5   of Leucolophides, and there seemed to be some others; but I
couldn't catch from outside what they were talking about, though
I was very eager to hear Prodicus—for I think that he is a wonderful
316a   man, and very learned—but his deep voice made such a booming
noise in the room that the words themselves were indistinct.

We had just come in, when there came in behind us the
5   handsome Alcibiades, as you call him, and I agree, and Critias the
son of Callaeschrus.

When we came in we spent a few moments looking at all this, and
b   then we went over to Protagoras, and I said, 'Protagoras, Hippocrates
here and I have come to see you.'

'Do you want to talk to me alone', he said, 'or in the presence of
the others?'

5   'As far as we're concerned,' I said, 'it makes no difference. You
decide once you've heard what we've come about.'

'What is it, then, that you've come about?' he asked.

'Hippocrates here is an Athenian, the son of Apollodorus, of a
10   great and wealthy family, and in natural ability he seems the equal
c   of anyone of his age. I think that he wants to become eminent in
public life, and he thinks that that would be most likely to happen
if he were to become a pupil of yours. So perhaps you would now
consider whether you think you ought to talk to us about this in
private, or in the presence of others.'

8

'You show a very proper consideration for me, Socrates,' he said.   5
'A foreigner who comes to great cities and persuades the best of the
young men to abandon the society of others, kinsmen or acquain-
tances, old or young, and associate with himself for their own   d
improvement—someone who does that has to be careful. He
becomes as a result the object of a great deal of resentment and
hostility, and of many attacks. I maintain that the craft of the sophist
is an ancient one, but that its practitioners in ancient times, for fear   5
of giving offence, adopted the subterfuge of disguising it as some
other craft, as Homer and Hesiod and Simonides did with poetry,
and Orpheus and Musaeus and their followers with religious rites
and prophecies. Some, I have heard, went in for physical training,
like Iccus of Taras and, in our own day, Herodicus of Selymbria   10 e
(originally of Megara), as good a sophist as any. Your fellow citizen
Agathocles, a great sophist, used music and literature as a cover, and
so did Pythocleides of Ceos and many others. All of them, as I say,
used these crafts as a screen out of fear of resentment. But I   5
disagree with them all over this; for I don't think that they succeeded 317a
in their aim; they didn't deceive the people in power in the various
cities, which was the point of those subterfuges, since the mass of
the people don't really notice anything, but just repeat whatever   5
their rulers tell them. If you can't escape by running away, but
merely bring yourself out into the open, then it's foolish even to
try, and bound to make people much more hostile to you, for they   b
think that someone who behaves like that is a scoundrel on top of
everything else. So I have gone quite the opposite way from these
others, and I admit that I am a sophist and that I educate people;   5
I think that an admission of that kind is a better precaution than
a denial. And I've taken other precautions as well, so that, touch
wood, I've never come to any harm through admitting to being a   c
sophist. And yet I've been practising the craft for many years (and
indeed I'm a good age now, I'm old enough to be the father of any
of you). So I much prefer, if you please, to talk about these things
in the presence of all who are here.'   5
I suspected that he wanted to put on a performance in front of
Prodicus and Hippias and show off because we had turned up to   d
admire him, so I said, 'Why don't we ask Prodicus and Hippias and

the people with them to come over too, and listen?'
'By all means,' said Protagoras.

5   'Would you like us to put out some seats', said Callias, 'so that
you can talk sitting down?'
It was agreed that we should do that. We were all pleased at the
prospect of hearing wise men talk, and we took the benches and
10   beds ourselves and arranged them beside Hippias, as the benches
e   were set out there already; meanwhile Callias and Alcibiades fetched
Prodicus from his bed and came along with him and those who were
with him.

When we were all sitting down Protagoras said, 'Now that these
5   others are here, Socrates, you might say something about what you
mentioned to me a short time ago on your young friend's behalf.'
318a   'I'll begin', I said, 'just where I did last time, by saying what
we've come about. Hippocrates here is anxious to become your pupil;
so he says that he would be glad to know what benefit he will derive
5   from associating with you. That's the sum of our conversation so far.'
'Young man,' replied Protagoras, 'if you associate with me, this is
the benefit you will gain: the very day you become my pupil you
will go home a better man, and the same the next day; and every
day you will continue to progress.'
b   'There's nothing remarkable in that,' I said. 'It's just what you'd
expect, since even you, old and wise as you are, would become a
better man if someone taught you something that you happened
5   not to know. Don't just answer like that, but suppose that
Hippocrates suddenly changed his mind and was anxious to study
with that young man who has recently come to the city, Zeuxippus
c   of Heraclea, and came to him as he has now done to you, and heard
him say what you have just said, that every day he will improve
himself and become a better man through studying with him.
If he asked, "In what respect do you say that I'll be better? What
5   will I improve at?" Zeuxippus would say, "At painting". And if he
went to Orthagoras of Thebes and heard him say what you've said
and asked him in what respect he would become better day by day
through studying with him, Orthagoras would say "At flute-
playing". In just the same way, will you please answer the young

10

man and me, when I put the question on his behalf: "If Hippocrates   d
becomes a pupil of Protagoras, and goes away a better man on the
very day he becomes a pupil, and makes similar progress every day,
what will he be better at, and in what respect will he make
progress?" '

Protagoras answered, 'You have put a good question, Socrates,   5
and I like answering people who do that. If Hippocrates comes to me
he won't have the same experience as he would have had had he
gone to any other sophist. The others maltreat young men; they   e
come to them to get away from school studies, and they take
them and pitch them back into those studies against their will,
and teach them arithmetic and astronomy and geometry and music
and literature'—and as he said this he looked at Hippias—'but if he
comes to me he won't learn anything but what he came for. What   5
I teach is the proper management of one's own affairs, how best to 319a
run one's household, and the management of public affairs, how to
make the most effective contribution to the affairs of the city both
by word and action.'

'Have I understood you correctly, then?' I said. 'You seem to me
to be talking about the art of running a city, and to be promising to
make men into good citizens.'   5

'That, Socrates,' he said, 'is precisely what I undertake to do.'

'It's a splendid thing to have discovered,' I said, 'if you have in
fact discovered how to do it (for I shall not say, particularly to you,
anything other than what I really think). I didn't think that that   10
was something that could be taught, but since you say that you   b
teach it I don't see how I can doubt you. Why I think that it
can't be taught or handed on from one man to another, I ought to
explain. I say, as do the rest of the Greeks, that the Athenians are
wise. Well, I observe that when a decision has to be taken at the   5
state assembly about some matter of building, they send for the
builders to give their advice about the buildings, and when it
concerns shipbuilding they send for the shipwrights, and similarly
in every case where they are dealing with a subject which they   c
think can be learned and taught. But if anyone else tries to give
advice, whom they don't regard as an expert, no matter how
handsome or wealthy or well-born he is, they still will have none

11

5 of him, but jeer at him and create an uproar, until either the
would-be speaker is shouted down and gives up of his own accord,
or else the police drag him away or put him out on the order of the
presidents. That's the way they act in what they regard as a
d technical matter. But when some matter of state policy comes up
for consideration, anyone can get up and give his opinion, be he
carpenter, smith or cobbler, merchant or ship-owner, rich or poor,
5 noble or low-born, and no one objects to them as they did to those
I mentioned just now, that they are trying to give advice about
something which they never learnt, nor ever had any instruction in.
So it's clear that they don't regard that as something that can be
e taught. And not only is this so in public affairs, but in private
life our wisest and best citizens are unable to hand on to others the
excellence which they possess. For Pericles, the father of these
young men, educated them very well in those subjects in which
320a there were teachers, but he neither instructs them himself nor has
them instructed by anyone else in those matters in which he is
himself wise; no, they wander about on their own like sacred cattle
looking for pasture, hoping to pick up excellence by chance. Or
take the case of Cleinias, the younger brother of Alcibiades here.
5 Pericles, whom I mentioned just now, is his guardian, and no doubt
for fear he should be corrupted by Alcibiades he took him away
from him and sent him to be brought up in Ariphron's house; and
b before six months were up he gave him back to Alcibiades, not
knowing what to do with him. And I could mention many others,
good men themselves, who never made anyone better, either their
own families, or anyone else. So when I consider these facts,
5 Protagoras, I don't think that excellence can be taught. But then
when I hear you say that you teach it, I am swayed once again and
think that there must be something in what you say, as I regard you
as someone of great experience and learning, who has made
discoveries himself. So if you can show us more clearly that
c excellence can be taught, please don't grudge us your proof, but
proceed.'

'Certainly I shall not grudge it you, Socrates,' he said. 'But
would you rather that I showed you by telling a story (as an older
man speaking to his juniors) or by going through a systematic

exposition?'
Several of those who were sitting around asked him to proceed   5
in whichever way he preferred. 'Well,' he said, 'I think that it will
be more enjoyable to tell you a story.'

'Once upon a time there were just the gods; mortal beings did
not yet exist. And when the appointed time came for them to come   d
into being too, the gods moulded them within the earth, mixing
together earth and fire and their compounds. And when they were
about to bring them out into the light of day, they appointed
Prometheus and Epimetheus to equip each kind with the powers   5
it required. Epimetheus asked Prometheus to let him assign the
powers himself. "Once I have assigned them", he said, "you can
inspect them;" so Prometheus agreed, and Epimetheus assigned the
powers. To some creatures he gave strength, but not speed, while he   e
equipped the weaker with speed. He gave some claws or horns, and
for those without them he devised some other power for their
preservation. To those whom he made of small size, he gave winged
flight, or a dwelling underground; to those that he made large, he 321a
gave their size itself as a protection. And in the same way he
distributed all the other things, balancing one against another. This
he did to make sure that no species should be wiped out; and when
he had made them defences against mutual destruction, he devised
for them protection against the elements, clothing them with thick
hair and tough skins, so as to withstand cold and heat, and also to   5
serve each kind as their own natural bedding when they lay down to
sleep. And he shod some with hooves, and others with tough,   b
bloodless skin. Then he assigned different kinds of food to the
different species; some were to live on pasture, others on the fruits
of trees, others on roots, and some he made to prey on other
creatures for their food. These he made less prolific, but to those
on whom they preyed he gave a large increase, as a means of
preserving the species.
'Now Epimetheus, not being altogether wise, didn't notice that he   c
had used up all the powers on the non-rational creatures; so last of
all he was left with human kind, quite unprovided for, and he was
at a loss what to do. As he was racking his brains Prometheus came to

13

inspect the distribution, and saw the other creatures well provided
5   for in every way, while man was naked and unshod, without any
covering for his bed or any fangs or claws; and already the appointed
day was at hand, on which man too had to come out of the earth
to the light of day. Prometheus was at his wits' end to find a means
d   of preservation for mankind, so he stole from Hephaestus and
Athena their technical skill along with the use of fire—for it was
impossible for anyone to acquire or make use of that skill without
fire—and that was what he gave to man. That is how man acquired
5   his practical skill, but he did not yet have skill in running a city;
Zeus kept watch over that. Prometheus had no time to penetrate
the citadel of Zeus—moreover the guards of Zeus were terrible—but
he made his way by stealth into the workshop which Athena and
e   Hephaestus shared for the practice of their arts, and stole
Hephaestus' art of working with fire, and the other art which
Athena possesses, and gave them to men. And as a result man was
322a well provided with resources for his life, but afterwards, so it is
said, thanks to Epimetheus, Prometheus paid the penalty for theft.
      'Since man thus shared in a divine gift, first of all through his
kinship with the gods he was the only creature to worship them,
5   and he began to erect altars and images of the gods. Then he soon
developed the use of articulate speech and of words, and discovered
how to make houses and clothes and shoes and bedding and how to
b   till the soil. Thus equipped, men lived at the beginning in scattered
units, and there were no cities; so they began to be destroyed by
the wild beasts, since they were altogether weaker. Their practical
art was sufficient to provide food, but insufficient for fighting
5   against the beasts—for they did not yet possess the art of running a
city, of which the art of warfare is part—and so they sought to come
together and save themselves by founding cities. Now when they
came together, they treated each other with injustice, not possessing
the art of running a city, so they scattered and began to be destroyed
c   once again. So Zeus, fearing that our race would be wholly wiped
out, sent Hermes bringing conscience and justice to mankind, to be
the principles of organization of cities and the bonds of friendship.
Now Hermes asked Zeus about the manner in which he was to give
5   conscience and justice to men: "Shall I distribute these in the same

14

way as the arts? These are distributed thus: one doctor is sufficient
for many laymen, and so with the other experts. Shall I give
justice and conscience to men in that way too, or distribute them to
all?"

‘ "To all," said Zeus, "and let all share in them; for cities could   d
not come into being, if only a few shared in them as in the other
arts. And lay down on my authority a law that he who cannot
share in conscience and justice is to be killed as a plague on the   5
city." So that, Socrates, is why when there is a question about how
to do well in carpentry or any other expertise, everyone including
the Athenians thinks it right that only a few should give advice, and
won't put up with advice from anyone else, as you say—and quite   e
right, too, in my view—but when it comes to consideration of how
to do well in running the city, which must proceed entirely through 323a
justice and soundness of mind, they are right to accept advice from
anyone, since it is incumbent on everyone to share in that sort of
excellence, or else there can be no city at all. That is the reason for
it, Socrates.

'Just in case you still have any doubts that in fact everyone thinks   5
that every man shares in justice and the rest of the excellence of a
citizen, here's an extra bit of evidence. In the case of the other
skills, as you say, if anyone says he's a good flute-player or good at
any other art when he isn't, they either laugh at him or get angry at   b
him, and his family come and treat him like a madman. But in the
case of justice and the rest of the excellence of a citizen, even if they
know someone to be unjust, if he himself admits it before everyone,
they regard that sort of truthfulness as madness, though they called   5
it sound sense before, and they say that everybody must say that he
is just whether he is or not, and anyone who doesn't pretend to be
just must be mad. For they think that everyone must possess it to
some extent or other, or else not be among men at all.   c

'On the point, then, that they are right to accept advice from
anyone about this sort of excellence in the belief that everyone
shares in it, that is all I have to say. I shall next try to show that   5
they think that it does not come by nature or by luck, but that
it can be taught, and that everyone who has it has it from deliberate
choice. In the case of undesirable characteristics which people think

d   are due to nature or chance, nobody gets annoyed at people who
        have them or corrects or teaches or punishes them, to make them
        any different, but they pity them; for instance, is anyone silly
        enough to try treating the ugly or the small or the weak in any of
5   those ways? No, that sort of thing, I think, they know comes
        about, fair and foul alike, by nature and by chance. But when it
        comes to the good qualities that men acquire by deliberate choice,
e   and by practice and teaching, if someone doesn't have them, but the
        opposite bad qualities, it's then that people get annoyed and punish
324a   and correct him. One such quality is injustice and impiety and in a
        word whatever is the opposite of the excellence of a citizen. There
        everyone gets annoyed with anyone who does wrong, and corrects
        him, clearly because it's something which you acquire by deliberate
        choice and learning. For if you care to consider, Socrates, the effect
5   which punishment can possibly have on the wrongdoer, that will
        itself convince you that people think that excellence is something
        which can be trained. For no one punishes a wrongdoer with no
b   other thought in mind than that he did wrong, unless he is
        retaliating unthinkingly like an animal. Someone who aims to
        punish in a rational way doesn't chastise on account of the past
        misdeed—for that wouldn't undo what is already done—but for the
5   sake of the future, so that neither the wrongdoer himself, nor anyone
        else who sees him punished, will do wrong again. This intention
        shows his belief that excellence can be produced by education; at
        least his aim in punishing is to deter. Now this opinion is shared by
c   everyone who administers chastisement either in a private or in a
        public capacity. And everyone chastises and punishes those whom
        they think guilty of wrongdoing, not least your fellow citizens, the
        Athenians; so according to this argument the Athenians are among
5   those who think that excellence can be trained and taught. It
        seems to me, Socrates, that I have now adequately shown that your
        fellow citizens are right to accept the advice of smiths and cobblers
        on political matters, and also that they regard excellence as
d   something that can be taught and trained.
            'That still leaves us with your problem about good men, why it
        is that they teach their sons and make them knowledgeable in
5   those subjects where there are teachers, but as far as concerns

16

that excellence which they themselves possess, they don't
make their sons any better than anyone else. On this point, Socrates,
I shan't tell any more stories, but rather give a literal exposition.
Look at it this way; is there or is there not one quality which every
citizen must have, if there is to be a city at all? On this point,   e
and this alone, depends the solution of this problem of yours.
For if there is, and this one quality isn't skill in carpentry or in
metalwork or in pottery but justice and soundness of mind and 325a
holiness—human excellence, in a word—if this is the quality which
everyone must have and always display, whatever else he wants to
learn or to do, and anyone who lacks it, man, woman or child, must   5
be taught and punished until he reforms, and anyone who doesn't
respond to teaching and punishment must be regarded as incurable
and banished from the city or put to death—if that's the way things   b
are, but none the less good men have their sons taught other things,
but not this, then think how astonishing their behaviour is. For we
have shown that they regard it both in the private and in the public   5
sphere as something that can be taught. So though it can be taught
and fostered, nevertheless they have their sons taught other things,
do they, where ignorance doesn't carry the death penalty, but in that
sphere where their own sons must suffer death or exile if they are
not taught and brought up to be good, not to mention the confis-   c
cation of their goods and in a word the absolute ruin of themselves
and their families, they don't take the utmost care to have them
properly taught? No, Socrates, you ought to realize that they   5
begin when their children are small, and go on teaching and
correcting them as long as they live. For as soon as a child can
understand what is said to him, his nurse and his mother and his
teacher and his father himself strive to make him as good as possible,   d
teaching and showing him by every word and deed that this is right,
and that wrong, this praiseworthy and that shameful, this holy and   5
that unholy, "do this" and "don't do that". If he obeys voluntarily,
so much the better; if not, they treat him like a piece of wood which
is getting warped and crooked, and straighten him out with threats
and beatings. And then when they send him to school they tell the
teachers to pay much more attention to the children's behaviour   e
than to their letters or their music. The teachers do that, and then

17

when they have learned their letters and are going on to understand
the written word, just as they did with speech before, they set

5   before them at their desks the works of good poets to read,

326a and make them learn them by heart; they contain a lot of
exhortation, and many passages praising and eulogizing good men
of the past, so that the child will be fired with enthusiasm to imitate
them, and filled with the desire to become a man like that. The
music teachers, too, do just the same, and see to it that the children

5   are well behaved and don't do anything bad. Moreover, once
they have learned to play the lyre, they teach them the poems of

b   other good poets, lyric poets in this case, which they set to music
and make the children's souls habituated to the rhythms and the
melodies, so that they become gentler, more graceful, and better

5   adjusted, and so better in word and action. For every aspect of
human life requires grace and proper adjustment. And then they
send them to a trainer as well, so that once their minds are properly
formed their bodies will be in a better condition to act under their

c   direction, and they won't be forced by physical deficiency to act
the coward in battle or in any other situation. The people who are

5   best able to do it—I mean, the wealthiest—do this especially, and their
sons begin to go to school at the earliest age and stay there the
longest. And when they have left school the city itself makes them

d   learn the laws and live according to their example, and not just act
in any way they like. Just as, when a child is still learning to write,
the teacher draws lines on his book with his pencil and then makes

5   him write the letters following the lines, so the city lays down laws,
devised by good lawgivers of the past, for our guidance, and makes
us rule and be ruled according to them, and punishes anyone who
transgresses them. This punishment is called correction, both here

e   and in many other cities, since the law corrects. Considering, then,
that such trouble is taken about excellence both by the state and by
private individuals, are you really surprised, Socrates, and doubtful
that it can be taught? You ought not to be; it would be far more

5   surprising if it could not be taught.

*   'Why, then, do good men often have worthless sons? The reason
is this; it's not at all surprising, if it's true what I said before,

327a that excellence is something of which no one must be ignorant, if

there is to be a city at all. If, then, it's as I say—and it most certainly
is—think of any pursuit or branch of knowledge that you care
to take as an example. Suppose that there could not be a city unless   5
we all played the flute to the best of our ability, and everyone was
in the habit of teaching the next man this both privately and publicly,
and reproving him when he played badly, and not refusing to share
his knowledge with him, just as at the moment no one refuses to
share his knowledge of what is right and lawful, or conceals it,   b
as in the case of other crafts—for we benefit, I believe, from one
another's justice and goodness, which is why everyone is eager to
teach the next man and tell him what is right and lawful. If, then,
we were all so willing and eager to teach one another to play the   5
flute, do you think, Socrates, that the sons of good flute-players
would themselves turn out to be better players than the sons of poor
players? I think not, but whoever had a son with the greatest
natural talent for the flute, his son would grow up to be famous,   c
and if anyone had a son with no talent, he would remain unknown.
And often the son of a good player would turn out poor, and the son
of a poor player good. But all the same they would all be competent
players, compared with people who can't play at all. And similarly,
as things stand, you must realize that even the wickedest man who   5
has been brought up in a society governed by laws is a just man, an
expert in this sphere, if you were to compare him with men without   d
education, or courts, or laws, or any coercion at all to force them
to be good; they would be savages like those in the poet Pherecrates'
play at last year's Lenaea. My goodness, once you were among   5
people of that sort, like the misanthropes in that play, you'd be glad
to fall in with Eurybatus and Phrynondas, and you'd weep with
longing for the wickedness of people here. But now you are   e
acting like a spoiled child, Socrates; everybody is a teacher of
excellence, to the best of his ability, and yet you can't find anyone
who is. Why, just as if you were looking for a teacher of Greek, you 328a
wouldn't find one, nor, I imagine, if you were looking for someone
to teach the sons of craftsmen the craft they learn from their
father, in so far as he and his friends in the craft can teach them,   5
would it be easy to find a teacher, though it's perfectly easy to
find someone to teach complete novices; it's just the same with

b
5
c

excellence and all the rest. But if there is anyone of us who is even a little better than others at helping people to attain it, so much the better. I claim to be one such man, and to excel other men in making people fine and good, and to be worth the fee I charge and even more, as my pupils agree. For this reason I have devised the following system of charging; whenever anyone has completed his study with me, if he is willing, he pays me the fee I charge, but if not he goes to a temple, states on oath how much he thinks what he has learnt is worth, and pays down that amount.

5
d

'So much, Socrates, by way of story and argument, to show that excellence can be taught, and that the Athenians are of that opinion, and also that it isn't at all surprising that the sons of good men turn out bad, and the sons of bad men good, since even the sons of Polycleitus, the same age as Paralus and Xanthippus here, are not to be compared with their father, and similarly in the case of other experts. But as yet it's not right to find fault with these two; one can still hope for something for them, for they are young yet.'

5
e
5
329a
5

So Protagoras concluded this lengthy exhibition of his skill as a speaker. I stayed gazing at him, quite spellbound, for a long time, thinking that he was going to say something more, and anxious to hear it; but when I saw that he had really finished, I collected myself with an effort, so to speak, and looked at Hippocrates. 'Son of Apollodorus,' I said, 'I am most grateful to you for suggesting that I should come here; for what I've learnt from Protagoras is something of great importance. Previously I used to think that there was no technique available to men for making people good; but now I am persuaded that there is. I've just one small difficulty, and it's obvious that Protagoras will explain it too without any trouble, since he has explained so much already. Now if you went to any of the orators about this question, you would perhaps get a similar speech from Pericles, or from some other able speaker; but if you ask them any question, they are no more capable of answering or asking anything themselves than a book is. Ask them anything about what they've said, no matter how small a point, and just as bronze, once struck, goes on sounding for a long time until you

take hold of it, so these orators spin out an answer a mile long to   b
any little question. But Protagoras can not only give splendid long
speeches, as he has shown here, but he can also answer questions
briefly, and when he asks one himself he waits and listens to the
answer, which is a gift that few possess. Now, Protagoras, I've very   5
nearly got the whole thing, if you would just answer me this. You
say that excellence can be taught, and I should accept your view
rather than anyone else's; just satisfy me on something which   c
surprised me when you said it. You said that Zeus bestowed justice
and conscience on mankind, and then many times in your discourse
you spoke of justice and soundness of mind and holiness and all the   5
rest as all summed up as the one thing, excellence. Will you then
explain precisely whether excellence is one thing, and justice and
soundness of mind and holiness parts of it, or whether all of these
that I've just mentioned are different names of one and the same   d
thing. This is what I still want to know.'

'That's an easy question to answer, Socrates,' he said. 'Excellence
is a single thing, and the things you ask about are parts of it.'

'Do you mean in the way that the parts of a face, mouth, nose,   5
eyes, and ears, are parts of the whole,' I asked, 'or like parts of gold,
none of which differs from any of the others or from the whole,
except in size?'

'The former, I take it, Socrates; the way the parts of the face   e
are related to the whole face.'

'So do some men possess one of these parts of excellence and
some another,' I asked, 'or if someone has one, must he have them
all?'

'Not at all,' he said. 'There are many who are courageous but   5
unjust, and many who are just but not wise.'

'So are wisdom and courage parts of excellence as well?' I said. 330a
'Most certainly,' he replied. 'Wisdom is the most important part.'
'But each of them is something different from any of the others?'
'Yes.'

'And does each of them have its own separate power? When we
consider the face, the eye is not like the ear, nor is its power the   5
same, nor is any other part like another in power or in other ways.
Is it the same with the parts of excellence, that none is like any other,   b

either in itself or in its power? Surely it must be, if it corresponds to our example.'

'It is so, Socrates.'

'So then,' I said, 'none of the other parts of excellence is like
5   knowledge, none is like justice, none like courage, none like soundness of mind, and none like holiness.'

'No.'

'Well now,' I said, 'let's consider together what sort of thing each
c   one is. Here's the first question: is justice something, or not a thing
at all? It seems to me that it is something; what do you think?'

'I think so too.'

'Well, then, suppose someone asked us, "Tell me, is that thing
5   that you have just mentioned, justice, itself just or unjust?" I should
reply that it is just. How would you cast your vote? The same as
mine, or different?'

'The same.'

'So my reply to the question would be that justice is such as to
d   be just; would you give the same answer?'

'Yes.'

'Suppose he went on to ask us, "Do you say that there is also
such a thing as holiness?" we should, I think, say that we do.'

'Yes.'

' "And do you say that that too is something?" We should say
so, don't you agree?'

5   'I agree there too.'

' "And do you say that this thing is itself such as to be unholy,
or such as to be holy?" I should be annoyed at the question, and
say, "Watch what you say, sir; how could anything else be holy,
e   if holiness itself is not to be holy?" What about you? Wouldn't you
give the same answer?'

'Certainly,' he said.

'Suppose he carried on with his questioning: "Well, what was it
that you were saying a moment ago? Didn't I hear you correctly?
5   You seemed to me to be saying that the parts of excellence are
related to one another in such a way that none of them is like any
other." I should say, "Yes, you heard the rest correctly, but you
must have misheard if you think that I said that. It was Protagoras

22

who said it in answer to a question of mine." Suppose he said, "Is **331a**
that right, Protagoras? Do you say that none of the parts of
excellence is like any of the others? Is that your opinion?" What
would you say?'
　'I should have to agree, Socrates,' he said.   5
　'Well, once we've agreed to that, Protagoras, how shall we deal
with his next question? "So holiness is not such as to be something
just, nor justice such as to be holy, but rather such as to be not holy;
and holiness such as to be not just, and so unjust, and justice   **b**
unholy?" What shall we reply? For my own part I should say both
that justice is holy and holiness just; and, if you let me, I should
give the same answer on your behalf too, that justness is either the   5
same thing as holiness or very similar, and above all that justice is
like holiness and holiness like justice. Is that your view too, or had
you rather that I didn't give that answer?'
　'It doesn't seem to me quite so simple, Socrates,' he said, 'that I   **c**
should agree that justice is holy and holiness just. I think that there
is a distinction to be made. But what does it matter? If you like, let
us say that justice is holy and holiness just.'
　'Oh, no,' I said. 'I don't want to examine any "If you like's" or   5
"If you think so's" but rather to examine you and me. I emphasize
"you and me" because I think that one can best examine the   **d**
question by getting rid of any "Ifs".'
　'Very well then,' he said. 'Justice resembles holiness in a way;
since in fact anything resembles anything else in some way or other.
There is a respect in which white resembles black, and hard soft, and   5
all the other things that seem completely opposite to each other.
We said before that the parts of the face have different powers and
are not like one another. Well, in a way each one does resemble and
is like the others. So by this line of argument you could prove, if   **e**
you wanted to, that these too are all similar to one another.
But it isn't right to call things "similar" just because they have
some point of similarity, however small, nor "dissimilar" if they
have some dissimilarity.'
　I was astonished. 'Do you really think', I said, 'that the just   5
and the holy have nothing more than some slight similarity to one
another?'

332a   'Not exactly,' he said, 'but then again it isn't as you seem to
       suppose.'

       'Well anyway,' I said, 'since you seem to find discussion of this
       point uncongenial, let's leave it and turn to something else that you
       said. Do you believe that there is such a thing as folly?'
       'Yes.'
5   'And the very opposite of that is wisdom, is it not?'
       'So it seems to me.'
       'And when men act rightly and usefully, do you consider that
       they act sensibly in so acting, or the opposite?'
       'They act sensibly.'
b   'And surely it's with good sense that they act sensibly.'
       'Most certainly.'
       'And surely those who act wrongly act foolishly and do not act
       sensibly in so acting?'
       'I agree.'
       'So acting foolishly is the opposite of acting sensibly?'
       'Yes.'
5   'And surely foolish acts are done with folly, and sensible ones
       with good sense?'
       'I agree.'
       'Now surely something done with strength is done strongly, and
       something done with weakness is done weakly.'
       'Yes.'
       'And something done with speed is done quickly, and something
c   with slowness, slowly.'
       'Yes.'
       'And something done in the same way, is done from the same, and
       something the opposite way from the opposite.'
       'That's right.'
       'Well now,' I said, 'is there such a thing as the beautiful?'
       'Yes, there is.'
       'And does it have any opposite except the ugly?'
       'No, none.'
5   'Is there such a thing as the good?'
       'There is.'

24

'Does it have any opposite apart from the bad?'
'No.'
'Is there such a thing as the high-pitched in sound?'
'Yes.'
'And that has no opposite apart from the low-pitched?'
'None.'
'So,' I said, 'each member of an opposition has only one opposite, not many.'
'I agree.'
'Well now,' I said, 'let's take a look at what we've agreed. We've   d
agreed that each thing has only one opposite, and not more.'
'Yes, we have.'
'And that what is done in the opposite way is done from the opposite.'
'Yes.'
'And we've agreed that something done foolishly is done in   5
the opposite way to something done sensibly.'
'Yes.'
'And something done sensibly is done from good sense, and something done foolishly from folly.'
'That is so.'   e
'Surely if it's done in the opposite way, it's done from the opposite.'
'Yes.'
'The one is done from good sense, the other from folly.'
'Yes.'
'In opposite ways?'
'Certainly.'
'So from opposites?'
'Yes.'
'So folly is the opposite of good sense?'   5
'So it appears.'
'Now do you remember that we previously agreed that folly is opposite to wisdom?'
'Yes, I do.'
'And that each thing has only one opposite?'
'Yes.'   333a

'Which of our theses shall we give up, then, Protagoras? The thesis that each thing has only one opposite, or the one that said that wisdom is distinct from good sense, both being parts of
5 excellence, and not only distinct but dissimilar in themselves and in their powers, like the parts of the face? Which shall we give up? For the two are not altogether harmonious; they are not in tune, nor do they fit together. How could they be in tune, if on the one hand
b each thing must have only one opposite, and no more, and on the other folly, a single thing, turns out to have both wisdom and good sense as its opposites? Is that the way it is, Protagoras, or not?' I asked, and he very reluctantly admitted that it was.

'So good sense and wisdom would seem to be one and the same,
5 would they not? And previously, you recall, we saw that justice and holiness were virtually the same.'

'Well now, Protagoras,' I said, 'don't let's give up, but let's complete
c our inquiry. Do you think that a man who acts unjustly is sensible in so acting?'

'I should be ashamed to assent to that, Socrates,' he said, 'though many people say so.'

'Would you rather that I pursued the question with them', I asked, 'or with you?'

5 'If you will,' he said, 'deal with that popular opinion first.'

'I don't mind, provided that you answer the questions, whether you believe the answers or not. It is chiefly the thesis that I am testing, but all the same it perhaps turns out to be a test for me too, as I ask the questions, and for whoever is answering.'

d   At first Protagoras began to make difficulties, saying that it was an uncongenial thesis, but in the end he agreed to answer the questions. 'Come then.' I said, 'answer from the beginning. Do you agree that some people act sensibly in acting unjustly?'

'Let's say so.'

'And by acting sensibly you mean thinking well?'

5 'Yes.'

* 'And by thinking well you mean planning their unjust acts well?'

'Let's say so.'

26

'And do they plan well if they do well in their unjust acts, or
if they do badly?'

'If they do well.'

'Do you call some things good?'

'I do.'

'Now,' I said, 'are those things good which are beneficial to
men?'

'My goodness, yes,' he said, 'and there are things I call good even   e
though they aren't beneficial to men.'

I could see that Protagoras was annoyed by this time, and that
he was ready for a verbal battle and keen to get to grips; so when
I saw that, I took care to put my questions in a mild manner. 'Do
you mean things that aren't beneficial to any man, Protagoras,' 334a
I asked, 'or things that aren't beneficial at all? Do you call things
like that good too?'

'Not at all,' he said. 'I know of many things which are harmful
to men, food and drink and drugs and a thousand other things, and   5
of some which are beneficial. Some things have neither effect on
men, but have an effect on horses; some have no effect except on
cattle, or on dogs. Some have no effect on any animal, but do affect
trees. And some things are good for the roots of the tree, but bad for
the growing parts, for instance manure is good if applied to the   b
roots of all plants, but if you put it on the shoots and young
twigs it destroys everything. Oil, too, is very bad for all plants and
most destructive of the hair of animals other than man, but in   5
the case of man it is beneficial to the hair and to the rest of the
body. So varied and many-sided a thing is goodness, that even here
the very same thing is good for the outside of the human body, and   c
very bad for the inside. That is the reason why doctors all forbid
sick people to use oil in their food except in the smallest quantities,
just enough to cover up any unpleasant smell from the dishes and   5
garnishes.'

When he had finished the audience shouted their approval of his
speech, and I said, 'Protagoras, I happen to be a forgetful sort of
person, and if someone speaks to me at length, I forget what he is   d
talking about. It's just as if I were a trifle deaf; in that case you

27

would think it right to speak louder than usual, if you were going
to talk to me. So now, since you are dealing with someone with a
5   bad memory, cut your answers short and make them briefer, if I
am to follow you.'
'What do you mean by telling me to give short answers?' he asked.
'Are they to be shorter than the questions require?'
'By no means,' I said.
'The right length, then?'
e   'Yes.'
'So are they to be the length that I think right, or that you do?'
5   'Well, I've heard', I said, 'that you can speak at such length, when
you choose to, that your speech never comes to an end, and then
335a again you can be so brief on the same topic that no one could be
briefer, and as well as doing it yourself you can teach someone else
how to do it. So if you are going to have a discussion with me,
use the latter method, that of brevity.'
'Socrates,' he said, 'I've had verbal contests with a great many
5   people, and if I had done what you tell me to do, and spoken
according to the instructions of my antagonist, I should never have
got the better of anyone, nor would the name of Protagoras have
become known in Greece.'
b   I knew that he was dissatisfied with his previous replies, and that
he wasn't willing to take the role of answerer in the discussion, so I
felt that there was no point in my continuing the conversation.
5   'Well, Protagoras,' I said, 'I too am not happy about carrying on the
conversation in a way that is unacceptable to you. But whenever you
wish to have a discussion of the kind that I can follow, then I shall
take part with you. You can carry on a conversation, so they say,
and indeed you say so yourself, either by long speeches or by short
c   question and answer—you are such an able man—but I can't make
these long speeches, though I wish I could. As you can argue in both
styles, you should have made me some concession, so that we could
have had a conversation. But now, since you are not willing to do so,
5   and I have an engagement, and couldn't wait for you to spin out
these long speeches—I have to go somewhere—I shall go. Though I
should no doubt have been glad to hear what you have to say.'
At the same time I got up to go. And as I was getting up Callias

grasped my hand in his right hand, and with his left took hold of   d
this old cloak of mine, and said, 'We shan't let you go, Socrates; for
if you leave, our discussion won't be the same. So I beg you to
stay with us; there's nothing I'd rather listen to than a discussion
between you and Protagoras. Please oblige us all.'   5

By this time I had got up to go. 'Son of Hipponicus,' I said,
'I've always had a high regard for your love of learning, but now   e
I praise and love it, so that I should like to oblige you, if you asked
me something possible. But now it's as if you were asking me to keep
pace with Crison, the runner from Himera, at his peak, or keep up
in a race with some middle-distance runner or long-distance courier.
I should reply that I am far more eager than you to keep pace with   336a
them, but I can't, so if you want to watch Crison and me running
together, ask him to come down to my level; for I can't run fast, but 5
he can run slowly. So if you want to listen to Protagoras and me, ask
him to answer now the way he did at first, briefly, and sticking to
the question. If not, what sort of discussion will we have? I thought b
that a discussion was something quite different from a public speech.'

'But, you see, Socrates,' he said, 'Protagoras seems quite right
in asking to be allowed to speak as he likes, and for you to speak as 5
you like.'

Alcibiades broke in; 'That's not fair, Callias. Socrates admits that
he doesn't go in for speech-making, and concedes victory in that
sphere to Protagoras, but when it comes to discussion and ability   c
to handle question and answer, I should be surprised if he yields to
anyone. So if Protagoras admits that he is inferior to Socrates in
discussion, Socrates is content; but if he disputes it, let him conduct
a discussion by question and answer, and not make a long speech in   5
reply to every question, staving off objections and not giving answers, d
but spinning it out until most of the people listening forget what
the question was. Except Socrates, of course; I bet that he won't
forget, but he's only joking when he says he has a bad memory.
I think, then, that what Socrates says is fairer; and each of us ought 5
to give his own opinion.'

After Alcibiades, I think it was Critias who spoke. 'Prodicus
and Hippias, Callias seems to me very much on the side of Protagoras, e
while Alcibiades takes a partisan view of anything he is keen on.

But there is no reason for us to take sides either with Socrates or with Protagoras; instead we should ask both of them not to break off the conversation in the middle.'

337a   Then Prodicus said, 'I agree, Critias. Those who attend a discussion like this should listen to both speakers impartially, but not without discrimination—that's not the same thing. For one ought

5   to listen to both impartially, while not assessing each equally, but putting the abler man above the less able. For my own part, Socrates and Protagoras, I think that you should agree tó argue, but

b   not wrangle—for an argument can be between friends in a spirit of good will, a wrangle is between those who are hostile and unfriendly to one another—and so we should have a splendid conversation.

5   For in that way you who speak would gain the most esteem, though not praise, from us who listen—for esteem is something genuine in the minds of one's hearers, while praise is often mere deceitful

c   words contrary to their real opinion—while we who listen would derive in that way the most enjoyment, though not pleasure—for one derives enjoyment from learning and the exercise of intelligence purely in the mind, but pleasure from eating or some other pleasant experience purely in the body.'

5   Very many of those present agreed with these remarks of Prodicus'. And then the wise Hippias said, 'Gentlemen, I regard you

d   as all related, all akin, all fellow citizens—by nature, not by convention. For like is by nature akin to like, but convention, a tyrant over mankind, ordains many things by force contrary to nature. Surely, therefore, it is shameful if we, who understand the

5   nature of things and, being the wisest of the Greeks, have for that very reason come together to the very shrine of wisdom in all Greece and to this, the greatest and most magnificent house of that very

e   city, should achieve nothing worthy of our reputation, but quarrel among ourselves like the most worthless of men. I beg and counsel you

338a   then, Protagoras and Socrates, to regard us as arbitrators and come to an agreement. For your part, Socrates, I advise you not to seek that sort of precision in the discussion which involves excessive brevity, if that is not agreeable to Protagoras, but to let go and slacken the reins of the discourse, so as to give it more dignity

5   and elegance. And on the other hand I advise Protagoras not to

crowd on all sail and run before the wind into a sea of words out of
sight of land; both of you should take a middle course. So do as I
suggest, and choose an umpire, chairman, or president to see that   b
each of you keeps to the proper length in what he says.'

This was agreeable to the company; everyone indicated his
approval, and Callias refused to let me go and they asked me to
choose a chairman. I then said that it was quite improper to choose
a referee for an argument. 'For if the person chosen is inferior to   5
ourselves,' I said, 'it would not be right for an inferior person to
preside over men better than he, and if he is our equal, even then
it wouldn't be right; for someone who is our equal will do just the
same as we should, so it will be a waste of time to choose him.   c
All right, then, you will choose someone superior to us. But in fact
I think that it's impossible to choose anyone wiser than Protagoras.
And if you choose someone who is in no way superior, while
pretending that he is, then that too is an insult to Protagoras, to have
a chairman chosen for him as if he were of no account. As far as I am   5
concerned, it makes no difference. But here's what I am willing to
do, so that we can have a discussion as you are anxious to do. If
Protagoras is not willing to answer, let him put the questions, and   d
I shall answer, and at the same time I shall try to show him how, in
my opinion, one ought to answer questions. And when I have
answered all the questions he wants to ask, let him in turn undergo   5
questioning from me in the same way. So if he doesn't seem anxious
to stick to the question in his replies, you and I together will ask
him, as you asked me, not to ruin the conversation. There's no need   e
for any single chairman to be appointed for that; instead you will all
act together as chairmen.'

Everyone agreed that that was what we should do. Protagoras
was altogether unwilling, but none the less he was obliged to agree
to put the questions, and when he had asked sufficient, to submit   5
to questioning in his turn and give short replies.

So he began to put his questions something like this: 'I consider,
Socrates, that a most important part of a man's education is
being knowledgeable about poetry. By that I mean the ability to 339a
grasp the good and bad points of a poem, to distinguish them and

to give one's reasons in reply to questions. And in fact the question
5   that I am now going to ask concerns the very thing we are discussing
now, excellence; the only difference is that it is transferred to the
sphere of poetry. Simonides in one of his poems says to Scopas the
son of Creon of Thessaly that

b   It is hard, rather, to become a truly good man,
Foursquare in hand and foot and mind, fashioned without fault.

Do you know this poem, or shall I recite it all for you?'
5   'There's no need,' I said. 'I know it, and as it happens I've studied
it closely.'
'Good,' he said. 'Do you regard it as a fine, properly written
poem, or not?'
'Very fine and properly written.'
10   'Do you count it a fine poem, if the poet contradicts himself?'
'No.'
c   'Then look at it more closely.'
'But, my dear sir, I have studied it sufficiently already.'
'You know, then, that later on in the poem he says

Nor do I hold as right the saying of Pittacus,
5   Wise though he was; he says it is hard to be noble.

Do you think it is the same man who says that and the lines I quoted
earlier?'
'I know that it is.'
'You think, then, that the two are consistent?'
'Personally, I do,' I said (though at the same time I was afraid he
might be right). 'Don't you?'
d   'But how could anyone be thought to be consistent in saying
both these things? First of all he himself asserts that it is hard to
become a truly good man, and then a little further on he forgets
5   that and attacks Pittacus for saying just what he has said, that it
is hard to be noble, and refuses to accept it, though it's the same
as his own view. But in attacking someone for saying just what he
says, he is obviously attacking himself, so either the earlier or
the later statement must be wrong.'
10   This produced a shout of approval from many of the audience.

At first, what with his argument and the applause of the others, my   e
eyes went dim and I felt giddy, as if I had been hit by a good boxer.
But then—to tell you the truth, it was to gain time to consider what
the poet meant—I turned to Prodicus and addressed him. 'Prodicus,   5
Simonides is a fellow citizen of yours; you ought to come to his 340a
assistance. So now I'm resolved to call on you for help. Just as
Homer says Scamander called on Simoeis for help when he was
attacked by Achilles, in these words,

> Dear brother, let both of us restrain the man's strength,   5

so I call on you to help stop Protagoras utterly demolishing
Simonides. And certainly the defence of Simonides requires your
special skill, which enables you to distinguish wishing from desiring,   b
and all those splendid distinctions you made a short time ago. Now
see whether you agree with me. For Simonides doesn't seem to me
to contradict himself. But please give your opinion first, Prodicus;
do you think that becoming and being are the same thing, or   5
different?'
  'Different, of course.'
  'Now in the first passage doesn't Simonides give his own opinion,
that it is hard to become a truly good man?'   c
  'That's correct.'
  'But he attacks Pittacus,' I said, 'not, as Protagoras thinks, for
saying the same as he does, but for saying something different.
For it's not *becoming* noble that Pittacus says is difficult, as   5
Simonides does, but *being* noble. And as Prodicus says, Protagoras,
being and becoming are not the same thing. And if being is not the
same as becoming, Simonides does not contradict himself. Perhaps
Prodicus and many others would say in the words of Hesiod that it   d
is difficult to become good,

> For the gods have placed sweat on the path to excellence,

But when you reach the top,

> Thereafter it is easy to keep, hard though it was to achieve.'   5

  Prodicus indicated his agreement, but Protagoras said, 'Your
defence, Socrates, involves a worse mistake than the one you are

defending him against.'

e   'Well then, Protagoras, it seems I've done harm,' I said, 'and I'm
a ridiculous sort of doctor, for my treatment makes the disease
worse.'

'Well, that's the way it is.'

'How do you mean?'

5   'It would show great stupidity on the poet's part if he says that
it is so easy to keep excellence once you have it, when that's
the most difficult thing of all, as everyone agrees.'

'My goodness,' I said, 'it's lucky that we have Prodicus taking
341a   part in our discussion. You know, Protagoras, that skill of his
must be a marvellous and ancient one, originating with Simonides,
or even earlier. But though you are learned in so many other things,
you don't seem to be acquainted with it, as I am through being
5   Prodicus' pupil. And in the present case you don't seem to me to
see that by "hard" Simonides perhaps didn't mean what you mean.
It's like "terrible"; whenever I say in praise of you or anyone else
that Protagoras is a terribly wise man, Prodicus corrects me and
b   asks if I'm not ashamed to call something good terrible. For what
is terrible, he says, is bad; at least no one ever talks of "terrible
wealth" or "terrible peace" or "terrible health", but "terrible
5   disease" and "terrible war" and "terrible poverty", which shows
that what is terrible is bad. So perhaps it's the same with "hard";
perhaps Simonides and the Ceans use it in the sense of "bad", or
some other sense which you haven't grasped. So let's ask Prodicus;
c   it's reasonable to ask him about Simonides' dialect. What did
Simonides mean by "hard", Prodicus?'

' "Bad" ' he replied.

'So that's the reason', I said, 'why he attacks Pittacus for saying
5   "It is hard to be noble", as if he had heard him saying "It is bad to
be noble".'

'You surely don't imagine, Socrates,' he said, 'that Simonides
means anything else. He is censuring Pittacus for not distinguishing
the sense of words correctly, coming from Lesbos as he did and
having been brought up to speak a foreign language.'

10   'Well, Protagoras,' I said, 'you hear what Prodicus says. Have you
d   anything to say to that?'

'It's not that way at all, Prodicus,' answered Protagoras. 'I know
perfectly well that by "hard" Simonides means what we all mean,
not "bad" but what is not easy, and can't be attained without a great   5
deal of trouble.'

'Well I think so too, Protagoras,' I said. 'That's what Simonides
means, and Prodicus knows it as well, but he's having a joke and
testing you to see whether you can defend your position. That
Simonides doesn't mean "bad" by "hard" is shown quite clearly   e
by what he says immediately afterwards. He says

> That gift would belong to a god alone.

Now clearly he isn't saying "It is bad to be noble", and then going
on to say that the gods alone would possess that gift, and to assign   5
it to them alone. Prodicus would be making Simonides out to be
some sort of scoundrel, never a Cean. But I am willing to tell you
what I think Simonides means in this poem, if you want to have a   342a
sample of my knowledge of poetry, as you call it. Or if you like,
I shall listen to your explanation.'

When I had finished Protagoras said, 'If *you* like, Socrates.'
Prodicus and Hippias told me to go ahead by all means, and so did   5
the others.

'Well,' I said, 'I shall try to explain my own view of this poem.
The most ancient learning of Greece, and the most copious, is to
be found in Crete and in Sparta, and there are more wise men   b
there than anywhere else on earth. But they deny this and pretend
to be ignorant, so as not to betray their superiority in wisdom
over the rest of Greece, like those whom Protagoras described as
sophists. Instead, they try to make it look as if they excel in
courage and in fighting, for they think that if their real superiority   5
were discovered, everyone would seek to acquire wisdom. Up
to the present they have concealed this and deceived their
admirers in other cities, who imitate them by putting on boxing-   c
gloves, getting cauliflower ears, going in for gymnastics and wearing
short cloaks, in the belief that those are the things that make the
Spartans superior to other Greeks. But the Spartans themselves,
whenever they get tired of concealment and want to consult their   5
wise men openly, expel any foreigners, those admirers of theirs as

35

well as anyone else who happens to be in the country, and so
consult the wise men unknown to foreigners; and they don't allow
d   any of their young men to go abroad, and neither do the Cretans,
to make sure they don't forget what they are taught at home. And
in those cities you find not only men who take pride in their
education, but women too. This is how you'll see that what I say
5   is true, that the Spartans have the best education and the greatest
skill with words: if you meet the most ordinary Spartan, for most
e   of the conversation he strikes you as a dull fellow, and then, no
matter what you are talking about, he flings in some memorable,
brief, pithy saying like a skilful javelin-thrower, making the man he is
5   talking to look no more than a child. Now there are some, both of
earlier times and of our own day, who have seen that admiration of
Sparta is much more a matter of learning than of gymnastics, and
343a who know that the ability to utter sayings of that kind is the mark
of a perfectly educated man. Thales of Miletus was one, Pittacus
of Mytilene another, Bias of Priene, our own Solon, Cleobulus of
5   Lindos, Myson of Chen(ae); the Spartan Chilon was counted as the
seventh. All of these were admirers, devotees, and students of the
Spartan education, and you can see that their own wisdom is of
that kind, as each is the author of some brief, memorable sayings.
b   And not only that, but they joined together to make an offering
to Apollo at his temple in Delphi of the fruits of their wisdom,
and inscribed there those familiar maxims "Know thyself" and
"Nothing in excess". What, then, is the point of all this? The point
is that that was the form of expression of the wisdom of former
5   times, a Laconian brevity. And one of Pittacus' sayings which circu-
lated privately and won the approval of the wise was this one, "It is
c   hard to be good." So Simonides, who was anxious to get a reputation
for wisdom, saw that if he could bring down that saying then, just
as if he had defeated a famous athlete, he would himself become
famous among the men of his time. That was his object, I believe,
5   and it is that saying that he has in mind throughout the whole poem,
with the aim of discrediting it.
    'Let's all examine it together, then, to see whether what I say is
true. For right away the beginning of the poem would seem quite
crazy, if he wanted to say that it is hard to become a good man,

and then added "rather". For that phrase does not seem to have   d
been added for any purpose, unless one understands Simonides as
arguing against the saying of Pittacus. When Pittacus says that it is
hard to be noble, Simonides replies, "No, but rather to *become* a   5
good man, Pittacus, is hard in truth"—he doesn't say "a truly good
man", or apply truth to that, as if there were some men who are   e
truly good, and others who are good indeed, but not truly so (that
would strike people as silly and not something that Simonides
would say). You have to take the phrase "in truth" as transposed
in the poem, and as it were prefix the saying of Pittacus, as if we
were to imagine Pittacus himself speaking and Simonides replying,   5
thus: "It is hard to be noble", (Simonides in reply) "Pittacus, what **344a**
you are saying is not true: for it is not to *be*, but rather to *become* a
good man, foursquare in hand and foot and mind, fashioned without
fault, that is hard in truth." Taken like that, "rather" appears to   5
have been added for some purpose, and "in truth" put in its proper
place at the end; and everything that follows supports that way of
taking it. Now there are many things which one could say about
each of the expressions in the poem to show that it is well written—   b
for it is a quite delightful, carefully composed work—but it would
take a long time to go through it like that. Let's just examine the
outline of the piece as a whole and its intention, which is above all
to criticize the saying of Pittacus throughout the poem.   5

'For a little later, as if he were developing his argument, he says
that to become a good man is truly difficult, but possible, for a time
at least; but having become one, to remain in that state and be a   c
good man, as you say, Pittacus, is impossible and beyond human
power, but only a god could have that gift.

> And it is impossible for the man not to be bad,
> Whom helpless disaster overthrows.   5

Now in controlling a ship, who is it whom helpless disaster overthrows? Clearly not the man without knowledge of sailing; for he
has been overthrown from the start. So just as you can't throw a
man who is already down, but you can throw a man who is on
his feet, and put him down, but not if he's down already, similarly   d
helpless disaster can sometimes overthrow the resourceful man, but

not the man who is always helpless, and a helmsman can be struck
and rendered helpless by a great storm, and a farmer made helpless
5   by the onset of a bad season, and the same with a doctor. For the
noble man can become bad, as we learn from another poet who says

> Now a good man is sometimes bad and sometimes noble;

e   but the bad man can't become bad, but must always be so. So when
helpless disaster overthrows the resourceful, wise, and good man, it
is impossible for him not to be bad. But you, Pittacus, say that it is
5   hard to be noble; but in fact to become noble is hard, but possible,
but to be noble is impossible,

> For when he does well every man is good,
> But bad when he does badly.

345a Now as regards reading and writing, what counts as doing well, and
what kind of doing makes a man good at that? Obviously, having
learned his letters. And what is the doing well that makes a man
a good doctor? Obviously, having learned how to care for the sick.
5   "But bad when he does badly." Now who could become a bad doctor?
Obviously, someone who is first of all a doctor, and then a good
doctor—for he is the man who could become bad—but the rest of
us who are ignorant of medicine could never in doing badly become
b   doctors or carpenters or anything else of the kind; and someone
who could never in doing badly become a doctor could obviously
not become a bad doctor either. So it is that the good man too could
sometimes become bad, either through age or toil or disease or
5   some misfortune—for doing badly is nothing other than being
deprived of knowledge—but the bad man could never become
bad—for he is bad all the time—but if he is to become bad he must
first become good. So this part of the poem too points to the same
c   conclusion, that it is impossible to be a good man, good all the time,
that is, but it is possible to become good and for the same man to
become bad. And the best, who are good for longest, are those
whom the gods love.
5   'So all of this was written against Pittacus, and the next section
of the poem shows that even more clearly. For he says

Therefore never shall I cast empty away my share of time
On a vain hope, seeking what cannot be, an utterly blameless
Man, of us who reap the fruit of broad earth,   10
And when I find him, I shall tell you,

he says—so fierce is his attack on Pittacus' maxim throughout the   d
poem—

>   But I praise and love all
>   Who do nothing shameful freely;
>   But against necessity not even gods fight.   5

And this too was directed at the same target. For Simonides was not
so uneducated as to say he praised those who do nothing bad of
their own free will, as if there were some people who do bad things
freely. For I am pretty much of this opinion, that no intelligent man   e
believes that anyone does wrong freely or acts shamefully and badly
of his own free will, but they well know that all who do shameful
and bad things do so other than freely. And Simonides, for his part,
doesn't say that he praises those who do nothing bad freely, but he   5
applies this term "freely" to himself. For he thought that an honest
man often forces himself to be a friend and praise someone; for   346a
instance, it often happens that a man has an unnatural father or
mother, or country, or something like that. When that happens to a
bad man he views it almost with pleasure and makes a great display
of castigating and blaming the shortcomings of his parents or his   5
country, in order that he himself may not incur any blame or
reproach for his neglect of them, so he berates them even more
than need be, and deliberately makes new enemies on top of those   b
he can't avoid. But a good man conceals it all and forces himself to
praise them, and if he gets angry at his unjust treatment by his
parents or his country he calms himself down and makes friends
again, forcing himself to love and praise them.   5
   'Often, I think, Simonides considered that he himself was
praising and eulogizing a tyrant or someone else, not freely, but
under compulsion. It is this that he has in mind when he says to
Pittacus, "For my part, Pittacus, it's not because I am a fault-finder   c
that I censure you, since

>   He suffices me who is not bad nor

5
Altogether wicked, a sound man who knows
Justice that benefits the city.
Him I shall not censure—

for I am not one who loves to censure—

For the generation of fools is endless.

10   (So if anyone likes finding fault, he could have his fill on them.)

Now all things are fair, which are not mingled with foul."

d   When he says that, it's not as if he were saying "All things are white,
which are not mingled with black"—that would be absurd for many
reasons—but that he himself accepts the middle state as free from
censure. "I do not seek", he says, "an utterly blameless man, of us
5   who reap the fruit of broad earth, and when I find him I shall tell
you. So I shan't praise anyone for being such a man; it is enough
for me if he is in between and does nothing bad, for I praise and love
e   all"—and here he uses the Mytilenean dialect, since it is against Pittacus
that he says, "I praise and love all freely"—it's there, at "freely",
that one must divide the phrase—"who do nothing shameful, but
there are some whom I praise and love against my will. So if you,
347a   Pittacus, said what was even partly right and true, I should never
find fault with you. But since you give the appearance of speaking
the truth when in fact you are totally wrong on things of the greatest
importance, for that reason I blame you." That, gentlemen,' I said, 'is
5   what Simonides seems to me to have meant in writing this poem.'

'Socrates,' replied Hippias, 'you too seem to me to have given a good
b   account of the poem. I, too, though, have a good interpretation of
it, which I shall expound to you all, if you like.'

'Yes, Hippias,' said Alcibiades, 'some other time. But now it's
right that Protagoras and Socrates should honour their agreement,
and if Protagoras wants to ask any more questions, Socrates should
answer, or if Protagoras wants to answer, Socrates should ask the
questions.'

And I said, 'For my part, I concede to Protagoras whichever he
prefers; and if he is willing, let's leave the discussion of lyric and
c   other kinds of poetry, but I should be very glad, Protagoras, to

complete our examination of the question I asked you at first.
For the discussion of poetry strikes me as very like a drinking-party
of common, vulgar fellows; for people of that sort, who for lack of   5
education can't entertain one another over the wine with their own
conversation, put up the price of flute-girls, and pay large sums to   d
hear the sound of the flute instead of their own talk, and entertain
each other that way. But in a party of well-bred, educated people,
you never see flute-girls or dancers or harp-girls, but they can   5
entertain one another with their own conversation without any such
childish trifles, speaking and listening in turn in a dignified fashion,
even if they drink a great deal. Similarly gatherings of this kind, if   e
they are made up of the sort of men that most of us claim to be,
have no need of anyone else to take part and in particular no need
of poets; you can't question them about what they say, but in most
cases when people quote them, one says the poet means one thing   5
and one another, and they argue over points which can't be established with any certainty. No, they leave that kind of conversation
alone, and entertain one another by their own efforts and test   348a
each other's mettle in mutual argument. It seems to me that you and
I should rather follow the example of that sort of person, leave
the poets aside and conduct our argument independently, testing   5
the truth of the matter and our own capacities. And if you want to
carry on asking the questions, I'm prepared to reply; but if you're
willing, oblige me by completing the discussion which we broke
off in the middle.'

In reply to this and similar things Protagoras gave no clear   b
indication of which he was going to do. So Alcibiades looked at
Callias and said, 'Callias, do you think that Protagoras is being
fair now, not telling us whether he'll answer or not? I don't think   5
so, anyhow. So let him either join in the discussion or tell us that
he's not willing to, so that we know where he stands, and Socrates,
or anyone else who wants to, can take up a discussion with someone
else.'

And Protagoras, shamed, so it seemed to me, by these words of   c
Alcibiades and by the entreaties of Callias and practically everybody
else, was at length induced to take part, and told me to put the
questions and he would answer.

5   Then I said, 'Protagoras, please don't think that I have any
other aim in our discussion than to get to the bottom of the
problems that always puzzle me. For I think that Homer certainly
has a point when he talks of

d   Two going together, and one noticed it before the other.

For somehow we all do better that way, whatever has to be done or
said or thought out. "And if he notices it alone", he immediately
5   goes about looking for someone to show it to, to find confirmation,
and doesn't stop till he finds someone. It's for just this reason
that I had rather have a discussion with you than with anyone
e   else, for I think that you are best able to examine the questions that
it is right for an upright man to consider, especially questions about
excellence. For who other than yourself? It's not just that you
regard yourself as a worthy man; others are upright themselves
without the ability to make others so. You are both good yourself
5   and capable of making others good, and have such self-confidence
349a that, whereas others make a secret of this profession, you give
yourself the name of sophist and proclaim yourself openly to the
whole of Greece as a teacher of culture and excellence, and have
been the first to ask a fee for this. So should I not have called on
5   you to explore these matters and consulted and questioned you?
Of course I should. And now, with regard to my original question,
I should like you to remind me once again from the beginning of
what we said, and also to examine some further points together with
b   me. The question, I think, was this: are "wisdom", "soundness of
mind", "courage", "justice", and "holiness" five names for the one
thing, or does there correspond to each of these names some separate
5   thing or entity with its own particular power, unlike any of the
others? Now you said that they are not names for the one thing,
c   but each is the name of a separate thing, and all of these are parts
of excellence, not as the parts of gold are like one another and the
whole of which they are parts, but as the parts of the face are unlike
5   one another and the whole of which they are parts, each having its
own separate power. If you still think now as you did then, please
say so; but if at all differently, please explain how, since I shan't
hold you to anything if you've now changed your mind in any way.

For I shouldn't be surprised if you were saying that then just to   d
test me out.'

'Well, Socrates,' he said, 'I maintain that all of these are parts of
excellence, and four of them resemble one another fairly closely, but
courage is altogether different from all the rest. And this is how you   5
will know that what I say is true: you will find many men who are
totally unjust and irreligious and wanton and ignorant, but most
outstandingly courageous.'

'Stop there;' I said, 'it's worth taking a look at what you are   e
saying. Do you call courageous men daring or something else?'

'Yes, daring,' he said, 'and ready for what most men fear.'

'Tell me then, do you regard excellence as something fine, and
is it as something fine that you offer to teach it?'   5

'The finest of all things, unless I'm quite mad.'

'Is part of it shameful, and part fine, or is it all fine?'

'It's all as fine as anything can be.'

'Now, do you know who it is who are daring at diving into wells?' **350a**

'Yes, divers.'

'Because of their knowledge, or something else?'

'Because of their knowledge.'

'And who are daring at fighting on horseback? Cavalrymen, or
people who can't ride?'

'Cavalrymen.'

'And in skirmishing? Is it trained skirmishers, or untrained?'   5

'Trained skirmishers,' he said. 'And in every other case, if this is
the answer you are looking for, those who have knowledge are more
daring than those who lack it, and once they have acquired it they   b
are more daring than they themselves were before.'

'And have you ever', I asked, 'seen people who are ignorant of all
these things, but daring in each of them?'

'I have,' he said. 'Too daring.'

'So, are these daring men courageous as well?'

'In that case courage would be something shameful; for such   5
people are mad.'

'Well now, what do you say about the courageous? Isn't it that
they are (the) daring?'

'Yes, I stick to that.'

c   'So these people who are daring in that way seem not courageous
but mad, isn't that so? And on the other hand these people who are
wisest are also most daring, and being most daring are most
courageous? And according to this argument wisdom would be the
5   same as courage?'
       'You are not correctly recalling,' he said, 'what I said in answer to
your question, Socrates. You asked me if the courageous are daring,
and I agreed that they are; but you didn't ask me if, in addition, the
daring are courageous—for if you had asked me that, I should have
d   said that not all are. You have nowhere shown that I was wrong in
what I did agree, viz. that the courageous are daring. Then you
show that people when they have knowledge are more daring than
when they lack it, and also than others who are ignorant, and on
5   that basis you conclude that courage and wisdom are the same thing;
but if you go about it that way you might think that strength is the
same thing as wisdom. For if you proceeded that way and began
e   by asking me if the strong are capable, I should say yes; and then,
if those who know how to wrestle are more capable than those who
don't know how to wrestle, and themselves more capable after
they have learnt than before, I should say yes; and once I had
5   agreed to that you would be able, using the very same arguments,
to conclude that according to what I had agreed wisdom was the
same thing as strength. But I neither here nor anywhere else admit
that the capable are strong, but rather that the strong are capable;
351a   for capability and strength are not the same thing, but the former
comes from knowledge indeed, but also from madness and animal
boldness, while strength results from a good natural condition and
nurture of the body. And similarly in the other case daring and
5   courage are not the same, so that it happens that the courageous are
daring, but that not all the daring are courageous. For daring results
b   both from skill and from animal boldness and madness, like
capability, but courage from a good natural condition and nurture
of the soul.'

       'And do you maintain, Protagoras,' I said, 'that some men live
well and others badly?'
       'I do.'

44

'Well, now, do you think a man would live well if he lived in   5
misery and suffering?'

'No.'

'And what if he had a pleasant life to the end? Don't you think
that he would have lived well like that?'

'Yes, I do.'

'So to have a pleasant life is good, and to have an unpleasant life   c
bad?'

'Provided one takes pleasure in praiseworthy things.'

'What's that, Protagoras? Surely you don't go along with the
majority in calling some pleasant things bad and some painful
things good. What I say is, in so far as things are pleasant, are they
not to that extent good, leaving their other consequences out   5
of account? And again it's the same with painful things; in so
far as they are painful, are they not bad?'

'I don't know, Socrates,' he replied 'whether I should give such
a simple answer to your question and say that all pleasant things   d
are good and all painful things bad. Rather it seems to me safer,
having regard not only to what I say now but also to all the rest of
my life, to reply that some pleasant things are not good, and again   5
that some painful things are not bad, while some are, and a third
class is neutral, neither good nor bad.'

'And don't you call pleasant', I said, 'things which are character-   e
ized by pleasure or which produce pleasure?'

'Certainly.'

'Well, that's what I'm saying; in so far as they are pleasant, are
they not good? I'm asking whether pleasure itself is not good.'

'As you always say, Socrates,' he replied, 'let's investigate it. And
if the question seems to the point and it appears that pleasant and   5
good are the same, then we shall be in agreement. But if not, we shall *
argue about it then.'

'Do you wish to lead the investigation,' I asked, 'or shall I?'

'You ought to,' he said, 'as it's you who are in charge of the   10
discussion.'   *

'Well, then,' I said, 'perhaps things might become clear if we   352a
go about it like this. Imagine someone looking at a man and trying

45

to assess his health or some other bodily function from his appearance, and saying, once he had seen his face and hands, "Come now,
5   uncover your chest and back and let me see them, so that I can examine you more thoroughly." I too want something of the sort as regards our question. I've seen that your view about the good and the pleasant is as you say, and now I want to say something like this:
b   "Come now, Protagoras, uncover for me this part of your mind as well; how do you stand as regards knowledge? Do you agree with the majority there too, or do you think otherwise? The opinion of the majority about knowledge is that it is not anything strong,
5   which controls and rules; they don't look at it that way at all, but think that often a man who possesses knowledge is ruled not by it but by something else, in one case passion, in another pleasure, in another pain, sometimes lust, very often fear; they just
c   look at knowledge as a slave who gets dragged about by all the rest. Now are you of a similar opinion about knowledge, or do you think that it is something fine and such as to rule man, and that if
5   someone knows what is good and bad, he would never be conquered by anything so as to do other than what knowledge bids him? In fact, that intelligence is a sufficient safeguard for man?" '

'My opinion is indeed as you say, Socrates,' he replied, 'and
d   moreover it would be an especial disgrace to me of all people not to maintain that wisdom and knowledge is the mightiest of human things.'

5   'That's splendid,' I said, 'and quite true. Now you know that the majority of people don't agree with us, but hold that many people who know what is best to do are not willing to do it, though it is in their power, but do something else. And those whom I've asked about the cause of this say that people who act in that way do so
e   because they are overcome by pleasure or pain or under the influence of one of the things I mentioned just now.'

'Yes, Socrates,' he said, 'people have many other wrong ideas too.'

5   'Join me, then, in trying to win them over and to teach them the real nature of the experience that they call being overcome by
353a pleasures and for that reason failing to do what is best, when one knows what it is. For perhaps if we told them that they are wrong

and mistaken they would ask, "Well, if this experience isn't being   5
overcome by pleasure, what is it then? What do you call it? Tell
us."'

'But why, Socrates, must we examine the opinion of the mass of
people, who say whatever comes into their heads?'

'I think', I replied, 'that this is relevant to our question of how   b
courage is related to the other parts of excellence. So if you are
willing to abide by what we just agreed, that I should conduct
the discussion in the way that I think best suited to make the matter   *
clear, please follow my lead. But if not, if you had rather, I'll let the   5
matter go.'

'You're quite right,' he said. 'Go on as you've begun.'

'Well once again,' I said, 'if they asked us, "What then do you   c
say this thing is, which we were calling being weaker than pleasures?"
I should answer as follows: "Listen, and Protagoras and I shall try
to explain. Don't you maintain that it happens that in some   5
circumstances, often for instance when you are conquered by the
pleasures of food and drink and sex, you do things though you
know them to be wrong?" "Yes." So we in our turn should ask,
"In what respect do you say they are wrong? Is it because they   d
provide this immediate pleasure, and because each of them is
pleasant, or because later on they lead to diseases and poverty and
many other things like that? Or even if they lead to none of these
later, but merely cause pleasure, would they still be bad, just   5
because they cause pleasure in one way or another?" Do you
suppose, Protagoras, that they would give any other answer than
that they are bad not because they produce immediate pleasure, but   e
because of what comes later, diseases and the like?'

'For my part,' said Protagoras, 'I think that that is what most
people would say.'

'"And surely in causing diseases they cause pains, and in
causing poverty they cause pains." They would agree, I think.'

Protagoras agreed.   5

'"Don't you think that, as Protagoras and I maintain, the only
reason these things are bad is that they result in pains and deprive 354a
one of other pleasures?" They would agree.'

We both agreed on that.

47

'Suppose, now, we asked the opposite question, "When you also say that some painful things are good, don't you mean such things
5 as athletic training and warfare and medical treatment by cautery and amputation and drugs and starvation diet? It's these that are good, but painful?" Would they say so?'

'Yes.'

b   ' "Now do you call them good because at the time they cause the most extreme suffering and anguish, or because later on they produce things like health and good bodily condition and the safety
5 of the city and rule over others and wealth?" They would agree, I think.'

'Yes.'

' "And are these things good for any other reason than that they result in pleasures and the relief from and avoidance of pains?
c Or can you point to any result by reference to which you call them good, other than pleasures and pains?" They would say no, I think.'

'I think so too,' said Protagoras.

5   ' "So you pursue pleasure as good, and avoid pain as evil?" '
He agreed.

' "So it's pain which you regard as evil, and pleasure as good, since you even call enjoyment itself bad when it deprives you of greater pleasures than it has in itself, or leads to pains which are
d greater than its own pleasures. For if you call enjoyment itself bad for any other reason and by reference to any other result, you would be able to tell us what it is. But you can't." '

'I don't think so either,' said Protagoras.

5   ' "And again, surely it's the same about suffering pain itself. Don't you call suffering pain itself good when it gets rid of greater pains than it has in itself, or when it leads to pleasures which are greater than the pains? For if you refer to any other result when
e you call suffering pain itself good than the one I say, you will be able to tell us. But you can't." '

'You are quite right,' said Protagoras.

*   ' "Well once again," ' I said, ' "if you asked me, 'But why are you
5 going on at such length and elaboration about this?' I should say, 'I beg your pardon. First of all, it isn't easy to show the real nature of what you call being weaker than pleasures; secondly the whole

argument depends on this. But even now you are at liberty to
withdraw, if you can give any other account of the good than 355a
pleasure, or of evil than pain. Or are you content to say that it is a
pleasant life without pains? Now if you are content with that, and
aren't able to call anything good or bad except what results in 5
that, listen to what follows. I maintain that, if that is your position,
it is absurd for you to say that a man often does bad things though
he knows they are bad and could refrain from doing them, because
he is driven and overwhelmed by pleasures. And then again you say b
that though a man knows what is good, he is not willing to do it,
because he is overcome by immediate pleasures. Now that this is
absurd will become perfectly clear if we stop using many terms all 5
at once, "pleasant", "painful", "good", and "bad", and instead,
since there turned out to be just two things, we use just two names
for them, first of all "good" and "bad", and then "pleasant" and c
"painful". Let's agree on that, then, and say, "Though a man knows
that some things are bad, he does them all the same." Now if
someone asks "Why?" we shall say "Because he is overcome".
"Overcome by what?" he will ask. And we can no longer say "By 5
pleasure", for it has got another name, "good", instead of
"pleasure", and so when he says "Overcome by what?" we shall
answer, if you please, "Overcome by the good". Now if our
questioner happens to be an ill-mannered fellow, he'll burst out d
laughing and say "What an absurd thing to say! That somebody
should do bad things, though he knows they are bad, and doesn't
have to do them, because he is overcome by good things. Well," he'll
say, "are the good things in your view worth the bad, or not?" 5
Obviously we shall answer, "Not worth the bad. Otherwise the man
whom we describe as weaker than pleasures would not have acted
wrongly". "What is it then", he will perhaps ask, "which makes
good things not worth bad things or bad not worth good? Is it
anything apart from the one's being larger and the other smaller; or e
the one's being more and the other fewer?" We shan't be able to
suggest anything else. "It's clear, then", he will say, "that what you
mean by being overcome is taking fewer good things at the cost of
greater evils". So much for that. Now let's restore the names 5
"pleasant" and "painful" for these very same things, and say "A

man does—before we said bad things, but now let's say painful
356a things, in the knowledge that they are painful, because he is
overcome by pleasant things, which are, of course, not worth it."
And what other way is there for pleasure not to be worth pain,
except that one should be more and the other less? And that is a
5   matter of being larger and smaller, or more and fewer, or more and
less intense. For if someone said, "But, Socrates, there is a great
difference between immediate pleasure and pleasure and pain at a
later time," I should say, "Surely not in any other respect than
b   simply pleasure and pain; there isn't any other way they could
differ. Rather, like someone who is good at weighing things, add
up all the pleasant things and all the painful, and put the
element of nearness and distance in the scale as well, and then
say which are the more. For if you weigh pleasant things against
pleasant, you always have to take the larger and the more, and if
5   you weigh painful against painful, you always have to take the less
and the smaller. And if you weigh pleasant against painful, if the
painful are outweighed by the pleasant, no matter which are nearer
and which more distant, you have to do whatever brings the pleasant
c   about, and if the pleasant are outweighed by the painful, you have
to avoid doing it. Isn't that the way it is?" ' I should say." I'm sure
that they would not be able to disagree.'

He himself agreed.

5   ' "Now since that is so," I shall say, "answer me this. Do the
same magnitudes look bigger when you see them from near at hand,
and smaller at a distance, or not?" They will say that they do. "And
similarly with thicknesses and numbers? And the same sounds are
d   louder near at hand and softer at a distance?" "Yes." "So if our
well-being had depended on taking steps to get large quantities, and
avoid small ones, what should we have judged to be the thing that
saves our lives? The art of measurement or the power of appearances?
5   The latter, as we saw, confuses us and makes us often change our
minds about the same things and vacillate back and forth in our
actions and choices of large and small things; but measurement would
have made these appearances powerless, and given us peace of mind
e   by showing us the truth and letting us get a firm grasp of it, and so
would have saved our lives." In the face of this would they agree

that it is the art of measurement that would save us, or some other?'
  'Measurement,' he agreed.   5
  ' "And what if the preservation of our life had depended on a
correct choice of odd and even, whenever one had to make a correct
choice of a larger number or a smaller, either each kind against
itself or one against the other, whether near at hand or at a
distance? What would have preserved our life? Knowledge, surely. 357a
And surely some sort of measurement, since that is the art concerned
with larger and smaller quantities. And since we are concerned with
odd and even, it would surely have been none other than arithmetic."
Would our friends agree, or not?'
  Protagoras, too, thought that they would agree.   5
  ' "Well then, gentlemen; since we have seen that the preservation
of our life depends on a correct choice of pleasure and pain, be it
more or less, larger or smaller or further or nearer, doesn't it seem b
that the thing that saves our lives is some technique of measurement,
to determine which are more, or less, or equal to one another?"
"Yes, certainly." "And since it's measurement, then necessarily it's
an art which embodies exact knowledge." "Yes." "Now *which* art,   5
and *what* knowledge, we shall inquire later. But this suffices to show
that it is knowledge, and to provide the demonstration that
Protagoras and I are required to give in reply to your question.   c
You raised it, if you remember, when we were in agreement that
nothing is more powerful than knowledge, and that no matter where
it is it always conquers pleasure and everything else. You then said
that pleasure often conquers even the man who is in possession of   5
knowledge, and when we didn't agree, it was then that you asked us,
'Well, if this experience isn't being overcome by pleasure, what is it
then? What do you call it? Tell us.' If we had then straight away   d
said 'Error' you would have laughed at us; but now, if you laugh at us
you will be laughing at yourselves. For you have agreed that those
who go wrong in their choice of pleasures and pains—which is to   5
say, of good and bad things—go wrong from lack of knowledge, and
not merely of knowledge, but, as you have already further conceded,
of measurement. And you surely know yourselves that wrong action
done without knowledge is done in error. So this is what being   e
weaker than pleasure is, the greatest of all errors, for which

Protagoras here and Hippias and Prodicus claim to have the cure.
5   But because you think that it is something other than error you
neither consult these sophists yourselves nor send your sons to them
to have them taught this; you don't believe that it can be taught, so
you hang on to your money instead of giving it to them, and as a
result you do badly both as private individuals and in public affairs."

358a That's what we should have said in reply to the majority. And now,
on behalf of Protagoras and myself, I ask you, Hippias and Prodicus
(for you can answer jointly), whether you think that what I am
saying is true or false.'
5   They were all completely satisfied that it was true.
'You agree, then,' I said, 'that what is pleasant is good, and what
is painful bad. I leave aside our friend Prodicus' distinction of names;
for whether you call it "pleasant" or "delightful" or "enjoyable", or
b   however you care to apply such names, my dear Prodicus, give your
answer according to the sense of my question.'
Prodicus laughed, and indicated his agreement, and so did the rest.
'Well, gentlemen,' I said, 'what about this? Aren't all actions
5   praiseworthy which lead to a painless and pleasant life? And isn't
praiseworthy activity good and beneficial?'
They agreed.
'So if what is pleasant is good,' I said, 'no one who either knows
c   or believes that something else is better than what he is doing, and
is in his power to do, subsequently does the other, when he can do
what is better. Nor is giving in to oneself anything other than error,
nor controlling oneself anything other than wisdom.'
They all agreed.
'Well now. Is this what you mean by error, having false opinions
5   and being mistaken about matters of importance?'
They all agreed to that as well.
'Now surely,' I said, 'no one freely goes for bad things or things
d   he believes to be bad; it's not, it seems to me, in human nature to be
prepared to go for what you think to be bad in preference to what
is good. And when you are forced to choose one of two evils,
nobody will choose the greater when he can have the lesser. Isn't
that so?'

52

All of us agreed to all of that.

'Well, then,' I said, 'is there something that you call fear and   5
apprehension? And is it the same thing as I mean? (This is a
question for you, Prodicus.) I mean by this an expectation of evil,
whether you call it fear or apprehension.'

Protagoras and Hippias thought that that's what fear and apprehension are, while Prodicus thought it was apprehension, but not   e
fear.

'Well, it doesn't make any difference, Prodicus,' I said. 'The
point is this. If what has just been said is true, will any man be
willing to go for what he fears, when he can go for what he doesn't
fear? Or is that impossible, according to what we have agreed? For
if anyone fears something, it was agreed that he thinks it bad; and   5
no one who thinks anything bad goes for it or takes it of his own
free will.'

That too was agreed by everyone.   359a

'On that basis, then, Prodicus and Hippias,' I said, 'let Protagoras
defend the correctness of his first answer to me. I don't mean what
he said right at the beginning; for at that point he said that while   5
there are five parts of excellence none is like any other, but each
has its own separate power. I don't mean that, but what he said
later. For later he said that four of the five resemble one another
fairly closely, but one is altogether different from the others, namely   b
courage. His evidence was the following: "You will find, Socrates,
men who are totally irreligious, unjust, wanton, and ignorant, but
very courageous; that's how you will know that courage is very
different from the other parts of excellence." I was very surprised
at his answer at the time, and even more now that I have gone
into the question together with you. So I asked him if he called
courageous men daring. "Yes, and ready," he said. Do you recall   c
that answer, Protagoras?' I said.

'I do.'

'Well, now,' I said, 'tell us, what are courageous men ready for?
The same things as cowards?'

'No.'

'Different things, then.'

'Yes,' he said.

5   'Do cowards go for things which they are confident about, and
courageous men for fearful things?'

'So it's generally said, Socrates.'

d   'True,' I said, 'but that isn't what I'm asking. What do *you* say
the courageous are ready for? Fearful things, in the belief that they
are fearful, or not?'

'But it's just been shown by what you've said,' he replied, 'that
that's impossible.'

5   'That's true as well,' I said. 'So if that demonstration was correct,
no one goes for things that he regards as fearful, since giving in to
oneself turned out to be error.'

He agreed.

'But now everyone, coward and courageous alike, goes for what

*e   he is confident about, and in this way, at any rate, cowards and
courageous go for the same things.'

'But, Socrates,' he said, 'the things that cowards go for are
exactly the opposite of those that the courageous go for. For
instance, courageous men are willing to go to war, but cowards
aren't.'

5   'Is it praiseworthy to go,' I said, 'or disgraceful?'

'Praiseworthy.'

'So if it's praiseworthy, we agreed previously that it is good; for
we agreed that all praiseworthy actions are good.'

'That's true; I remain of that opinion.'

360a   'You are right,' I said. 'But which of them is it you say are not
willing to go to war, though that is something praiseworthy and
good?'

'Cowards,' he said.

'Well, now,' I said, 'if it's praiseworthy and good, is it also
pleasant?'

'Well, that's what was agreed,' he said.

'So cowards are unwilling, in full knowledge of the facts, to go

5   for what is more praiseworthy and better and pleasanter?'

'But if we agree to that,' he said, 'we shall contradict our
previously agreed conclusions.'

'And what about the courageous man? Does he not go for what
is more praiseworthy and better and pleasanter?'

'I have to agree,' he said.

'Now in general, when a courageous man is afraid, his fear is not   b *
something disgraceful, nor his confidence when he is confident?'

'That's right,' he said.

'And if not disgraceful, are they not praiseworthy?'

He agreed.

'And if praiseworthy, good as well?'

'Yes.'

'Now by contrast the fear and the confidence of cowards,
madmen, and the foolhardy are disgraceful?'   5

He agreed.

'And is their confidence disgraceful and bad for any other reason
than ignorance and error?'

'It's as you say,' he said.   c

'Well, now, do you call what makes a man a coward, cowardice or
courage?'

'I call it cowardice,' he said.

'And didn't it turn out that they are cowards as a result of their
error about what is to be feared?'

'Certainly,' he said.

'So it's in consequence of that error that they are cowards?'

He agreed.   5

'And you agree that what makes them cowards is cowardice?'

He assented.

'So cowardice proves to be error about what is to be feared and
what isn't?'

He nodded.

'But now,' I said, 'the opposite of cowardice is courage.'   d

'Yes.'

'Now wisdom about what is to be feared and what isn't is the
opposite of error about that.'

At that he nodded once again.

'And error about that is cowardice?'

With great reluctance he nodded at that.

'So wisdom about what is to be feared and what isn't is courage,   5
since it is the opposite of error about that?'

At this he wasn't even willing to nod agreement, but remained

silent. And I said, 'What's this, Protagoras? Won't you even answer
yes or no?'

'Carry on yourself,' he said.

e   'I've only one more question to ask you,' I said. 'Do you still
think, as you did at the beginning, that some men are altogether
ignorant, but very courageous?'

'I see that you insist, Socrates,' he said, 'that I must answer.
5   So I'll oblige you; I declare that from what we have agreed it seems
to me impossible.'

'Indeed I've no other object', I said, 'in asking all these questions
than to try to find out the truth about excellence, and especially
361a what it is itself. For I know that once that were apparent we should
become perfectly clear on the question about which each of us has
had so much to say, I maintaining that excellence can't be taught,
and you that it can. And it seems to me that the conclusion we have
5   just reached is jeering at us like an accuser. And if it could speak, it
would say "How absurd you are, both of you. You, Socrates, began
b   by saying that excellence can't be taught, and now you are insisting
on the opposite, trying to show that all things are knowledge,
justice, soundness of mind, even courage, from which it would
follow that excellence most certainly could be taught. For if
excellence were anything other than knowledge, as Protagoras was
5   trying to make out, it would obviously not be teachable. But now,
if it turns out to consist wholly in knowledge, as you insist, Socrates,
it will be astonishing if it can't be taught. Protagoras, on the other
hand, first assumed that it can be taught, but now seems to be taking
c   the opposite view and insisting that it turns out to be practically
anything rather than knowledge; and so it most certainly couldn't
be taught." For my part, Protagoras, when I see all this in such
terrible confusion, I am desperately anxious to have it all cleared up,
5   and I should like to follow up our discussion by considering the
nature of excellence, and then returning to the question of whether
or not it can be taught. I shouldn't like that Epimetheus (After-
d   thought) of yours to fool us with his tricks in our discussion, the
way he neglected us in distributing his gifts, as you said. I preferred
Prometheus (Forethought) to Epimetheus in the story; it's because
5   I have forethought for my life as a whole that I go into all these

questions. And as I said at the beginning, if you were willing I should be most happy to examine them with you.'

'For my part, Socrates,' said Protagoras, 'I applaud your enthusiasm and the way you pursue your arguments. I don't think I'm an inferior person in any respect, but in particular I'm the last   e man to bear a grudge; for I've said to many people that of all those I've met I like you far the best, especially of those of your age. And I declare that I should not be surprised if you became famous for your wisdom. As to these questions, we shall pursue them some   5 other time, whenever you wish; but now it's time to turn to something else.'

'Indeed that's what we should do,' I said, 'if you prefer. In fact, **362a** quite a while ago it was time for me to go where I said, but I stayed to oblige our friend Callias.'

That was the end of the conversation, and we left.   *

ABBREVIATIONS

I. *Ancient Authors*

Ar.	Aristotle
+*EN*	*Nicomachean Ethics*
Met.	*Metaphysics*
Phys.	*Physics*
+*Pol.*	*Politics*
Rhet.	*Rhetoric*
Top.	*Topics*
Arist.	Aristophanes
+*Lys.*	*Lysistrata*
+*Thesm.*	*Thesmophoriazusae*
D.L.	Diogenes Laertius
Diod.	Diodorus Siculus
+Hdt.	Herodotus
	Homer
+*Il.*	*Iliad*
+*Od.*	*Odyssey*
Pind.	Pindar
+*Ol.*	*Olympian Odes*
+*Pyth.*	*Pythian Odes*
	Plato
Alc. I & II	*Alcibiades I & II*
+*Apol.*	*Apology*
+*Charm.*	*Charmides*
Clit.	*Clitophon*
Crat.	*Cratylus*
+*Crit.*	*Critias*
+*Euth.*	*Euthyphro*
+*Euthyd.*	*Euthydemus*
+*Gorg.*	*Gorgias*
+*Hipp. Maj.*	*Greater Hippias*

+*Hipp. Min.*	*Lesser Hippias*
+*Lach.*	*Laches*
+*Ph.*	*Phaedo*
+*Phaedr.*	*Phaedrus*
+*Phil.*	*Philebus*
Pol.	*Politicus* (*Statesman*)
+*Prot.*	*Protagoras*
+*Rep.*	*Republic*
Soph.	*Sophist*
+*Symp.*	*Symposium*
+*Theaet.*	*Theaetetus*
+*Tim.*	*Timaeus*
+*Ep.*	*Letters*
Plut.	Plutarch
+*Alc.*	*Life of Alcibiades*
Lyc.	*Life of Lycurgus*
+Th.	Thucydides
Xen.	Xenophon
Lac. Pol.	*Spartan Constitution*
+*Mem.*	*Memorabilia* (*Memoirs*) *of Socrates*
+*Symp.*	*Symposium*

All the above are available with English translations in the Loeb Classical Library series, and those marked + in Penguin Classics (at time of going to press). Translations of Plato are also available in Jowett[4] and in Hamilton and Cairns eds. (see Bibliography under 'Translations'), and of Aristotle in Jonathan Barnes ed., *The Complete Works of Aristotle*, Princeton, NJ, 1984. For Theognis see J. M. Edmonds, *Elegy and Iambus* vol. I (Loeb), London and New York, 1931.

II. *Modern Works*

AGP	*Archiv für Geschichte der Philosophie*
AP	*Ancient Philosophy*
BCH	*Bulletin de Correspondance Hellénique*
BICS	*Bulletin of the Institute of Classical Studies, London University*

ABBREVIATIONS

CJPhil	*Canadian Journal of Philosophy*
CQ	*Classical Quarterly*
CR	*Classical Review*
CW	*Classical World*
DK	H. Diels and W. Kranz, *Die Fragmente der Vorsokratiker*, 7th and subsequent eds., Berlin, 1954–
DUJ	*Durham University Journal*
EA	E. N. Lee, A. P. D. Mourelatos, and R. M. Rorty eds., *Exegesis and Argument, Studies in Greek Philosophy Presented to Gregory Vlastos* (*Phronesis* Suppl. Vol. I), Assen, 1973
JHP	*Journal of the History of Philosophy*
JHS	*Journal of Hellenic Studies*
JPhil	*Journal of Philosophy*
LG	J. M. Edmonds, *Lyra Graeca* (Loeb), London and Cambridge, Mass., 1928
LSJ	Liddell and Scott, *Greek-English Lexicon*, 9th edn., revised Jones and McKenzie, Oxford, 1940
OCD²	*The Oxford Classical Dictionary*, 2nd edn., Oxford, 1970
OCT	Oxford Classical Text
OSAP	*Oxford Studies in Ancient Philosophy*
PAS	*Proceedings of the Aristotelian Society*
PBA	*Proceedings of the British Academy*
Phron	*Phronesis*
PMG	D. Page, *Poetae Melici Graeci*, Oxford, 1962
PR	*Philosophical Review*
PS	Gregory Vlastos, *Platonic Studies*, 2nd ed., Princeton, 1981
RE	*Realencyclopädie der classischen Altertumswissenschaft*, Stuttgart, 1894–
RM	*Review of Metaphysics*
SM	G. B. Kerferd, *The Sophistic Movement*, Cambridge, 1981.
TAPA	*Transactions of the American Philological Association*
YCS	*Yale Classical Studies* (cited by vol. number)

BIOGRAPHICAL NOTES ON THE MAIN CHARACTERS OF THE *PROTAGORAS*

SOCRATES 470/69–399 B.C. Born in Athens, where he spent all his life, apart from periods of military service, engaged in the informal discussion of philosophical (mainly ethical) topics. Though he never engaged in formal teaching, he gathered round himself a circle of mainly younger men, including Plato, many of whom were opposed to the extreme form of democracy current in Athens. He was put to death on vague charges of impiety and corruption of youth, which were probably politically inspired. His philosophical views and methods were a major influence on Plato, but the ascription of any specific doctrine to Socrates is a matter of much controversy. He wrote nothing himself, but in the fourth century many accounts of his personality and teaching were written, mostly friendly, but some hostile, with different degrees of approximation to historical truth. The most substantial element of this literature to survive is the dialogues of Plato; Socrates also figures in a number of works by Xenophon. The *Clouds* of Aristophanes, first produced in 423, gives a contemporary caricature.

PROTAGORAS c.490–420. From Abdera, on the north coast of the Aegean. The first professional sophist, i.e. itinerant professor of higher education. He had a long and successful career, travelling widely throughout the Greek world and making very large sums of money. He aimed to teach upper-class youths how to attain personal and political success, putting considerable emphasis on skill in speech and argument, in which he developed a systematic method of teaching. He is said to have written a number of works in this area, and on more general ethical and philosophical topics. A few quotations are preserved, expressing agnosticism on the existence of the gods and extreme subjectivism, according to which every belief is true for the person who holds it. The latter position is criticized at length by Plato in the *Theaetetus.*

HIPPIAS   From Elis in the north-west Peloponnese. His dates are uncertain, but Plato makes him describe himself in the *Greater Hippias* (282e) as considerably younger than Protagoras, while *Apol.* 19e indicates that he was still alive in 399. He too made a considerable reputation and fortune, and frequently represented his city on diplomatic missions. He was a polymath, who wrote on and taught subjects including mathematics, science, history, rhetoric, literature, ethics, and a range of practical crafts. Nothing of his work survives. He appears in two Platonic dialogues, both entitled *Hippias*; the authenticity of one, the *Greater* (i.e. *Longer*) *Hippias*, is questioned by some scholars.

PRODICUS   From Ceos, an island off the southern tip of Attica. Dates uncertain, but still alive in 399 (*Apol.* 19e). Like Hippias, he used the opportunities provided by diplomatic missions to build up an international clientele. He was primarily a teacher of rhetoric, whose speciality was the distinction of near-synonyms; many examples are given in the *Protagoras* and elsewhere. In a number of places Plato makes Socrates say, sometimes apparently ironically, sometimes not, that he is indebted to this technique. Prodicus' other interests included ethics, theology, and science. All that survives of his work is a paraphrase by Xenophon (*Mem.* II.i.21–34) of his fable of the choice of Heracles between Virtue and Pleasure.

ALCIBIADES   c.450–404. Athenian. He rose to political prominence at an early age, and was one of the leaders of the policy of ambitious imperialism which led to the disastrous Sicilian expedition of 415, of which he was appointed one of the commanders. Implicated in an act of sacrilege committed shortly before the expedition sailed, he fled to Sparta to escape trial, and took an active part in the war against Athens. Subsequently reinstated at Athens he gained some military successes, but, once more attracting popular suspicion, went into exile a second time and was murdered with the connivance of the Athenian government. On his relations with Socrates see pp.64–5 below. The Platonic corpus contains two dialogues entitled *Alcibiades*, of doubtful authenticity. He plays a prominent part in the *Symposium*.

CALLIAS c.455–c.370. Member of a distinguished Athenian family, he was chiefly known for his lavish expenditure, including large sums spent on sophists, which dissipated the family fortune. His sister married Alcibiades subsequently to the dramatic date of the *Protagoras.*

CRITIAS c.460–403. Athenian, first cousin of Plato's mother. An associate of Alcibiades, he was opposed to the Athenian democracy, and was one of the most extreme among the Thirty Tyrants, the oppressive dictatorship which seized power in Athens from 404 to 403. He was killed in the fighting which accompanied the overthrow of the tyranny. He was a poet, dramatist, and prose writer, of whose works some fragments survive (DK 88). He has a prominent part in the *Charmides.*

For information on others appearing or mentioned in the dialogue, see Commentary.

Full biographical information is given for all the characters of the dialogue in *RE*, and for Socrates and the sophists in Guthrie III, chs. 11 and 13. Briefer information is available for the main characters in *OCD*[2] and for the sophists in Kerferd *SM* ch. 5 and in Rankin ch. 2. The ancient evidence for the sophists is collected in DK II, sections 80 (Protagoras), 84 (Prodicus), and 86 (Hippias); an English translation is given in Sprague ed. A more recent collection of the evidence for Protagoras is that by Capizzi.

COMMENTARY

309a1–310a7 *Introductory conversation between Socrates and an unnamed friend.*

The dramatic date of the dialogue is shortly before the outbreak of the First Peloponnesian War, probably about 433; see Morrison *CQ* 41. Socrates is about 37, Alcibiades about 17.

309a2 Alcibiades: it is clear that the charge of 'corrupting the young men', which was one of the accusations on which Socrates was put to death (Xen. *Mem.* I.i.1, D.L. II.40), was based at least partly on his supposed responsibility for the subsequent political careers of some of his young associates, notably Alcibiades and Critias (see Biographical Notes). Plato makes Socrates allude to this in the *Apology* (33a–b) without mentioning names, since a recent amnesty had made it impossible for his accusers to bring a direct charge. Xenophon, writing some years later, refers directly (*Mem.* I.ii.12–16) to the accusation (probably made explicitly by the fourth-century pamphleteer Polycrates, who wrote an *Accusation of Socrates* containing charges which could not be made openly at the trial) that 'Critias and Alcibiades, after having been associates of Socrates, inflicted a great number of evils on the state'. *Rep.* VI, 494b–495b contains a clear allusion to the career of Alcibiades and his relations with Socrates. Cf. Guthrie III, pp.345, 378–83.

Socrates is regularly represented by Plato as being physically and emotionally attracted to young men of fine appearance and intelligence. The most striking and explicit description of his feelings is given (in the first person) at *Charmides* 155c–e, but other references abound, e.g. *Symp.* 216d, *Alc. I* 103a–104d, *Gorg.* 481d. There is no reason to doubt Plato's explicit statements, nor his equally explicit testimony that Socrates gave his feelings no physical expression, but rather sought to promote the moral and intellectual development of the young men who attracted him; cf. especially Alcibiades' account of his relations with Socrates at *Symp.* 215a–219d. This is consistent with the theory of love which Socrates puts into the mouth of the wise woman Diotima at *Symp.* 201d–212a. The fundamental desire of the lover is for immortality, in its lower form by the begetting of children, in its higher by the production of the things of the spirit, especially in artistic creation and in education. Hence a lover who meets someone physically and spiritually attractive will satisfy himself by leading the other to a state

64

of moral and intellectual excellence (209a–c). Socrates' remark that his interest in the discussion with Protagoras made him forget Alcibiades, as 'what is wisest is always finer', recalls Diotima's account (210a–212a) of 'erotic education'; the lover proceeds from love of the physical beauty of a single individual via the love of physical beauty in general to beauty of soul (moral and intellectual), thence to more abstract forms (e.g. the beauty of the sciences), finally reaching the crowning vision of beauty itself. Socrates seems here to exemplify the third stage, love of beauty of soul. For further discussions of Socrates' attitude to sex and love see Guthrie III. pp.390–8, Dover, *Greek Homosexuality*, pp.153–70.

309a3 'still a fine-looking man, but a man all the same'. Homosexual attractiveness was considered to fade with maturity; cf. *Alc. I* 131d, Dover op. cit., pp.85–7. Hence Alcibiades, who is now a man, is (from the erotic point of view) 'past his best', though still handsome.

309b1 The reference is to *Il.* XXIV. 348 and *Od.* X. 279.

310a8–314c2 *Socrates narrates how a young friend, Hippocrates, called on him early in the morning to ask for an introduction to Protagoras. He questions Hippocrates on what he hopes to learn from Protagoras and finds that he has no clear idea of what the sophist has to teach. The only suggestion Hippocrates makes, that Protagoras teaches one how to be an effective speaker, does not, Socrates argues, differentiate sophists from other experts, e.g. musicians. Socrates warns Hippocrates of the dangers of submitting to education without an adequate conception of its content.*

310a9 Hippocrates is probably a historical person, as are most of the characters in Plato's dialogues, but nothing is known about him beyond what is said in this dialogue.

311b6 Hippocrates of Cos, a contemporary of Socrates, was the founder of the most influential school of Greek medicine. A large number of works ascribed to the school survives, but none can be ascribed with any confidence to Hippocrates himself.

311c3 Polycleitus and Pheidias were the two most celebrated sculptors of the fifth century.
Socrates shows, by contrasting the present case with two hypothetical cases of seeking tuition from experts, that what Hippocrates

expects from Protagoras is not vocational instruction. The contrast requires that the payment to the doctor be payment for medical tuition, not medical treatment, and similarly in the case of the sculptor.

311e4 'a sophist'. The Greek *sophistēs* lacks the specific pejorative implication (of dishonesty in argument) which attaches to its English derivative. From its original use as equivalent to *sophos* 'expert' or, more specifically 'sage', it had by this period acquired the technical sense 'itinerant purveyor of higher education'. See Guthrie III, pp.27–36, with refs. p.27, n.1, and Kerferd *SM* ch.4.

312a2–7 Hippocrates' embarrassment at the thought of becoming a sophist himself reflects the ambivalent attitude of contemporary opinion towards the profession. On the one hand they became extremely wealthy and were received in the houses of the great. On the other, not merely were they gravely suspect to conservative opinion as a potential source of corruption for the young (*Prot.* 316c–d, *Meno* 91c, Arist. *Clouds passim*, see Dover's introduction, pp.xxxii–lxiv), but even such an exponent of 'advanced' ideas as Callicles, himself an associate of the rhetorician Gorgias, who had much in common with the sophists, dismisses them as 'worthless fellows' (*Gorg.* 520a). Hippocrates' attitude suggests that even the devotees of sophists may have regarded the profession, while all right for foreigners, as not quite respectable for a citizen of good family; most of the well-known sophists were non-Athenian.

312b1 The reading-master taught not only reading and writing, but also gave instruction in the works of the poets, laying much emphasis on their ethical content (cf. 325e–326a). This, together with music and physical training, was the staple of elementary education, the only formal education available until the advent of the sophists. For Plato's view of its inadequacies, see especially *Rep.* II, 376e–III, 412b.

312b8 In view of its theological connotations, 'soul' has a narrower sense than the Greek *psuchē*, which signifies the self in its non-bodily aspects, embracing intellect, will, desires and emotions. Here the most natural translation would be 'entrust yourself', but since at 313a we have the specific contrast between bodily and non-bodily aspects of the self, for which 'body' and 'soul' are the best pair of contrasting English terms, 'soul' is used for *psuchē* here too.

312c5 'as the name implies'. Hippocrates derives the noun *sophistēs* (wrongly) from *sophos* = 'wise, learned' + the root of the verb 'to know', *epistasthai.* It is in fact derived, via the regular 'agent' termination, from the verb *sophizesthai,* 'to be wise'.

312d5–e6 Socrates' attempted demonstration of the inadequacy of the account of the sophist's expertise as skill in oratorical training is itself inadequate. He relies on a single example, that of the music teacher, to establish the implied general proposition that, whenever *A* makes *B* an effective speaker, he does so by imparting to *B* some specialized knowledge which is to be the subject-matter of *B*'s speeches. The establishment of a general conclusion on the basis of two or three key instances is a characteristic feature of Socrates' argumentation in Plato's dialogues, occurring many times in this dialogue (e.g. 332c, 349e–350a) and elsewhere; Aristotle indicates (*Met.* M4, 1978b27–9) that this kind of argument was characteristic of the historical Socrates. While no universal conclusion about an open class follows logically from any enumeration of particular propositions about members of that class, nevertheless the method has heuristic value, in that some well-chosen instances can lead one to see that some generalization is true, whether necessarily or contingently, of the class as a whole. The chief danger of the method is that the instances chosen may be atypical. That is so in this case. Socrates ignores the possibility that *A* may make *B* an effective speaker, not by imparting some specialized knowledge to speak about, but by training him in techniques of effective presentation of any subject-matter. This, the standard conception of rhetorical training, is the account of his practice given by Gorgias in the dialogue named after him (456a–457c). Instruction in techniques of rhetoric and argument was in fact an important part of Protagoras' curriculum, though not the whole of it (see Biographical Note and notes on 318e5–319a7, pp.71–2 below). On Socratic inductive arguments, see Robinson, ch. 4.

312d5 'master of'. *Epistatēs,* from the verb *ephistasthai,* 'to stand, be set over', means 'controller, overseer, etc.' By punning on the resemblance to the verb *epistasthai,* 'to know', Socrates gives it the sense 'one who is in control by virtue of his knowledge'.

*

312e3–4 'about what he knows'. The reading translated here is that of the manuscripts. The OCT adopts an emendation by Stahl, 'about what he teaches you' (see Additional Note on 312e1). Since either reading gives perfectly good sense, there seems no good reason to depart from the MSS.

313b4—5 'Entrust yourself' is clearly synonymous with 'entrust your soul' at 312b8 and 313b1—2 (cf. c2—3).

313c4—7 The definition of a sophist as one or another of different kinds of salesman of learning is one of several alternative definitions given in the *Sophist*; see 223c—224e and 231d.

314a4 'another container': sc. than that in which the goods are set out for sale. Adam and Adam take it in the sense 'other than our own bodies' (p.90), but while that fits b1 better than the interpretation given here (since learning is not set out for sale in any sort of container, and hence *'another* container' in b1 has no point), it can hardly be understood here; 'another container' presupposes a reference to some actual container, which can be none other than that in which the goods are offered. The phrase is presumably repeated in b1 in the sense 'you can't do that with learning', without strict attention to logical detail.

314c3—317e2 *Arrival of Socrates and Hippocrates at the house of Callias; description of the scene. Introductory conversation with Protagoras.*

314e5—315a1 Callias' mother was formerly married to the famous statesman Pericles, by whom she had the two sons named here. Both, like their father, died in the great epidemic which struck Athens shortly after the beginning of the Peloponnesian War. On the dissolution of that marriage she married Callias' father Hipponicus. Plutarch, the only source on this point, reversed the order of the two marriages, as is shown by information on the relative ages of her children. See Davies pp.262—3.

315a1 Charmides: Plato's maternal uncle. He was associated with his cousin Critias in the oligarchic revolution of 404, and was killed in the fighting when it was overthrown. He is the principal character in the dialogue which bears his name.

315a3 Philippides: member of a distinguished Athenian family.
Antimoerus: known only from this passage. Mende, like Abdera, was a subject city of the Athenian empire on the N. Aegean coast.

* **315b9** *Od.* XI. 601.

315c2 Eryximachus: a doctor. He appears with his friend Phaedrus in the *Symposium*, where he discusses love in terms of medical theory. He was implicated in the sacrilege of 415 (see Biographical Note on Alcibiades).

315c3 Phaedrus: appears in the *Phaedrus* and *Symposium* as an amateur of oratory, with a particular interest in the theme of love. He too was exiled as having been implicated in the events of 415 (Davies p.201). Myrrinus was a district of Athens (cf. 'Cerameis' d7).

Andron: mentioned at *Gorg.* 487c as a friend of Callicles. He was a member of the oligarchic government of the Four Hundred, who held power briefly in 411. See Dodds ad loc., p.282.

315c7 'giving a detailed decision': the use of the verb *diakrinein*, used of legal judgements, and the description of the scene indicate that Hippias is seen as handing down authoritative pronouncements like a judge in court.

315c8 *Od* XI. 582.

315d7 Pausanias: appears in the *Symposium*. His relationship with Agathon is mentioned by Xenophon (*Symp.* viii. 32). Nothing else is known about him.

315e2 Agathon: at this time a boy of about 15, he became a prominent tragedian. The dinner-party in the *Symposium* is held at his house to celebrate his first victory in the dramatic competitions in 416. Some fragments of his plays survive. Aristophanes makes fun of him in *The Thesmophoriazusae*, produced in 411.

315e4 Adeimantus son of Cepis: otherwise unknown.

Adeimantus son of Leucolophides: another prominent Athenian implicated in the sacrilege of 415. He was subsequently a commander (sometimes together with Alcibiades) in the later campaigns of the war, and was accused of treachery after the final defeat of Athens in 404.

316d5 'for fear of giving offence': alternatively 'for fear of all that unpleasantness'. The Greek may refer either to feelings (of hostility etc.) aroused by the sophist in others or to the consequent unpleasant feelings experienced by him.

316d9 Iccus: a noted athlete and trainer, from Taras in south Italy (mod. Taranto). Cf. *Laws* VIII, 839e–840a.

316e1 Herodicus: a doctor and trainer, from Selymbria, a Megarian colony near Byzantium. On the severity of his regime see *Rep.* III, 406a–b; cf. *Phaedr.* 227d.

316e2–3 Agathocles and Pythocleides: prominent musicians and music teachers. Agathocles is mentioned at *Lach.* 180d, Pythocleides at *Alc. I* 118c.

317b3–c2 On Protagoras' long career and good reputation cf. *Meno* 91e, from which we learn that his career spanned forty years and that his good reputation lasted up to and well beyond his death. This is convincing proof of the falsity of the later tradition (DK 80 A 1–4 and 12) according to which he was forced to flee from Athens on a charge of impiety and was lost at sea in doing so. See Dover *Talanta* 76.

317c3 This, together with the *Meno* passage just mentioned, which tells us that Protagoras died about the age of 70, is the best evidence for his dates. He must have been twenty to thirty years older than Socrates, hence born some time between 500 and 490, and must therefore have died some time between 430 and 420. Since he is referred to as still alive in a comedy by Eupolis, *The Flatterers*, produced in 422/1 (DK 80 A 1 and 11), his dates must be approximately 490–420. He had therefore been practising as a sophist for close on thirty years and possibly more by the time of the dramatic date of the *Protagoras*.

317c4–5 'to talk about these things in the presence of all who are here': alternatively 'to talk about all these things in the presence of those who are here'.

317e3–320c1 *Socrates asks Protagoras what Hippocrates will learn from him. Protagoras replies that he will teach him how to attain success in public and private life. Socrates interprets this as a claim to be able to teach men how to be good citizens, an account of his activity which is accepted by Protagoras. Socrates then gives two reasons for thinking it impossible to teach that: (a) on matters of policy, as opposed to technical questions, the Athenians do not regard anyone as an expert; (b) men who are acknowledged to be outstandingly good citizens have failed to make their sons equally good.*

318b7 Zeuxis or Zeuxippus was one of the best-known painters of the period.

318c5   Orthagoras was a celebrated virtuoso of the *aulos*, a reed instrument resembling the modern oboe or clarinet. The conventional mistranslation 'flute' is adopted here, as sanctioned by time-honoured usage.

                                                       *

318e5–319a2   Protagoras claims to teach how to be successful in managing one's private affairs and in contributing by word and action to the affairs of the city. That this kind of instruction was what young men wanted, and the sophists claimed to provide, is also shown by *Meno* 91a–b; cf. *Gorg.* 520e, Xen. *Mem.* I.ii.15 and 64. While Hippocrates had not explicitly said that that was what he wanted to learn, Socrates had said so on his behalf at 316b8–c4. From this point nothing further is said about success in one's private affairs.

    Success in contributing to the affairs of the city might be measured in terms of success in achieving such purely personal goals as office or wealth, or in terms of success in so directing affairs that they tend to the advantage of the city. To be successful in the first sense is (on a cynical view) to be a good politician, in the second to be a good statesman. The distinction is likely to be overlooked, particularly in a democratic state where it is taken for granted that those who enjoy the highest reputation are those who have conferred the greatest benefits on the city. That that assumption is false was a central theme of Plato's criticism of Athenian democracy (e.g. *Gorg.* 515b–519b).

319a3–7   'to make men into good citizens'. The Greek might also be rendered as 'to make citizens into good men', or 'to turn out good citizens'. Nothing turns on the choice of rendering: see n. on 319e2, pp74–5 below.

    We find it startling that Socrates should equate teaching the art of how to run a city with making men into good citizens, and that Protagoras should accept this equation. Modern thought makes a clear distinction between the good politician and the good statesman on the one hand, who excel in the performance of (different) specific tasks, and the good citizen on the other. The goodness of the latter consists not in excellence in any specific task, but in his adequate fulfilment of various general obligations, e.g. to obey the laws, pay taxes, undertake military service. These obligations do indeed, on a normal view, include the obligation to take some part in political life, at the very least by voting at elections, but it is not normally considered part of the obligations of a citizen *qua* citizen to

participate directly in central government. This distinction was less clear-cut in an extreme democracy such as fifth-century Athens, where every adult male citizen was a member of the supreme deliberative assembly and might find himself obliged by lot to
* perform a variety of executive functions. Direct participation in government was thus one of the functions of the citizen as such; hence outstanding statesmen can naturally be described as 'wisest and best citizens' (319e1–2). But even when allowance has been made for the difference between an ancient democratic city-state and a modern democracy, the simple identification of the notions of good statesman and good citizen embodies a serious confusion. The formulation and execution of policy is at best *one* of the functions of a citizen in a participatory democracy, a function which requires special gifts of intellect such as judgement and breadth of vision, and of character such as courage and determination, together with attributes such as skill in negotiation and the ability to influence others. Those other functions of the citizen which may be summed up as the acceptance of general obligations require less by way of intellectual capacity; rather the citizen must possess such moral qualities as loyalty, public-spiritedness, and a sense of fairness. Hence being a good statesman is at best *a* necessary condition of being a good citizen, another necessary condition being the possession of the moral qualities just mentioned. Protagoras' initial claim is that he can teach one how to satisfy the first necessary condition; but in his defence of his claim against Socrates' objections he appears to shift his ground to the position that being a good citizen consists wholly in the satisfaction of the second condition, which is the aim of his teaching (see below, pp.81–3: for a fuller discussion see Adkins *JHS* 73).

319b3–d7   Socrates' first objection runs as follows (supplied steps in parentheses):

b3–4   1. The Athenians are wise.
          2. (Hence, their judgement is to be accepted as true.)
b5–c7   3. On any subject which the Athenians think can be taught, they allow only experts to speak.
c7–d6   4. On questions of running the city, they allow any citizen to speak.
d6–7   5. Hence, from 3 and 4, the Athenians consider that skill in running the city cannot be taught.
          6. (Hence, by 2 and 5, skill in running the city cannot be taught.)
Comments:
    (i) The argument depends on the understood proposition 2,

derived from 1. This proposition is neither explicitly stated by Socrates nor challenged by Protagoras.

(ii) The step from 4 to 5 requires the additional assumption 4´:
The Athenians consider that it is not the case that all citizens are experts on questions of running the city. Protagoras' defence consists in challenging this assumption (322a–323c). On the difficulties of that defence see below pp.82–3.

(iii) A more plausible defence would be to challenge the truth of either 2 or 3 by making a distinction between different skills. The difference between technical questions as conceived by Socrates, e.g. how best to build a temple, and policy questions is that in the former some goal is assumed and what is in question is the best way to achieve it. Here technical experts are alone qualified to speak, because they alone know the facts on which a decision depends. In policy questions, on the other hand, what is in dispute is the question of which goal is to be adopted, or perhaps more frequently which of a number of agreed goals are to be given higher priority. Here the ultimate question is not one of fact, but of preference, and hence there are no experts. (In fact Socrates greatly oversimplifies the dichotomy, since even questions of the former kind generally include non-technical questions calling for decision rather than a factual answer, e.g. which of a number of proposed temples is the more beautiful, or whether it is better to spend more on an admittedly more beautiful temple than to build a cheaper one and use the balance for some other desirable purpose. On these questions experts have no special status.) Yet even though running the city involves making non-factual decisions, it does not follow that one cannot be taught how to do it. One can, for instance be trained in decision-making, e.g. by working through a number of practice situations and being made aware of the kinds of factor that have to be taken into account and the kind of mistakes that can be made; one can also be taught subsidiary skills such as oratory and diplomacy. Someone who had undergone that kind of training might reasonably claim to speak on matters of policy with a certain degree of authority, which would increase with wider experience of actual affairs. But since the element of preference is especially prominent in questions of policy it is reasonable that even those who lack this training should be listened to, just as it is reasonable that a layman should be heard on the aesthetic, social, and other non-technical aspects of a public works programme.

Someone who adopted this defence might wish to credit the Athenians with this distinction, or alternatively not to do so. If he did, he would argue that 3 is false. If he did not, he would argue that 2 is false, since, while indeed the Athenians consider that skill in running the city cannot be taught, in fact it can be. He would explain the Athenians' mistaken belief as a consequence of their failure to make the distinction just outlined. Of these two approaches, the former is the more convincing, since the only evidence which Socrates adduces in support of 3 consists of citing two cases of technical questions (cf. remarks on inductive arguments p.67 above). This provides some ground for the belief that in his presentation of the argument Socrates assumes that the only subjects which 'can be learned and taught' are technical subjects.

319d7–320b3 A fuller version of this argument occurs at *Meno* 93a–94d: cf. *Alc. 1* 118c–119b, *Lach.* 179a–d.

319e2 'Excellence' is used here and generally (see end of this note) to render the Greek *aretē*. This word functions as the abstract noun from the adjective 'good'; anything which is a good *x*, or (generally equivalently) which does well the activity which is characteristic of *x*'s *ipso facto* possesses the *aretē* of or appropriate to *x*'s. Thus Plato talks of the *aretē* of the eyes and ears, i.e. good sight and hearing (*Rep.* I, 353b), and says that a horse which has been injured or otherwise damaged is made worse 'with respect to the *aretē* of horses' (ibid. 335b), i.e. a damaged horse is not such a good horse as the same horse undamaged. Frequently an *x* has to possess not just one but a number of desirable attributes in order to be a good *x*; then each of those attributes can be called *an aretē* (of the sort appropriate to *x*'s) individually, and possession of all those attributes conjointly (i.e. the state of being a good *x*) is *the aretē* appropriate to *x*'s. For specific *aretai* see *Meno* 73d–74a, and for 'total' *aretē* see *Prot.* 324e–325a. Human *aretē* falls within this general schema; a man may achieve excellence in some specific role, e.g. as a boxer, or he may possess qualities in virtue of which he is a good or admirable *man*. In the former case his *aretē* is that of a boxer (e.g. Pind. *Ol.* vii. 89), in the latter it is human *aretē*. Greek conceptions of what made a man an excellent or admirable man differed widely at different periods: thus in Homeric society *aretē* consisted primarily of prowess in warfare and personal splendour, while the standard fifth-century conception placed much more emphasis on social attributes such as fair dealing and self-restraint (see Adkins, *Merit and Responsibility*, esp. chs. 3–4), at the same time assigning a central place to intellectual attainments (e.g. *Prot.* 329e–330a, Ar. *EN* VI). The conventional rendering 'virtue', with its specifically moral connotations, is thus highly misleading; while fifth-century Greeks did indeed count some moral virtues as prominent among the qualities that make a man a good man, they recognized much else besides. The excellence which is immediately in question is that of a citizen, of which the paradigm example is a statesman such as Pericles, who was successful both in attaining personal power and reputation and in enlarging the power and reputation of the city. The question of whether excellence can be taught, as originally introduced by Socrates in this passage, is the question whether it is possible to teach someone how to attain that sort of success. As was remarked above (pp.71–2), Protagoras shifts the discussion to the question of whether it is possible to teach someone to be a good citizen in the sense of a fair-minded and law-abiding citizen. No distinction is drawn between being a good citizen in that sense and being a good man; hence we find Protagoras using the expressions 'excellence of a citizen' (324a1) and 'excellence of a man' (325a2) as interchangeable. The rest of the dialogue is devoted to human excellence, i.e. what makes a man a good man, rather than to the specific question of what makes a man a good citizen. Similarly *Meno* 93a–94d makes no distinction between being a good man and being a good citizen (cf. *Apol.* 20b). That distinction naturally arises when one is concerned with the individual in a purely private capacity, e.g. in intimate personal relationships, or in situations where the claims of citizenship might be transcended, e.g. by a duty to humanity in general. Neither type of situation is considered in the main discussion, though Hippias' remarks on the artificiality of political distinctions (337c–d) point in the direction of the latter.

Aretē is generally translated as 'excellence', but sometimes, where the context demands it, as 'skill' (e.g. 323a7–8), and is sometimes rendered by a paraphrase (e.g. 322e2–323a1). All occasions where the rendering is other than 'excellence' are mentioned in the notes.

320a4   Cleinias: at *Alc. I* 118e Alcibiades bluntly describes his younger brother as a madman. Nothing is known of him apart from these two passages.

320a7   Ariphron: brother of Pericles, with whom he was joint guardian of Alcibiades and Cleinias (Plut. *Alc.* i. 1).

320b4–5   'I don't think that excellence can be taught'. It was agreed at 319a that Protagoras claimed to teach the art of running a city (*politikē technē*), i.e. how to become a good citizen. Here Socrates interprets him as claiming to teach excellence ([*politikē*] *aretē*; the specification is implicit). This illustrates the conceptual link between an art or craft (*technē*) and excellence (*aretē*); someone possesses a craft in the fullest sense only when he is good at it, i.e. possesses the corresponding skill or excellence, and hence the claim to teach an art is the claim to teach the appropriate *aretē*. Of course, not all *aretai* are acquired skills; e.g. good sight is not a skill possessed by the eyes. The question at issue is whether being a good citizen (not distinguished from being a good man) is an acquired skill; cf. *Meno* 70a.

320c2–7 *Protagoras asks whether he should reply to Socrates' objections by means of a story or of an argument. When the choice is left to him he opts to tell a story.*

320c2–4 A story (*muthos*) can be anything from a complete fiction to a parable which conveys a truth by means of a narrative which is not to be taken as literally true. The latter sort of story is frequently used by Plato in contexts where literal truth and rigour is not possible, as in theological contexts (e.g. *Tim.* 29c–d). By contrast, a factual statement or argument (the word *logos* has both senses) contains nothing but the literal truth; for the contrast see e.g. *Tim.* 26a, *Gorg.* 523a. In representing Protagoras as choosing between story and factual exposition purely on considerations of entertainment value rather than on grounds of appropriateness to the subject, Plato perhaps intends to suggest that the sophist has a somewhat cavalier attitude, not indeed to the essential truth of what he has to say, but to truth and rigour in matters of detail.

320c3 'as an older man speaking to his juniors'. In fact, Protagoras is virtually treating the audience like children. Cf. *Rep.* II, 377a, *Pol.* 268c–e; also 317c above.

320c8–328d2 *Protagoras' reply to Socrates' objections.*
    A.   *Reply to Obj. I (Athenians do not recognize experts in political matters):*
        (i) *Story of Prometheus (320c8–322d5),*
        (ii) *Explanation and expansion of story (322d5–324d1).*
    B.   *Reply to Obj. II (Good citizens do not teach their sons to be good): 324d2–328c2).*
    C.   *Summary: (328c3–d2).*
A (i). Prometheus and Epimetheus, who have been assigned by the gods responsibility for the creation of men and animals, distribute to the various species different capacities and means of protection. When it comes to the turn of man, Epimetheus, who had undertaken the distribution, finds that he has used up all the means of preservation, leaving man unprotected. Accordingly, Prometheus steals

from the gods knowledge of the practical crafts together with the use of fire, but without the knowledge of how to run a community. Thus equipped, men begin to develop the fundamentals of civilized life, religion, language, agriculture, and the provision of food and shelter. At first they live in scattered groups, and when the fear of wild animals drives them together into larger communities, they are unable, from ignorance of how to run a community, to prevent their mutual antagonisms from driving them asunder, leaving them at the mercy of the animals once again. Zeus then intervenes to save mankind from destruction; Hermes is sent to implant in men conscience and justice, thereby enabling them to live peaceably together, and is instructed to make sure that everyone receives these gifts, for only on that condition is community life possible. Anyone who is incapable of receiving them is to be put to death as a plague on the community.
A (ii) a. (322d5–323a4). The story shows why the Athenians are right to give everyone a voice in questions of how best to conduct the affairs of the city, since consideration of those questions must be entirely a matter of justice and soundness of mind, which amount to the excellence of a citizen, and unless everyone possessed that excellence there could be no organized communities.
   b. (323a5–c2). That everyone is expected to possess that excellence is further shown by the fact that anyone who maintains that he is totally lacking in it is held to be mad.
   c. (323c3–324d1). The fact that people are punished for acts of injustice etc. manifests the general belief that being a good citizen is not a chance natural gift like good looks, but something that can be inculcated and deliberately acquired, since there is no point in punishing someone for some fault of character unless he is able to rectify it.
B. The reply to the second objection is given not in story form but in a literal exposition. Everyone is taught to be a good citizen, not as a specialized subject, but as the general aim of the whole educational process, beginning in the nursery and continuing via the various kinds of schooling into adult life, where the process is continued by the influence of the laws. Differences of achievement are to be explained by differing natural aptitudes on the part of the pupils, as in any other field. For himself, Protagoras claims merely to possess greater skill than most in this universal educational task.
C. Protagoras claims to have shown (a) that one can be taught to be a good citizen, (b) that the Athenians believe that one can, and (c) that it is not surprising that the sons of outstanding men sometimes turn out badly and vice versa.
   The Greeks were familiar with two opposed accounts of human

development: (a) that represented here, the naturalistic tradition, developed in the fifth century from traditional antecedents, of progress from primitive beginnings; (b) the older Hesiodic tradition of progressive decline from an original state of innocence. See e.g. Lovejoy and Boas, and Dodds *Concept of Progress* ch. 1. Plato's own theory (*Pol.* 273–4, *Tim.* 72–3, *Crit.* 110–12, *Laws* III, 676–82) combines elements of both traditions.

There has been much discussion of the question whether Protagoras' defence is based on an actual work of his (see Guthrie III, p.64, n.1). In view of the considerable interest in the fifth century in the origins of civilization (see Guthrie III, pp.60–84 and Kahn in Kerferd ed.), and in view of the fact that the list of titles of works attributed to Protagoras includes one 'On the original state of things' (D.L. IX. 55), it is perfectly plausible that it is. On the other hand, nothing in the dialogue indicates that Protagoras' story might be familiar to his audience; contrast *Theaet.* 166c–d, esp. d1–2.

Much weight has also been put on the fact that ch. 6 of the *Dissoi Logoi* (i.e. *Arguments For and Against*, a short sophistic work, generally dated to the end of the fifth century) shows familiarity with some of the arguments dealt with in section B of Protagoras' defence, e.g. the argument that if excellence could be taught, then the great men would not have failed to teach their sons to be as good as they, with the counter-argument that Polycleitus did teach his son sculpture, but for all that he did not become a good sculptor, since he lacked the necessary talent (328c). If, as is generally believed, this pamphlet is earlier than the *Protagoras*, it is a reasonable inference that both its author and Plato used the same set of arguments for and against the thesis that excellence can be taught, and a further reasonable inference that the author of those arguments was Protagoras, who maintained that on any topic there are two arguments opposed to one another (DK 80 A 20, B 6a). It is not, however, impossible that the *Protagoras*, either in its present form or in an earlier version, was the earlier work. This possibility is generally held to be excluded on the grounds (a) that the *Dissoi Logoi* was written very soon after the end of the Peloponnesian War in 403, on the strength of a reference to that event in ch. 1 as 'very recent', and (b) that the *Protagoras* was in any case written after the death of Socrates in 399, and probably quite a few years later. Without going into the problems surrounding (b), it is sufficient to say that (a) is unsupported. In ch. 1 the author of the *Dissoi Logoi* prefaces a list of victories which were good for the victors and bad for the losers with the remark that he will begin with the most recent (*ta neōtata*: the expression, which is the most plausible emendation of a corruption in the manuscripts, may mean either 'the most recent' or 'something very recent'). It is clear that what is described as the most recent need not be thought of as very recent, particularly since the list runs 'Peloponnesian War, Persian Wars (490–480), Trojan War (remote antiquity)'. There is therefore no obvious *terminus ante quem* for the composition of the *Dissoi Logoi*, and hence no ground for the ascription of priority to the *Protagoras*, even if the latter is a work of the 380s. The most that can be said is that is a reasonable, but unprovable hypothesis that Protagoras' defence derives from some writings of his. (For details of the *Dissoi Logoi* see Guthrie III, pp.316–19; text in DK 90, translation, with bibliography, by Sprague in *Mind* 68, discussion in Barnes ch. 23(b).)

In reply to Socrates' first objection, viz, that the Athenians think that there are no experts on how to run the city, Protagoras argues that, on the contrary, they and everyone else regard all citizens as experts in that field. He supports this by giving, in the story, firstly an account of the nature of political expertise and secondly reasons why the possession of that expertise by everyone or nearly everyone is necessary for the existence of the community.

The nature of political expertise is revealed by its being placed in a threefold classification of powers or qualities, each set associated with a different divine or quasi-divine figure. Firstly there are the attributes which Epimetheus distributes to the beasts. Secondly, man, and man alone, is equipped by Prometheus with a set of skills which have been stolen from the gods. Finally, at a later stage in man's development, Zeus invests him via Hermes with the qualities necessary for organized community life, i.e. political expertise. Some difficulties have arisen from the attempt to specify the literal nature of the classification thus set out in terms of the story. The distinction between the gifts of Epimetheus and those of Prometheus is relatively unproblematic. The attributes (e.g. thickness of hide) and capacities (e.g. the ability to fly) on which animals depend for their survival do not require the exercise of intelligence, and are hence unlearned. They are assigned to the non-rational creatures (321c1). Man, on the other hand, survives by dint of his intelligence, which manifests itself in his invention (322a5–8) and his mastery by learning of practical skills. Problems arise when we come to the gifts of Zeus. It is fairly clear that, in the terms of the story, they are identified with political expertise itself, not with some pre-condition of it. Firstly, since that expertise is not itself mentioned in the story proper, unless we take it to be the actual gift of Zeus we have in the story itself no account of what it is. But immediately on the conclusion of the story proper (322d–323a) Protagoras says that that is the reason why the Athenians are right to take advice from everyone on matters of political expertise, since that advice must proceed entirely through justice and soundness of mind, implying that the story itself has given a sufficient account of the nature of political expertise. Secondly, a central point of the story is that unless conscience and justice, unlike the practical crafts, are universally distributed, the community cannot exist; precisely the same is said of political expertise at 323a2–3, 324d7–325a2 and 326e8–327a2 (cf. also 322d4–5 and 323b7–c2). Thirdly, at 329c2–3 Socrates says to Protagoras, 'You said that Zeus bestowed justice (*dikaiosunē*) and conscience (*aidōs*) on mankind', *dikaiosunē* being the regular word for one of the constituents of *aretē*, whereas Protagoras' actual terms (322c4, c7, d5) were *aidōs* and *dikē*. Clearly *dikē* and *dikaiosunē* are equivalent. This leaves the question of what is the literal signification of the gift of these attributes by Zeus, which will amount to a specification of the literal difference between those attributes and those signified by the gifts of Prometheus. According to Kerferd (*JHS* 53) the gift of *aidōs* and *dikē* by Zeus in the story represents the acquisition by the individual of political expertise by means of the educational processes of the city, as described at 325c–326e. Hence the difference between the skills given by Prometheus and the gifts of Zeus is that while the former were developed by men in a pre-political phase of their development, the possession of the latter requires the prior existence of political communities. If this is correct, Protagoras' position is radically confused, since the same condition is both a precondition of the existence of such a community and requires the prior existence of the community to account for its own existence. To avoid this difficulty, Kerferd also takes Protagoras as intending the gift of Zeus to be taken literally; since in order to found organized communities men required something which they could not have otherwise than via communities 'divine intervention was required to enable the process to start' (p.45). In view of Protagoras' notorious agnosticism about the gods, this view is surely impossible. While it is not impossible that Plato is himself confused on this point, or is deliberately representing Protagoras as confused, it is preferable to seek an interpretation which can dispense with either assumption.

Attention to the details of the story provides such an interpretation. Two features mark off the gifts of Zeus from those of Prometheus, firstly that men receive them at a later time and in response to a specific danger, viz. the danger of annihilation from failure to combine for their defence against the beasts, and secondly that they are distributed differently. Whereas the gifts of Prometheus were handed out one to one man and one to another (322c5–7), those of Zeus must be given to everyone. If we take Protagoras to be giving an account of the nature of political expertise via a speculative account of how it may be supposed to have developed in man, we find that these two features naturally coincide to constitute a major differentia. The essential feature of the reconstruction is that men, living naturally in small scattered groups, probably corresponding to families (see below on 322b1, pp.84–5) are driven by necessity to form larger communities, but find that hostility between different groups makes communal life impossible. What is lacking is a sense of social solidarity transcending the natural kinship group, which would enable every individual to see every other as possessing rights not in virtue of a natural bond of kinship, but merely as a member of the community, and which would in consequence generate habits of self-restraint and respect for others. That is to say, they lacked *dikē* and *aidōs* (or their prosaic equivalents *dikaiosunē* and *sōphrosunē*). Moreover, these dispositions must not be the preserve of a special élite, but must be shared by all, for anyone lacking in them is potentially disruptive of the community. Gradually, the story tells us, by a long process of trial and error, this universal habit of mind was built up, finally allowing organized communities to develop. The literal signification of the gift of these attributes by Zeus is simply the development of this social spirit (cf. Guthrie III, p.66). Protagoras is concerned to point out that this social spirit is non-primitive, in the sense that it requires the transcendence of what may reasonably be supposed to be primitive attachments to one's own kin. We have no justification for supposing him to make any distinction between that psychological sense of non-primitiveness, and the chronological sense, in which the social spirit develops at a later time than the primitive instincts. In singling out universal commitment to obligations transcending primitive ties as a defining characteristic of a community which recognizes moral, as opposed to merely tribal rules, Protagoras has indeed pointed out an important feature of social morality, but since he has done so in reply to a question about the teaching of political expertise he has implied that the two are identical.

The obvious inadequacy of that identification is its apparent neglect of the intellectual element. While the possession of justice, self-restraint etc. may be a necessary condition for being a good member of a democracy on the Athenian pattern, it is clearly not sufficient. In addition a good citizen (i.e. one who displays political expertise or excellence) will require experience, far-sightedness, good judgement, etc., i.e. everything that the Greeks summed up as *sophia* or *phronēsis*, understood in their practical aspects. Any reasonable list of the qualities which make up total human excellence has to include this, as is taken for granted in the discussion of the

81

interrelation of the various constituents of excellence from 329c.
It is possible, however, that Protagoras presupposes rather than
ignores *sophia.* Political expertise is introduced in the story as an
extra endowment which man, already in possession of technical
skill, required to enable him to live in organized communities.
Thus in order to succeed in communal living he does not have to
learn how to deliberate, to profit from experience etc., since he
already knows how to do that *as far as concerns his own natural
group.* What he has yet to acquire is the goodwill to put his
practical wisdom at the service of the larger community. So practical
wisdom is not a skill specific to community life in the way that
justice and self-restraint are, but is rather presupposed as a skill
common to the political and the pre-political aspects of human
life. Thus Protagoras' failure to mention *sophia* as a part of political
expertise may indicate, not that he thinks that one can be a good
citizen without it, but that he takes it for granted as an obvious
prerequisite, like good health. (Cf. his original account of his
programme of study as the good management of one's own affairs
and those of the city (318e–319a).) This would fit in well with his
position on the universality of political expertise. In addition to the
reason given above for believing that everyone must be just and
self-restrained, he has the best of reasons for believing that everyone
must be wise, since the wisdom which he has in mind is just that
practical intelligence with which every rational adult has to conduct
his own affairs, directed outwards, as it were, by his sense of community with other citizens. Thus, just as everyone has to possess
justice to some extent or other, or else not live among men
(323b7–c2), so everyone has to possess wisdom to some extent or
other, or else not be a fully adult, responsible member of the
community. The qualification 'to some extent or other' is important.
Just as Protagoras does not say that everyone is equally just or self-
restrained (see Kerferd p.43), and allows that some pretty despicable
characters nevertheless display those qualities to that minimal extent
which allows them to live as members of the community (323b,
327d), so he should not be taken as maintaining that everyone is
equally wise, but rather as allowing that some pretty stupid people
nevertheless meet the minimum standard of wisdom necessary for
membership of the community. Naturally, such people are unlikely
to have much success in influencing policy; but for all that, they are
at least entitled to a hearing, purely in virtue of being rational adults.

If this, admittedly charitable, view of Protagoras' position is
accepted, then rather than accuse him of shifting from one
conception of being a good citizen to another (see above, pp.71–2),
we can say that he has a constant conception, embracing both

intellectual and moral excellence, and that he shifts from emphasizing the former to the latter. Yet this is explanation rather than
defence, since the shift of emphasis is so marked as to leave the
actual nature of his instruction quite obscure. Further, if everything
above mere moral and intellectual imbecillity is counted as excellence,
then the concept is so diluted as virtually to vanish. Protagoras
claims to make his pupils politically expert in the ordinary sense of
pre-eminent; Socrates' objection that there can be no experts in that
sense is not met by the argument that, in common belief, every
normal adult is an expert in some much reduced sense.   *

A further objection is that Protagoras nowhere explains why one
has to have special expertise to be entitled to speak on technical
matters, but nothing beyond mere adulthood and rationality to
speak on matters of public policy. Since this point is not raised in
the dialogue, Protagoras naturally gives no answer. It is, however,
hard to see how a satisfactory answer could fail to embody the view
that, while a technical expert is one who knows how best to attain
an agreed end, questions of policy are themselves largely questions
about what ends are to be pursued, or which among a number of
agreed ends are to be accorded the greatest importance. On this
view, these questions are not susceptible of right and wrong answers,
and hence there can be no one who is especially qualified to answer
them. Rather, each individual has to make up his mind how he
wants to live and what sort of community he wants to live in.
In so far, then, as each man must make up his own mind on these
questions, a common policy should be arrived at by consulting (as
far as possible) everyone's judgement, which has the consequence
that everyone must be given a voice in decision-making. It appears,
then, that the familiar doctrine of the subjectivity of the ultimate
value-judgements governing human life has to be seen as the
unacknowledged and unchallenged basis of Protagoras' position.
See Bambrough in Laslett ed.

That doctrine would follow naturally from the more general
subjectivist thesis which Protagoras maintained. Since he held that
in general what each man believes is true for him, which I take to
imply that the notion of impersonal truth, according to which a
belief is true or false *simpliciter*, is an empty one, it will follow that
what each man believes on matters of public policy is true for him,
and that no view can be said to be just true or false. So much can
with reasonable confidence be ascribed to Protagoras. Further, we
might reasonably conjecture that this position could be applied to
political theory in the following way. Since no opinion on how to
conduct affairs is truer than any other, no one can claim any special
authority for his opinion. But the *polis* must act in some way or

other. Hence the most sensible rule is to let all opinions be heard and to act on the one which wins the most general assent. Hence Protagorean subjectivism might quite naturally (though not, of course, necessarily) lead to support for democracy. As we can be reasonably sure that the historical Protagoras held the former position, and as we find him represented by Plato in this dialogue as maintaining the latter, it is not unreasonable to suppose that Plato intended the reader to see a connection between the two. If that hypothesis is accepted, then the tension between Protagorean subjectivism and the features of Protagoras' defence in this dialogue which are inconsistent with that general position (see pp.100–3 below) would become correspondingly more marked. It may well have been Plato's intention to undermine Protagoras' credibility as a teacher of *aretē* by the indirect suggestion of that fundamental inconsistency.

NB. The above account of Protagorean subjectivism is not universally accepted; see Kerferd in Edwards ed.

321e2 Athena was associated with spinning and weaving, with pottery, and with the cultivation of the olive. The reference may be to any of these crafts.

322a3–8 'first of all ... then'. The order may be temporal, or merely that in which different items are mentioned. In the former case, the story would have the peculiar feature that the origin of religion precedes the development of language.

322a4 'through his kinship with the gods'. This phrase must be understood as continuing the reference to the divine gift, since the only respect in which man, as distinct from the other animals, is akin to the gods is that he shares the divine attribute of practical intelligence. The sentence should be taken: 'Since man shared in a divine gift, through *the resulting* kinship with the gods he alone worshipped them.' Some editors suggest deleting the phrase as an interpolation, but the thought is quite clear as the text stands.

* **322b1** 'in scattered units': i.e. small groups. There is no suggestion that in the pre-political phase men lived as isolated individuals, since the development of such institutions as language and religion presupposes at least a rudimentary form of community. No doubt we are to think of the primitive social units as something like families; cf. *Laws* III, 680a ff. and Aristotle's similar account (*Pol.* I.2), where the primitive unit is the family, which develops into the village, from which the city is formed. It may reasonably be objected to Protagoras that even family life requires the co-operative

84

virtues, which on his account mankind does not acquire until the dispensation of Zeus. He might perhaps reply that fairness and self-restraint within the family are instinctive and determined by affection, while as social virtues they must be accepted as obligatory independently of such feelings. The latter proposition is true, the former obviously false. The essential distinction for his purpose is that between a rudimentary form of the virtues, where obligations are recognized as due only to members of one's own family or other natural group, and the developed political form, where obligations are recognized as transcending natural bonds.

'Cities': essentially, a *polis* was an organized community big enough to be self-sufficient (Ar. *Pol.* I.2, 1252b27–30), self-sufficiency generally connoting political independence. Here 'community' would be the most natural rendering, while in other contexts 'city', 'state', 'country', or 'city-state' would be more appropriate. In order to bring out the conceptual and linguistic links with *politēs* (member of a *polis*, citizen) and *politikē technē* (art of running a city or community), which are essential to the argument, it has seemed best to render *polis* by 'city' throughout, at the cost of introducing into this passage misleading associations of size and complexity, attaching to the English 'city' but absent from the Greek *polis*.

322c2 'conscience'. *Aidōs* has connotations of self-respect, shame, modesty, and respect or regard for others; in different contexts one or other connotation may predominate. It is virtually synonymous with *sōphrosunē*, when the latter term is used in the sense of that soundness of mind which makes a man accept his proper role in society and pay due regard to the rights of others (cf. n. on 332a7, pp.122–4 below). Hence the close connection between the words, in this passage and elsewhere (e.g. Th. I.84.3, *Charm.* 160e). One of the primary manifestations of this soundness of mind is self-restraint; one refrains from doing what one would like to do because it would be disgraceful to oneself, or hurtful to someone else, or a breach of social norms. Hence there is a close connection with the other main aspect of *sōphrosunē*, viz. self-control, in particular mastery of bodily appetite (for fuller discussion see n. previously referred to). The renderings 'soundness of mind' and 'good sense' adopted for *sōphrosunē* are to be understood in that way. The choice of the words *aidōs* and *dikē*, rather than *sōphrosunē* and *dikaiosunē*, to designate the gifts of Zeus is probably dictated more by stylistic considerations than by any distinction of sense; the former pair, which have a more archaic sound, suggestive of poetic personification, are more appropriate to the poetic style of the story than their more abstract and prosaic variants. Cf. Hesiod, *Works and Days* 190–201.

322d1–5 As regards the words of Zeus' decree, there is no contradiction in his ordering that conscience and justice are to be distributed to all, while at the same time saying what is to be done to those who are incapable of receiving these gifts. Analogously the commander of a besieged town might order, 'Arms are to be distributed to all citizens; anyone incapable of using them is to be put to dig trenches.' But consideration of the literal sense of the decree reveals a difficulty; the literal sense is that social life requires that a sense of moral obligation be possessed by everyone or virtually everyone, not merely by an élite. Yet there may be moral defectives, who are incapable of this moral sense. The situation is similar in the case of language. In fact the great majority of humans are capable of using language, and community life would be impossible if that were not so, but a small minority is incapable of doing so. The literal sense of the rider to the decree is that social life requires the elimination of moral defectives, once their deficiency manifests itself. This appears to be an excessively strong requirement; while it is plausible that social life requires that moral defectives be restrained, it is not necessary that they be eliminated. Society can in fact get along provided that there are not too many such, just as the language-using community can get along provided that there are not too many who cannot use language. It is possible that Protagoras does not distinguish between the two positions (i) social life requires (a) that virtually everyone in fact have a moral sense and (b) that those without one should be restrained, and (ii) social life requires (a) that literally everyone have a moral sense and therefore (b) that those without one should be eliminated. Position (ii) contains the internal difficulty that during the time before the moral defective is eliminated, when unsuccessful efforts are being made to reform him (325a), a condition for the possibility of social life is unfulfilled; hence strictly speaking no community could exist during that time. As this is obviously unacceptable, the correct requirement for the existence of communities must be (ia) rather than (iia); but in that case it is not clear why moral defectives must be eliminated, rather than merely restrained. Hence position (i) appears considerably stronger than either position (ii) or the compromise position (ia) + (iib). The difficulty of distinguishing between positions (i) and (ii) arises from uncertainty whether 'everyone' is to be taken strictly, or more loosely as 'everyone or nearly everyone'. The reason for entertaining the latter possibility is that the only ground given for the assertion 'everyone must share in

86

moral sense', viz. that community life would be impossible if only a few did (d2–4), is in fact a ground for the looser assertion that everyone or nearly everyone must. Plato may indeed have overlooked this fact, and have treated 'everyone' and 'a few' as exhaustive alternatives, but on the other hand he may have meant 'everyone or nearly everyone'. See n. on 323a2–3, pp.87–8 below.

322d7–8 'when there is a question about how to do well in carpentry or any other expertise': lit. 'when there is a question about excellence in carpentry or any other technical (sc. excellence)'.

322e2–323a1 'when it comes to consideration of how to do well in running the city': lit. 'when there is consideration of excellence concerning the city'.

323a1 'which must proceed'. The antecedent is probably 'consideration' rather than 'excellence'; consideration of how to do well can more naturally be said to proceed by means of justice etc. than can doing well itself. The sense of the whole is unaffected, since it is assumed that advice on how to attain some excellence may properly be given by all and only those who actually possess it. Hence the reason why consideration of how to attain excellence in civic matters must proceed wholly via justice etc. is precisely that that excellence itself consists in the possession of those qualities. Similarly, consideration of how to be a good carpenter must proceed wholly via knowledge of carpentry, since possession of that knowledge is just what being a good carpenter is.

The above assumption is mistaken. Since many skills require physical attributes such as strength and balance in addition to 'know-how' it is possible that someone who lacks the former and therefore lacks the skill itself may yet possess the latter, and hence be able to advise on how to acquire a skill; a trainer of athletic champions need not be a champion himself. Conversely, a 'star' might be incapable of formulating his 'know-how', and so incapable of giving good advice on how to acquire the skill.

323a2–3 Protagoras' position here (repeated at 324d7–325a5 and at 326e8–327a2) is prima facie inconsistent with his common-sense admission (329e5–6, 349d5–8) that not every member of a civilized community is a good man. He would presumably reply that men who are unjust etc. by conventional standards are none the less good in the minimal sense required for participation in social life (327c4–e1). But while that defence removes the inconsistency, it prevents Protagoras from meeting Socrates' objection to his claim to teach excellence in the accepted sense (see above, pp.82–3). It seems likely that Protagoras fails to distinguish the propositions (a) civilized life requires that everyone *be required* to be good (i.e. be subject to penalties if he fails etc.), and (b) civilized life requires that everyone *be* good. (a) is, arguably, true, (b) obviously false. If that is so, then Protagoras will have failed to distinguish a universal normative requirement from a universal factual one. In that event, a sense of the truth of the normative requirement may have led him to give the factual requirement a sense in which it could be true, thus leading to the minimal interpretation. The use of the expression 'it is incumbent' (*prosēkon*) may indicate that Protagoras has a normative requirement somewhere in mind, though the argument needs the requirement to be factual. In the later passages where the thesis is repeated the modal expressions are 'necessary' and 'must', which less strongly indicate the normative requirement. The syntax of the sentence allows 'since it is incumbent . . . at all' to express either Protagoras' own view or that of the Athenians *et al.* The point is immaterial, since Protagoras endorses the judgement of the latter.

323a5–c2 This argument is affected by the same confusion, in addition to other obscurities. (1) The man who admits to being unjust is so in fact (b3–4). Is he unjust in the sense of being totally lacking in the moral sense which everyone must have if society is to hold together, or merely unjust in the sense of being by ordinary standards dishonest etc., while not altogether devoid of moral sense (see preceding n.)? Common sense suggests that conventional standards must be in question, but the argument requires that injustice must be taken as total lack of moral sense, since the crucial sentence (b7–c2) has been established only for the minimal conception of justice. (2) The crucial sentence is itself ambiguous. It may mean (a) 'Everyone must possess (justice) to some extent or other, or else be banished or put to death' or (b) 'Everyone must possess (justice) to some extent or other, for unless he did he could not live in a community.' On the first interpretation the wicked man would be mad to admit his wickedness because in so doing he would be condemning himself to death or exile from human society. On the second he would be mad because he would be saying something manifestly false. The first interpretation follows directly from the words of Zeus at 322d4–5, and is supported by the reference to the capital punishment of moral ineducables at 325a7–b1; the second fits better with 327c–d, which implies that there can be no moral ineducables in a civilized community. While the first interpretation appears more strongly supported, there is inconsistency in the views which Plato attributes to Protagoras in these passages. It is unclear whether Plato was aware of this.

323a8 'Skills' translates *aretai*, since 'excellences' is too artificial.

323b1 'Treat' renders *nouthetein*, which may mean 'advise, admonish', or 'punish'. As there is little point in lecturing someone you take to be mad, it is presumably implied that they lock him up or otherwise treat him roughly until he comes to his senses.

323c3–8 Protagoras has so far attempted to show (a) what political expertise consists in and (b) that it is universally believed that everyone possesses it. He now attempts to show that there is also a universal belief that it is not a natural endowment, but a skill acquired through teaching.

323c5–6 'by nature or by luck'. The two phrases are equivalent in this context, both having the implication 'without conscious purpose or choice'; cf. *Laws* X, 889a–c. Their conjunction is here roughly equivalent to the English 'by accident of birth'. 'By luck' translates *apo tautomatou*, lit. 'by means of the self-moving' (whence 'automatic'); 'chance' at d1 and 5 translates *tuchē*. Though Aristotle distinguishes *tuchē* from *tautomaton* (*Phys.* II.6), they are frequently interchangeable, as is clearly the case here.
'From deliberate choice': lit. 'from care'. The thesis is that a good citizen is so because he or others have taken care to see that he is.

323d1 'Correct' parallels the duality of sense in *nouthetein* (see n. on b1).

323d7 'practice'. *Meno* 70a distinguishes practice as a possible source of excellence from both nature and teaching: cf. *Clit.* 407b. The contrast is presumably between on the one hand instruction in the form of systematic verbal exposition and on the other discipline or habituation which might contain little or no formal instruction: cf. Aristotle's distinction between teaching and habituation (*EN* I.9, 1099b9–11; X.9, 1179b20ff.). Clearly there is a continuous scale between the extremes; most systems of teaching include both instruction and practice in different proportions, and it is clear that here practice and teaching are seen as different aspects of a single process rather than as alternatives. This is consistent with the views of the historical Protagoras; see DK 80 B 3: 'Teaching requires nature (i.e. talent) and practice', and 10: 'P. used to say that there is no skill (*technē*) without practice and no practice without skill.' Xenophon reports Socrates as maintaining that courage is a natural endowment which can be developed by teaching and practice (*Mem.* III. ix.1–3); cf. the view of Protagoras at 351b1–2. The whole educational programme of the *Republic*, moral and intellectual, consists of the development of natural talent through practice and systematic instruction; see O'Brien *Soc. Paradoxes* ch. 4.

323e7 'Impiety' renders *asebeia*, 'having an improper attitude to the gods', which is synonymous with *to anosion einai.* An equivalent English term is 'irreligion'; see n. on 325a1, pp.96 –7 below.

324b1 'retaliating unthinkingly like an animal'. The verb *timōreisthai* has the senses 'retaliate, revenge oneself' and 'punish'. These senses are not clearly differentiated, reflecting the close association in traditional thought between punishment on the one hand and private vendetta and divine retribution on the other (see Adkins chs. 3–4). (While Aristotle distinguished *timōria* = 'revenge' from *kolasis* = 'punishment' (*Rhet.* I.10, 1369b12–14), this is clearly a sharpening of ordinary usage.) In this passage the former sense seems to predominate in b1–3 and the latter thereafter. b1 requires the sense 'retaliate', since rational punishment is being contrasted with the instrinctive behaviour of an animal, which cannot properly be called 'punishment'. The next sentence (b1–4) runs 'Someone who aims to punish (*kolazein*) in a rational way does not *timōreisthai* on account of a past misdeed . . . but (sc. he *timōreitai*) for the sake of the future'; the first occurrence of the verb suggests 'retaliate', the second (understood) suggests 'punish', i.e. the shift in predominant sense occurs at this point. b7–c1 clearly requires the sense 'punish', since it is impossible to talk of 'those who retaliate in a public capacity', while in the next sentence (c1–3) the verb appears to be used synonymously with *kolazein* (= 'punish'). In an attempt to reproduce the doublet I have translated the verb as 'chastise' from b3 to c1.

323c8–324d1 Modern discussions of punishment (see Hart ch. 1) distinguish three main areas of dispute:
(i)   The definitional question
       What is the definition of the concept of punishment?
(ii)   Questions of justification
       (a) What is the aim of the practice of punishment?
       (b) Does that aim show the practice to be rationally or
           morally justified?
(iii) Questions of distribution

(a) What class of person is in general liable for punishment?

(b) What amounts of punishment are appropriate either in general or in particular cases?

Protagoras says nothing about (i). He is best understood as giving, in undifferentiated form, answers to qq. (ii) and (iii) as follows:

(ii)   (a) The aim of the practice of punishment is the discouragement of socially undesirable behaviour.

      (b) That aim shows the practice to be justified.

(iii)   (a) (?All and) only those offenders should be punished whose punishment may be expected to prevent further wrongful acts on the part either of those punished or of others.

      (b) The appropriate amount of punishment is in every case that which may be expected to be most effective in preventing further wrongdoing.

In describing Protagoras as answering these questions in undifferentiated form, I mean that he does not explicitly distinguish (ii) from (iii), nor (a) from (b) within either (ii) or (iii). Nor does he make the distinction between moral and rational justification required by (iib). He describes punishment administered with the aim of preventing further wrongdoing as done 'in a rational way' (324b1–2), i.e. as rationally justified, without considering the further question whether a practice which is rationally justified may none the less lack moral justification.

The institution which Protagoras is concerned to justify is the punishment of wrongdoers; the infliction of harm on the innocent with a view to the prevention of future wrongdoing (e.g. by judicial frame-up, or by the punishment of hostages) is not considered. Hence we cannot credit him with any view, however implicit or undifferentiated, on the question of whether the infliction of harm on the innocent can be justified by its effectiveness in preventing wrongdoing. On the question with which he does concern himself, the punishment of offenders, his words do not allow us to differentiate between the following formulations:

1.   All and only those offenders should be punished whose punishment may be expected to prevent further wrongful acts on the part of those punished or of others.

2.   Only those offenders should be punished whose punishment may be expected . . .

According to 1, presumed effectiveness of punishment in preventing further wrongdoing is the sole necessary and sufficient condition for the justified punishment of an offender. According to 2, it is a necessary condition of justification, but it is left open whether any further condition is necessary.

These distinctions assume some importance when the question

is raised to what extent Protagoras' position is incompatible with retributive theories of punishment. This question is itself complicated by the fact that the term 'retributive theory' can be used to designate a variety of positions:

I.   As a theory of the definition of punishment (q. (i)), retributive theory is the thesis that punishment is by definition harm inflicted by a recognized authority on a person believed guilty of an offence.

II. As a theory of the general justifying aim of the practice of punishment (q. (ii)), retributive theory is the thesis that the aim of the practice is the fulfilment of the requirements of justice by the infliction of harm on those guilty of offences against some specified legal or moral code, and that that fulfilment of the requirements of justice justifies the practice both rationally and morally.

III. As a theory of the distribution of punishment (q. (iii)), retributive theory is either the thesis (a) that the guilt of the person punished is the sole necessary and sufficient condition of the punishment's being justified, or the thesis (b) that the guilt of the person punished is a necessary condition of justification. Retributive theory may also be applied to questions as to the appropriate amount, method, etc. of punishment, in the form of the doctrine that the punishment should fit the crime.

Since Protagoras says nothing about the definition of punishment, no question arises with regard to I. His position on the general justifying aim of punishment is clearly incompatible with the form of retributive theory represented by II. Of the two formulations which might represent Protagoras' position on the distribution of punishment (p.91), both are inconsistent with III (a) but not with III (b). III (b) is clearly consistent with 2, since both state a necessary condition of a punishment's being justified. It might appear to be inconsistent with 1, since the latter states a necessary and sufficient condition independent of that specified as necessary in III (b). But III (b) states a necessary condition for the justification of the punishment of *anyone*, while 1 states a necessary and sufficient condition for the justification of the punishment of *an offender*. It may be true both that one is justified in punishing X only if X is an offender, and that provided that X is an offender, one is justified in punishing him if and only if his punishment may be expected to be effective in preventing further wrongdoing. This may be expressed symbolically as follows:

where J $=$ 'the punishment of . . . is justified',

O $=$ '. . . is an offender',

and   E $=$ 'the punishment of . . . may be expected to be

effective in preventing further wrongdoing'
the following formulae are consistent:

> (a) $(x)\,(Jx \rightarrow Ox)$
>
> and   (b) $(x)\,(Ox \rightarrow (Jx \leftrightarrow Ex))$.

III(a) is clearly inconsistent with both 1 and 2, since III (a) states a single necessary *and sufficient* condition of the justification of the punishment of anyone, viz. that he is an offender, while on Protagoras' view in addition to the satisfaction of that condition the satisfaction of a further condition is both necessary and sufficient (by 1) or merely necessary (by 2). The position attributed to Protagoras on the amount etc. of punishment ((iiib), p.91) is inconsistent with the retributivist doctrine that the punishment should fit the crime, since the latter assumes a correspondence between the intrinsic natures of the punishment and of the crime, independent of any considerations of the consequences of punishment, which in Protagoras' view provide the sole criterion of appropriateness in punishment.

As a theory of the general justifying aim of punishment, the position attributed to Protagoras appears stronger than the retributivist position. The former sees the aim of punishment as something readily intelligible, viz. the prevention of social harm, and moreover represents the practice as tending towards the realization of that goal in a reasonably intelligible way, viz. by discouraging potential offenders and/or conditioning them against the desire to offend (see below pp.94—5). On the latter view the aim of the practice is to fulfil a requirement of justice. But it is hard to see why it is a requirement of justice that undesirable conduct should be punished. It might be argued that if it is not punished then those who abstain from such conduct are being treated unfairly, in that they are being given like treatment to offenders in respect of unlike conduct. But this presupposes that the respect in which undesirable conduct differs from acceptable conduct is such that those who act in the former way ought to be punished as opposed to being specially treated in some other way, e.g. being smiled at, which is precisely what this argument is intended to establish. A reason can indeed be given why at least certain sorts of undesirable conduct ought to be punished, viz. that it is desirable that they be discouraged by the creation of sanctions against those who do them, but that is to adopt the Protagorean position. Failing that, the retributivist appears obliged to fall back on obscure metaphors such as that of restoring a moral balance which has been upset by the undesirable act; when analysed, these advance the discussion no further than the original claim that punishment of undesirable conduct is a requirement of justice.

93

On the question of the distribution of punishment, we have seen (p.92) that Protagoras has no dispute with the retributivist who maintains merely that any infliction of punishment is justified only if the person punished is in fact guilty of the offence for which he is punished (i.e. III (b)). There is, however, a dispute between either version of his position and the stronger form of retributivism, according to which punishment is justified if and only if the person punished is guilty of the offence for which he is punished. Here the retributivist's case is stronger than in the previous argument. If it is desirable that certain kinds of acts be discouraged by prohibitions which in turn require to be supported by sanctions, then the fact that an act of the kind in question has been done must be in itself sufficient justification for the putting of the sanction into effect, otherwise it will lose its effectiveness as a threat. The point of the prohibition is indeed to discourage acts of that kind, as Protagoras may be taken to emphasise, but the point of the punishment is not directly to influence future conduct, but rather to maintain the prohibition via the coercive force of the sanction. Thus Protagoras is right to urge that a rationally based prohibition must aim at and have a reasonable chance of imposing a restriction on undesirable conduct, while the retributivist is right to urge that, given a rationally based prohibition, in determining the legitimacy of punishment it is irrelevant to inquire into the likely efficacy of punishment in any particular instance. Yet considerations of the *amount* etc. of punishment require a further modification of the retributivist position, since the circumstances of a particular case may make it desirable to modify a punishment legitimately imposed for breach of a rationally based prohibition, either in the direction of severity, as in exemplary sentences, or in the direction of leniency, down to the limiting case where the punishment is waived altogether (e.g. a suspended sentence). Considerations of the likely effect of the particular punishment will figure prominently in most decisions of this kind. Leaving aside questions of definition, a comprehensive theory of punishment must incorporate elements of both the Protagorean and the retributivist positions: Protagoras shows that the point of punishment as an institution is as a sanction to enforce prohibitions against undesirable behaviour, and that consideration of the amount etc. of punishment in a particular case must take account of factors including the likely effect of the particular punishment. The retributivist shows that a breach of a rationally based prohibition is itself at least a *prima facie* ground for the infliction of punishment, independently of any consideration of the consequences, i.e., given that the prohibition is one which it is desirable to maintain in force, the fact that it has been broken is *a* reason for punishing the offender, though that reason may be overridden by considerations relating to the particular circumstances. While this may appear to be a minimal element of retributivism, it is nevertheless significant, since a theory which regards punishment as undertaken exclusively 'for the sake of the future' (324b4) is unable to say why the fact that a prohibition has been broken is even a reason for inflicting punishment. A comprehensive theory must contain the insight, due to the retributivist, that the discouragement of future wrongdoing requires the recognition of past wrongdoing as itself a ground, though not necessarily a conclusive ground, for coercive action.

Protagoras makes no distinction between a purely coercive function of punishment, i.e. that of deterring the potential wrong-doer from what he nevertheless remains inclined to do, and an educative function, i.e. that of so conditioning him against wrong-doing that he loses the inclination for it; see esp. 324b5—7. The belief that punishment leads to repentance refers to the latter function (cf. *Laws* IX, 862d), though one might wish to distinguish more clearly than Plato does a conditioned revulsion against some kind of conduct from a reasoned rejection of it. In thinking of the role of punishment in the bringing up of children it is difficult to separate these two functions in practice, since most acts of punishment are aimed at both short-term deterrence and long-term conditioning. We tend, however, to assume that the punishment of adults under legal and similar systems is primarily coercive, assigning the educational function to other institutions. This assumption reflects a minimal view of law, characteristic of liberal thought, as designed firstly to prevent encroachments on the freedom of the individual, and secondly to enable the state to provide a framework of services within which the individual is free to live as he chooses. While that tradition was not foreign to Greek thought (see Democritus, DK 68 B 181, and Aristotle's account of the views of the sophist Lycophron (*Pol.* III.9, 1280b10—12)), another probably more influential tradition regarded law as having the function of directing the citizens towards the best possible life; see e.g. Democritus, DK 68 B 248, *Apol.* 24d, *Crito*, esp. 51e, *Prot.* 326c—e, *Laws* I, 630—2, Ar. *EN* V.1, 1129b14—19, Xen. *Lac. Pol.* i.2, Plut. *Lyc.*, esp. xxxi. (In this tradition positive law was less sharply distinguished from custom than in modern thought, custom frequently having the force of law, and the word *nomos* designating both; see e.g. *Gorg.* 482c—483c, with Dodds's note on b4 (p.266), and Plut. *Lyc.* xiii.1.) Within this tradition it is less unnatural to see even legal punishment as having an educative function comparable to that which we recognize in the rearing of children.

For further reading on the theory of punishment see Acton ed. The account of punishment here ascribed to Protagoras has considerable affinities with Plato's own theory, as expressed in the *Gorgias* (476a–479e and 525a–d), *Laws* (V, 735d–e; IX, 854d–e, 862d–863a), and elsewhere. As in the *Protagoras*, the main functions of punishment are reformation and deterrence. As regards the former, the analogy with medicine occurs in the *Gorgias* (479a–c), *Republic* (III, 409e) and *Laws* (locc. citt.); the criminal is seen as suffering from a disorder of the soul which it is the function of punishment to cure. As Dodds points out (*Gorgias* p.254), this fits well with the Platonic view that all wrongdoing is involuntary (see below pp.203–4). The punishment of the incurably wicked is justified by its deterrent function; this provides a justification for capital punishment (*Laws* IX; cf. *Prot.* 322d, 325a and *Rep.* III, 410a) and for the eternal punishment of the worst sinners (*Gorg.* 525a–d; cf. *Rep.* X, 615c–616a). A third function, that of ridding the community of dangerous elements, which is stated in the *Laws* (locc. citt.), is not explicitly mentioned in Protagoras' exposition, but is implied by the wording of Zeus' decree (322d). Plato's discussion, while indeed including divine punishment within its scope, is the earliest known attempt at a theoretical treatment of punishment as a human institution serving a social purpose, as opposed to earlier views which see it within a context of ritual pollution and divine retribution; for references to subsequent discussions see Dodds (loc. cit.). There seems to me to be insufficient evidence to decide whether * Plato here reproduces the views of the historical Protagoras.

324d2 Protagoras now turns ostensibly to the second of Socrates' objections. It is not in fact directly answered till 326e6, since the answer requires a prior account of how the sons of good men are taught.

324d5–6 'that excellence which they themselves possess': lit. 'that excellence in which they themselves are good'.

325a1 'holiness'. As applied to persons *hosios* approximates to 'showing the proper attitude (sc. in thought, word, and action) towards the gods'. Its nearest English equivalents are perhaps 'pious' or 'religious'. The opposite *anosios*, 'manifesting an improper attitude towards the gods', corresponds fairly closely to 'irreligious', and is so rendered at 349d7 and 359b3. As applied to things *hosios* is roughly equivalent to 'required or permitted by the gods', hence in some contexts 'sacred', in others 'lawful'. It is the latter range of uses which makes it natural to describe the personal attribute itself (and the attribute of justice) as something *hosion*, which gives roughly the sense 'being just and religious are things required by the gods'. In order to reproduce the development of the argument it is necessary to use a single word for the personal attribute and for the attribute of things; 'holy' and 'holiness' are used (artificially) for this purpose.

325b5–6 'though it can be taught and fostered': not, at this point, an assertion of Protagoras' own, but a statement of the belief of the 'good'.

325c6 'correcting'. The verb is *nouthetousin*. Cf. notes on 323b1 and on 323d1, p.89 above.

326b1–6 As the reference to the children's souls indicates, the grace and adjustment in question are in the first instance psychological states. The various modes and rhythms of Greek music were supposed to tend to the production of various states of character; see *Rep*. III, 398d–402a on the psychological role of the arts, especially music, in education. This psychological conditioning would also produce external manifestations such as proper deportment (*Rep*. 400c–e).

326d2–5 The traditional view (disputed by Adam and Adam pp.122--3) that the reference is to horizontal lines drawn on the writing-tablet to guide the pupil's writing is confirmed by the discovery of a tablet containing an exercise to be copied between horizontal lines; see Turner *BICS* 65.

326d8–e1 'correction': lit. 'straightening'. The verb is that used at 325d7. The regular sense of the noun is 'examination' or 'audit', used primarily of the examination of the accounts of public officials; it does not appear to be used with the sense 'punishment', but the verb and cognate forms are used occasionally in that sense.

327b2 'Goodness' translates *aretē*.

327d2–3 'force them to be good': lit. 'force them to take care about excellence'.

327d3–4 Pherecrates: a writer of comedies, of which only a few quotations survive. His play *The Savages* was produced at the Lenaea (the earlier of the two great annual dramatic festivals at Athens, held in January) in 420. As the weight of evidence for the dramatic date points to about 433 (see p.64 above), it is best to treat this as an anachronism, of which there are other instances in Plato (e.g. *Symp.* 193a1–3; cf. Dover *Phron* 65).

327d6–7 Eurybatus and Phrynondas were apparently real persons, whose names became proverbial for wickedness. Cf. Arist. *Thesm.* 861; presumably Protagoras is recalling a similar mention of them in Pherecrates' play.

327e1 'you are acting like a spoiled child'. The basic meaning of the verb *truphan* is 'live in luxury'; hence it comes to mean 'be spoiled' (of children) and 'behave like a spoiled child, sulk'. Protagoras presumably means that, like a spoiled child, Socrates is being too choosy; with any number of teachers to choose from, he can't find one to suit him.

327e3–328a1 Cf. *Alc. I* 111a1–4.

328c3–d2 Summary of conclusions reached. Protagoras claims to have established (a) that one can be taught to be a good citizen, (b) that the Athenians believe that one can, and (c) that it is not surprising that the sons of good men sometimes turn out badly and vice versa.

Protagoras has argued for (b) at 323c5–324d1, and for (c) at 324d2–327c3. Previously, at 320c8–323c5, he has argued for the following three propositions: (i) the excellence of a citizen consists primarily in the possession of justice and soundness of mind, (ii) it is necessary for the existence of the community that those qualities be possessed by everyone, (iii) everyone, including the Athenians, believes (ii). Then, after his argument for (b) and (c), he contrasts the universality of excellence, thus conceived, in a civilized community with its total absence outside (327c3–e1), and concludes (e1–328c2) by setting his own position as a teacher of excellence in the context of the account of its inculcation by the whole community which formed part of his argument for (c). The question then arises where Protagoras argues for (a). It appears that the account of the teaching process (324d2–326e5) is intended to be taken as such an argument, since Protagoras concludes it (326e4–5) by saying that it shows that it would be astonishing if excellence could not be taught. The mere existence of a practice of teaching a given subject-matter does not of itself show that that subject-matter *can* be taught, but merely that certain people attempt to teach it in the belief that it can be taught. That belief might be mistaken, in which case those under instruction would either fail to master the subject-matter, or would master it independently of the teaching, e.g. by instinct. Protagoras' exposition rules out those possibilities in turn, the first at 320c8–323a4, where the story and its immediate expansion show that everyone must master the subject-matter in question, and the second at 327c3–e1, where it is asserted that those who have not undergone the teaching process (i.e. those who have not been brought up in a civilized community) do not master the subject-matter. Protagoras' argument for (a) then requires all three stages; 1 excellence (i.e. justice, soundness of mind etc.) is universal in civilized society (320c8–323c5), 2 excellence is taught in a civilized society (324d2–326e5), 3 excellence cannot be acquired outside a civilized society (327c3–e1). It is doubtful whether Protagoras can be thought of as clearly aware of the necessity for stage 3, since he appears to regard the argument as complete at 326e5. If so, he regards the existence of a practice of teaching as sufficient proof that the subject-matter can be taught, i.e. he fails to distinguish two senses of the expression 'can be taught', viz. 'is such that one can attempt to communicate it' and 'can be successfully communicated'. Then rather than crediting him with a complete argument for (a) we must say that he provides the materials for a complete argument.

I set out below the structure of the whole argument, divided with reference both to the three propositions which Protagoras maintains (left-hand side) and to Socrates' objections (right-hand side).

a	320c8–323a4	i Excellence = justice, soundness of mind etc.	Obj. I
		ii Excellence must be universal.	
		iii The Athenians believe that it must be universal.	
a	323a5–c5	Further argument for iii.	Obj. I
b	323c5–324d1	The Athenians believe that it can be taught.	Obj. I
a&c	324d2–326e5	Excellence is taught by the whole community.	Obj. I & II
c	326e6–327c3	The sons of good citizens fail through lack of aptitude.	Obj. II
a	327c3–e1	Those who do not live in a civilized community do not attain excellence.	
a	327e1–328c2	Protagoras is a specially gifted prac-	

titioner of the teaching undertaken
by the whole community.

From 327c3 Protagoras is no longer directly concerned with either of Socrates' objections. The reason is that Protagoras attempts to prove more than he is strictly required to in order to meet Socrates' challenge. Socrates has produced only two arguments against the teachability of excellence; the first, which assumes that what the Athenians believe is true (see pp.72–3 above), purports to show that they believe excellence not to be teachable, the second alleges that the failure of distinguished men to train their sons in excellence is a proof of its unteachability. In reply to the first Protagoras argues firstly that the facts which Socrates cites do not manifest the belief that excellence cannot be taught, but rather the belief that it is possessed by all civilized men, and secondly that certain practices, common to the Athenians and all other peoples, manifest the belief that it can be taught. In reply to the second, Protagoras argues that the phenomenon which Socrates appeals to is not a proof of the unteachability of excellence, since it can be explained by another factor, viz. lack of aptitude on the part of the pupil. Hence Protagoras could finish the argument at 327c3 in a strong position, since he has given some grounds for believing not merely that Socrates' evidence and assumptions do not support his conclusion, but that his fundamental assumption, viz. that what the Athenians believe is true, actually leads to Protagoras' conclusion. But Protagoras has throughout been concerned not merely to gain an *ad hominem* victory over Socrates by showing what the Athenians really think about excellence, but to refute him by showing what excellence really is and why it is in fact teachable. As the above analysis shows, from 320c8 to 323c5 that argument is bound up with the direct reply to the first objection. It reaches what Protagoras probably regards as its conclusion at 326e5, where the argument is embedded in the reply to the second objection, and on completion of that reply Protagoras returns to add some finishing touches, including a statement of his own role in the teaching process.

That role is sometimes interpreted (e.g. A.E. Taylor pp.246–7) as mere expertise in imparting the social traditions of whatever community Protagoras happens to find himself in, a conception which presupposes that 'there is no moral standard more ultimate than the standard of respectability current in a given society' (ibid.). Cf. *Theaet.* 167c and 172a, where Protagoras is represented as holding that what each city lays down or considers (*nomizei*) to be just and unjust, holy and unholy, etc. is so for that city so long as it continues to hold it, and that no such view can be called true or false *simpliciter*. But the story and its expansion make it clear that in Protagoras' view the social traditions of Athens or any other city reflect a universal ethical truth, viz. that the basic social virtues are justice and soundness of mind. It is entirely contrary to the basis of Protagoras' position to regard him as merely echoing a preference for these virtues which happens to prevail at Athens but which might be quite absent from the traditions of any other city. It is clearly his view (see above) that no such city could exist. The moral and legal code of any actual city must therefore already have passed the test of imposing on its citizens limitations on their freedom which satisfy basic requirements of justice (nowhere specified by Protagoras). Given the satisfaction of that minimum requirement, whatever the code of any city lays down as justified, obligatory, etc. is so until it is changed. This position is clearly unsatisfactory, as it leaves Protagoras no ground for moral criticism of the institutions of any state, no matter how cruel, unjust, etc., provided only that that state retains enough social cohesion to ensure its continued survival. But while that criticism of Protagoras' position is a serious one, it is distinct from Taylor's. Protagoras neither accepts the standards of respectability of any particular society as an *ultimate* moral standard (though his fundamental ethical objectivism is consistent with a wide degree of relativism, and in particular with the relativism of *Theaet.* 167c and 172a), nor does he simply impart a medley of traditions lacking any theoretical basis. Cf. Levi *Mind* 40, Loenen pp.75, 95, Moser and Kustas *Phoenix* 66, Gosling p.3, Nicholson *Polis* 80–1, Döring in Kerferd ed.

Another conception of Protagoras' role is proposed by Vlastos in Ostwald pp.xx–xxiv (cf. Cole *YCS* xxii). Vlastos takes Protagoras to claim in this dialogue the kind of expertise described at *Theaet.* 166d–167c, a passage which he believes to represent the views of the historical Protagoras. This expertise consists, not in imparting true beliefs, but in so conditioning the pupil that from a state of mind which he (the pupil) finds unsatisfactory (e.g. feeling himself unsuccessful in his affairs) he passes into a state which he finds satisfactory (e.g. feeling himself successful). This activity is parallel to that of the doctor, who finds his patient in a state where e.g. his food tastes unpleasant and brings him into one where it tastes pleasant. The test of the success of the process is the subjective judgement of the pupil or of the patient. If the patient feels better, then he is better, if the pupil believes that he is better at running things then he is; in neither case is the truth of the belief in question. While I agree with Vlastos that the passage of the *Theaet.* is intended by Plato to represent his understanding (not necessarily correct) of the views of the historical Protagoras (for the opposite view see McDowell pp.165, 169, 172–3; cf. Cole *YCS* xix), it does not seem to me that it provides an account of the activity of the sophist which is (a) internally consistent or (b) applicable to the programme of Protagoras in this dialogue in the way suggested by Vlastos. (a) McDowell points out (pp.166–7) that the account of the activity of the doctor is not in fact parallel to that of the politician and the sophist as it is supposed to be on Protagoras' thesis. The doctor makes the same food taste pleasant instead of unpleasant (and generalizing, he makes the same man have pleasant instead of unpleasant sensations, 166d–e); the politician makes different policies etc. seem right to a city, i.e. instead of harmful policies he makes useful policies seem right, and the sophist does the same for individuals (167c–d). This presupposes that harmful and useful policies are distinguished in fact, not merely by how they appear to a given city or individual. As McDowell says, a similar account could be given of the activity of the doctor, and may perhaps be in Plato's mind at 171e, viz. that the doctor makes healthy things pleasant to the patient instead of unpleasant and unhealthy things unpleasant instead of pleasant. But this account too presupposes an objective distinction between what is healthy and what is unhealthy. (In fact there is a hint of this at 167b, suggesting that the two accounts of the doctor's activity are not clearly separated.) (b) In our dialogue, Protagoras claims to teach his pupils to be successful in private and public affairs. That claim must be tested by actual results, the acquisition of wealth, position etc., not merely by the private feelings of the pupil. Protagoras * would not have had a public had he claimed merely to make his pupils find their lives more satisfactory in the belief that they were successful etc., without any claim that those beliefs were true. (Nor would a doctor, if his conception of a cure was simply that the patient felt better, without any claim that he was better, as defined e.g. by his objectively testable ability to do things.) Satisfaction on the part of the pupil could be at best a necessary condition of the success of Protagoras's teaching, not a necessary and sufficient condition (and similarly in the case of the patient).

Even granted that the historical Protagoras gave the defence of his programme attributed to him in the *Theaetetus*, there is no indication in the *Protagoras* that Plato represents him as intending his programme to be seen in that light. If, none the less, Plato did suppose that the reader would see it that way, his object may have been to indicate the inconsistency between the theoretical subjectivism of the defence and the requirement of objective truth contained in the actual programme. (It is clearly Plato's intention

COMMENTARY 328c3–329d1

in the *Theaetetus* itself to show that the defence is inconsistent.) In the absence of any definitive evidence, it is a perfectly plausible historical hypothesis that Protagoras did not in fact attempt any close integration of his popular teaching with his epistemological and meta-ethical theory. For a helpful discussion see Nill ch. 2.

For another attempt to reconcile the *Protagoras* with the *Theaetetus*, assuming a different interpretation of the latter, see Kerferd *DUJ* 49–50.

328d3–329d2 *Reaction of Socrates to the speech of Protagoras. He asks Protagoras whether the various virtues are distinct constituents of a total excellence, or whether they are identical with one another.*

328d4–5 'spellbound'. Cf. 315a7–b1. Plato frequently describes sophists as wizards (e.g. *Soph.* 235a1, *Pol.* 291c3–4) and as magicians (*Soph.* 235b5, 268d2), terms which also carry suggestions of 'trickster' 'charlatan', and 'showman'. Socrates' victims sometimes describe him in similar terms, e.g. *Meno* 80a–b.

328e2 'technique'. The word is the same as that occurring in the phrase translated 'by deliberate choice' at 323c6 and d6 and 324a2. Its basic meaning 'care' gives the derivative sense 'activity pursued with care', i.e. a systematic pursuit.

329a1 'Orators' here translates *dēmēgorōn* and at a6 translates *rhētores*. Both are in effect equivalent to 'politicians'; cf. *Gorg.* 466a–b.

329d1 'different names for one and the same thing'. This condition would be satisfied either if the names of the virtues had the same meaning (identity of sense), or if, while different in meaning, they nevertheless designated the same state of character. An example of the second situation is provided by *Gorg.* 506e–507c. Goodness in the soul depends on its possessing a certain order among its constituents to which we give the name *sōphrosunē*. Someone who has that order in his soul will always act as is fitting towards gods and men and will never pursue or avoid anything other than what he should, i.e. he will be just, holy, and courageous, and all these ways of acting will spring from the one state of soul. If we add, as the parallel with the *Republic* irresistibly suggests, that the crucial state of soul is one in which the elements of the soul are so ordered that the rational element predominates, then we can say that wisdom, *sōphrosunē*, courage, holiness, and justice are all one and the same state of soul. In view of the whole-hearted ontological

103

commitment with which Plato speaks of the virtues and their opposites in this dialogue (they are things (330c) which men share in (324e–325a), which have powers like the powers of the sense-organs (330a), and which account for or produce conduct of the appropriate kind (332d, 360c)), it would be most natural to interpret the thesis of the unity of the virtues as above, and highly unnatural to interpret it merely as the thesis that anyone who has one virtue necessarily has all the others. (Though that, of course, follows from the thesis as interpreted here.) On Vlastos's grounds for adopting that interpretation see below.

It remains unclear whether Plato thought that, in so far as the different kinds of conduct spring from the same state of the soul, any action which falls under one necessarily falls under all the others, or whether it is possible e.g. to act justly but not courageously in a situation where there is no danger. Further, there is no indication that at the time of writing this dialogue (if ever) Plato was aware of the fundamental meaning-reference distinction.

Neglect of this distinction is a major and basic defect of Vlastos's recent re-examination of the arguments on the unity of the virtues (*RM* 72, reprinted with emendations in *PS*, pp.221–69; page refs. are to the latter version; the distinction is also ignored by Allen pp.93–100 and by Santas *RM* 69). Vlastos argues as follows. At 329c–e Socrates puts forward what appears to be a single position by means of three theses:

1. The Unity Thesis, viz. that the names of the virtues are all names of one and the same thing.
2. The Similarity Thesis, viz. that the virtues resemble one another in all respects.
3. The Biconditionality Thesis, viz. that anyone who possesses any of the virtues necessarily possesses all the others.

Now since (1) and (2) are (according to Vlastos) obviously unacceptable, and must have been unacceptable, given their ordinary sense, to Plato, the position which Plato assigns to Socrates must be (3). But since the three theses apparently present a single doctrine, the first two must be reinterpreted in such a way that their meaning is identical with that of the third. Vlastos's basic ground for the assertion that (1) and (2) must have been unacceptable to Plato is his belief that in their ordinary sense both (1) and (2) imply that the names of the virtues are synonyms. This belief is indeed stated with regard to (1) in a qualified way: '(t)o ... affirm that ... each of the five (sc. names) "applies to one thing" would be normally understood as implying the claim that (i) the five virtues are *the same virtue* and perhaps even (ii) that their names are synonyms' (pp.226–7, author's italics). Thus Vlastos appears to consider the possibility that Socrates might maintain (i) without wishing to maintain (ii). But his only argument against (i) in fact depends on the assumption that (i) would itself commit Socrates to treating the names of the virtues as synonymous. This argument runs as follows (p.227):

1. Each virtue is a single nature or character (*idea*), which is manifested in acts characterized by the virtue-description and which can be used as a standard by looking to which one can tell whether an act falls under the virtue-description.

2. Plato cannot have thought that one could use the definiens of e.g. courage to determine whether an act falls under the description appropriate to e.g. piety.

3. But if the virtues are identical with one another, then Plato would be obliged to allow that possibility.

Therefore, Plato cannot have intended to assert that the virtues are identical with one another.

The defect in this argument emerges when step 2 is generalized. There appear to be two possible generalizations:

2a. Plato cannot have thought that one could use the definiens of any virtue to determine whether an act falls under the description appropriate to any *other* (i.e. non-identical) virtue.

2b. Plato cannot have thought that one could use the definiens of any virtue to determine whether an act falls under the description appropriate to any virtue designated by a different name.

If one understands Vlastos's step 2 in the former sense, the argument is question-begging, since it assumes the truth of the conclusion it is meant to establish, viz. that the virtues in question are not identical with one another. If, however, one understands it in the latter sense, then it is unacceptable. If the virtue designated by the name *a* is one and the same virtue as that designated by the name *b*, then why should one not use the definiens of *a* to determine whether an act falls under the description appropriate to *b*, and why should Plato have supposed that one could not? Even when the names are not synonymous, it may sometimes be perfectly proper to use the definiens of *a* to determine whether an act falls under the description appropriate to *b*. Thus, to return to our example (p.103), if *sophron* of an act means 'manifesting the proper order in the soul', and the proper order is that in which the rational element predominates, then it will be proper and indeed necessary to use the definiens of 'wisdom' (viz. 'the predominance of the rational element in the soul') as a standard to determine whether an act is *sōphrōn*. The Greek term which Vlastos renders as 'standard' is *paradeigma*, lit. 'exemplar'. One function of a *paradeigma* is to exhibit what it is that makes something F, what constitutes something as F, the properties through or in virtue of which (*kata, dia, tōi . . . einai*) it is F; examination of Plato's use of these terms makes it clear that they cover both cases where 'x is F in virtue of G' is analytic and where it is synthetic. Thus when Socrates says at *Rep.* V, 472d that 'we were constructing in discourse a *paradeigma* of a good city', he means that the ideal city is a model exhibiting those features which make a city a good one; it will hardly be claimed that the political arrangements of the ideal city merely elucidate the meaning of the expression 'good city'. If Vlastos were to insist that the function of a *paradeigma* must be to exhibit the features in virtue of which something is F, where 'in virtue of' is understood to signify a strictly analytic relation, then (a) he is imposing on Plato a restriction not warranted by the texts, and (b) his premiss 2 would have to be taken as

    2c. Plato cannot have thought that one could use the definiens of any virtue to determine whether any act falls by definition under the description appropriate to any virtue designated by a different name.

But that is simply to say that Plato cannot have thought that any two names of virtues are synonymous, i.e. to restate Vlastos's other arguments against the synonymy thesis. Vlastos, then, gives no arguments against taking the thesis of the unity of the virtues in the sense that the names of the virtues, while not necessarily synonymous, all designate the same state of character. One actual Platonic account of the virtues has been cited which appears to satisfy that description, while others could be suggested. In the examination of the particular arguments of the dialogue, this hypothesis will be considered further.

    In a footnote (n.12, p.227, not in the first published version) Vlastos mentions the sense-reference distinction, only to dismiss it on the ground that Plato did not have the distinction. His position is that, since Plato lacked the means to distinguish synonymy of names from any other way in which the various virtues might be said to be one and the same, he would be committed, and recognize himself to be committed, by any version of that thesis to the unacceptable consequences of the thesis that the names of the virtues are strictly synonymous, e.g. that those names are freely interchangeable in any transparent context (i.e. a context not introduced by an expression such as 'believes that', or containing the expressions 'necessary' or 'possible'). While I accept that Plato did not have the distinction I do not think that that justifies Vlastos's position. Rather, the lack of the meaning-reference distinction, and the consequent lack of a distinction between a clearly defined modern concept of synonymy (assuming there to be such a thing, see Quine *Word and Object* ch. 2) and a vaguer notion of 'standing for the same thing', might well account for Plato's declining to accept implications which apply only to the modern concept, or accepting them as unobjectionable, since they appear as objectionable only in the light of the modern concept. Thus if what Plato really believes is that it is possession of the knowledge of what is good and bad which is necessary and sufficient to account for one's giving everyone his due and for one's acting properly towards the gods, he might well accept (a) 'Knowledge of good and bad is that *eidos* in virtue of which all just actions are just' and (b) 'Knowledge of good and bad is that *eidos* in virtue of which all pious actions are pious', without feeling himself obliged to accept the consequence 'Justice is that *eidos* in virtue of which all pious actions are pious.' He would, moreover, be justified in so doing. for since 'accounts for' is a * non-symmetrical relation, '*A* accounts for *B*' and '*A* accounts for *C*' do not entail '*C* accounts for *B*'. The objectionable consequence follows only if (a) and (b) are considered as statements to the effect that certain expressions have the same meaning. Again, Vlastos argues that if the names of the virtues are synonyms, then they are interdefinable, which would be unacceptable to Plato. This consequence would be unacceptable only if the function of a definition is assumed to be the explication of the meaning of a term. But if a *logos* says, not what a word means, but what the thing named by the word really is (as *Meno* 87d–88d argues that *aretē*, i.e. what makes a man a good man, really is nothing other than knowledge, and *Prot.* 360c–d that courage, i.e. what makes a man act courageously, really is nothing other than knowledge), then Plato sees nothing objectionable in the thesis that the different virtues have the same *logos* (cf. Penner *PR* 73, esp. pp.39–42). If, as I believe, Socrates' position in the *Protagoras* is that all the specific *aretai* are one and the same in that different ways of behaving well all arise from the knowledge of what is good and bad (see below, pp.213–4 and cf. *Meno* 87b–89b, *Charm.* 173a–174d, *Lach.* 196d–199e, Xen. *Mem.* III.ix.5), then it is an imprecise one, since it takes no account of the ways in which these ways of behaving well are *different*, e.g. in that they presuppose different, though possibly overlapping areas of activity for their exercise. The fact that piety is described in the *Euthyphro* (11e–12e) as a part of justice rather than identified with justice suggests that in that dialogue Plato had that point more clearly in mind than when writing the *Protagoras*, but that of itself does not show (as Vlastos thinks, p.228) that the unity thesis is not maintained in the latter. For a complete statement of his theory, Plato requires both the thesis that good conduct is determined by knowledge of what is good and bad and the thesis that that knowledge is exercised in different areas, the different kinds of conduct thus produced being picked out by non-synonymous names. It does not appear that he ever stated his theory in this form; Aristotle's doctrine of *phronēsis* and its relation to the specific virtues of character embraces both aspects.

329d3–331b8   *Protagoras replies that the different virtues are distinct parts of a total excellence. Socrates gives an argument which attempts to reduce this position to absurdity.*

329d4–8   It is hard to see how the analogy of the different parts of a piece of gold could be supposed to apply to the different virtues. Protagoras has already said that he regards the virtues as states of character distinct from one another. The analogy indicates two ways in which the parts of a spatio-temporal object, which are themselves spatio-temporal objects, may be distinct from one another. (a) Each part may be something of a different kind, marked off by specific characteristics, from every other part and from the whole (e.g. a nose is specifically different both from an eye and from a face); (b) each part may be a thing of the same kind as every other part and as the whole (e.g. every part of a piece of gold is itself a piece of gold), distinguished from the whole and from the other parts only by its spatial position. (Plato says 'distinguished by size', but that is an error; while each part must indeed be smaller than the whole, all the parts may be identical in size (as in every other characteristic). No two parts, however, can occupy precisely the same space, nor can any part occupy precisely the same space as the whole; hence spatial position is the only necessarily differentiating characteristic. Since states of character have no spatial position, and since the discussion is in any case concerned with states of character considered in the abstract, not with particular instances (e.g. with the difference between courage and wisdom, not between Socrates' courage and wisdom), the second sort of difference has no application to the virtues. Protagoras is not, therefore, being invited to choose between different possible accounts of their interrelations. Presumably Plato wishes to make quite explicit the point that, if the virtues are to be differentiated from one another, it must be in virtue of their possessing specifically differentiating characteristics.

This indicates an error in the otherwise extremely helpful discussion by Gallop *Phron* 61. He points out, correctly, that Protagoras asserts four theses:

1. Justice, holiness etc. are distinct from one another (330a3).
2. None of the virtues is of the same kind as (*hoion*) any other (a4–b6).
3. One may possess one virtue without possessing all (329e5–6).
4. The virtues have 'powers' which differ in kind as do the virtues themselves (330a4–b1).

Asserting that, whereas the falsity of 1 entails the falsity of 2, 3, and 4, the falsity of 2, 3, or 4 does not entail the falsity of any of the others, he maintains that throughout the subsequent argument Socrates concentrates exclusively on 2, ignoring 1, 3, and 4. (Penner *PR* 73 p.51 takes the same view.) The falsity of 1 does indeed entail the falsity of 2, 3, and 4. But in addition the previous para. has shown that, provided *hoion* has the sense 'alike in every respect', 1 entails 2, from which it follows that the falsity of 2 entails the falsity of 1 (and hence of 3 and 4). Granted, where *hoion* has the sense 'alike in some respect(s)', 1 does not entail 2; but Socrates' argument depends on his failure to distinguish these senses of *hoion* (see n. on 330a6– 7, pp110–11 below). Thus, rather than agree that Socrates attacks 2 while ignoring 1, 3, and 4, we should say that he attacks 1 (and hence 3 and 4) by attacking 2.

329e5–6   See n. on 323a2–3, pp.87–8 above.
   The casual introduction of wisdom and courage strongly suggests that their contribution to total excellence has so far been taken for granted. On wisdom see pp.81–2 above.

330a2   Cf. 352c8–d3.

330a3–331b8   Socrates' argument proceeds as follows:
330a3   1. Each virtue is numerically distinct from every other.
330a4   2. Each virtue has its own specific power.
330a4–b6   3. No virtue is like any other, either in itself or with respect to its power.
330c1–2   4. Justice is something.
330c2–7   5. Justice is something just.
330c7–d1   6. Justice is such as to be just (from 5).
330d2–5   7. Holiness is something.
330d5–e2   8. Holiness is such as to be holy.
331a7–8   9. Holiness is not such as to be something just (from 3 and 5).
331a8   10. Justice is not such as to be holy (from 3 and 8).
331a8–9   11. Justice is such as to be not-holy (from 10).
331a9   12. Holiness is such as to be not-just (from 9).
331a9–b1   13. Holiness is such as to be unjust (from 12).

14. Justice is such as to be unholy (from 11).
331b1–3 15. But justice is holy and holiness is just.
331b3–6 16. Therefore justice and holiness are like one another
(i.e. 3 is false, by *reductio ad absurdum*).

330a4 'Power' renders *dunamis*. The analogy with the parts of the face, which are presumably thought of primarily as sense-organs, suggests that, as the organs are not mere dispositions to perform acts of seeing etc. but permanent parts of the person which enable him to perform such acts, so the virtues are not purely dispositional, but are permanent states of the person which enable him to perform acts of justice etc.; they are 'motive-forces' rather than 'tendencies' to use Penner's helpful distinction (*PR* 73 pp.44–9). This is consistent with the analysis given in the *Gorgias* and *Republic*, where the virtues are permanent organizational states of the soul, issuing in acts of the appropriate kinds. (Contrast *Lach.* 192b, where it is assumed that courage *is* a power.) I therefore disagree with Vlastos's assertion (*PS* p.229 n.20) 'The "power" ... of a particular virtue is
* that virtue itself, conceived as a dispositional quality manifesting itself in action'. The virtue is the permanent state which is in a man, as the eye is in a man; its power is the capacity to act well which it gives him, as the power of the eye is the capacity to see which the eye 'gives'. It does not seem that the distinction between virtues as permanent states and their powers plays any role in the argument; on Savan's interpretation, see below, pp.117–8.

330a6–7 'nor is any other part like another in power or in other ways'. Reflection on this sentence brings out the fact, on which the argument depends, that the word 'like' may have different implications in different contexts. x may be like y (i) in that x and y are qualitatively identical (i.e. have all characteristics except spatio-temporal position in common), (ii) in that x and y have most or a substantial number of their significant characteristics in common (roughly the ordinary sense of 'like', as in 'John is like his father'), (iii) in that x and y have at least one significant characteristic in common, or (iv) in that x and y have at least one characteristic in common. (It is in this minimal sense that, as Protagoras points out (331d2–3), anything may be said to be like anything else in some respect or other.) By 330a4–7 Protagoras is obviously committed to the position that the parts of the face (and hence by analogy the virtues) are not like one another in sense (i), and perhaps not in sense (ii) either, though that is less clear, since eyes, ears, etc. have some substantial similarities as well as substantial differences. On no ordinary understanding, however, is he committed to the view that the parts of the face are unlike in senses (iii) or (iv). Yet the crux of the argument, the derivation of steps 9 and 10 from 3 and 5 and 3 and 8 respectively, requires that 'like' be understood in sense (iii) or sense (iv). From 3 'No virtue is like any other' and 8 'Holiness is such as to be holy' it follows that 10 'Justice is not such as to be holy' only if 'No virtue is like any other' has the force of 'No virtue has any significant characteristic (or 'any characteristic whatever') in common with any other' (and similarly in the derivation of 9). It is indeed possible to take 330a6–7 as committing Protagoras to the view that the parts of the face are unlike in sense (iv) and hence in sense (iii), if the sentence is read as 'There is no respect in which any part resembles any other, whether power or any other respect whatever.' But to understand it in that way would not only amount to a violent departure from an ordinary understanding of Protagoras' view, but would turn the sentence into a manifestly illegitimate generalization from the immediately preceding instance. In the immediately preceding sentence (a4–6) Socrates asserts that the eye is not like the ears (sense (i) and perhaps sense (ii)) and that their power is not *the same* (explicitly sense (i) of 'like'). Clearly, the most that can legitimately be generalized from this is that the same holds of any two parts, and in fact this sentence may be given a natural interpretation in that sense, viz. 'Nor is any other part (sc. exactly) like any other, either in its power or in its other aspects (i.e. in its permanent character which gives it its power).' The application to the parts of excellence in the next sentence strongly suggests that this is how the sentence should be taken. The ambiguity of the sentence probably reflects a failure (? on the part of Socrates or of Plato) to distinguish between the different implications of 'like'.

*

330c1 'is justice something, or not a thing at all?'. If justice, holiness, etc. are literally nothing at all, then they cannot have any attributes, since there will be nothing for the attributes to apply to (cf. *Soph.* 237b–238a). Hence since the argument depends on the attribution of qualities to the virtues, this precondition must first be established. The precondition itself presupposes the generalization 'Whatever has any attributes must be', which covers the possibilities (i) 'Whatever has any attributes must be something' and (ii) 'Whatever has any attributes must exist.' Being and not-being are discussed at length in the *Sophist*, but the extent to which existence is distinguished from other sorts of being is disputed; see Ackrill *JHS* 57 and Owen in Vlastos ed. *Plato*. The suggestion which is ruled out appears to cover, also in undifferentiated form, both the following possibilities: (i) the names have no meaning, (ii) the names do not

111

pick out any feature of the real nature of things, but are used merely according to convention, e.g. nothing is really holy, though there is a convention according to which certain things are *called* holy (cf. Parmenides, DK 28 B 8, 38–41, Empedocles, DK 31 B 9). On the latter interpretation the view that holiness is not a thing at all amounts to the view that holiness does not exist in reality (*phusei*) but only by convention (*nomōi*); see n. on 337d1–3, pp.140–1 below.

330c2–7 The ascription of an attribute to itself (self-predication) is facilitated by the fact that in Greek attributes are regularly designated by the adjective preceded by the definite article, e.g. 'the beautiful' (= 'beauty'), 'the just' (= 'justice'). Hence 'The just is just' (i.e. the attribute justice *possesses* the attribute justice) is liable to be confused with 'The just is the just' (i.e. the attribute justice *is* the attribute justice). The confusion amounts to a failure to distinguish between being an attribute and having it, which in turn reflects an ontology lacking an adequate differentiation between attributes and the things that have them. Attributes are thought of in an undifferentiated way as 'things' (cf. c1), which are manifested in or by other things, but whose primary manifestation is in their own being. Hence it is natural for Plato to say (d8–e1) that unless holiness were itself holy, nothing else would be; if holiness were not manifested in its own being there would not be any such thing to be manifested in other things. In developing this line of thought Plato is led to the position (*Ph.* 74a–d, *Symp.* 211a–b, *Rep.* V, 476a–480a) that at least some important classes of attributes are completely manifested *only* by themselves, in contrast with their more or less imperfect or incomplete manifestation by observable instances, a position central to his theory of Forms. On that theory see e.g. Ross, Crombie II, ch. 3 and Vlastos in Bambrough ed.; on the role of self-predication in the theory see Vlastos *PR* 54 (but see his later view in *PS* pp.259–65).

It is frequently assumed (e.g. by Robinson p.234) that all propositions involving self-predication are necessarily false. This is not so. While some attributes, e.g. those possessed exclusively by physical objects, such as weight and solidity, or those possessed exclusively by living things, including all types of behaviour, cannot be truly predicated of any attribute, other attributes can be truly predicated of attributes. Thus both Socrates and wisdom may be interesting, or admired by the Greeks. Within this class some attributes are necessarily true of themselves; thus unity is a unitary attribute. In other cases the truth or falsity of a self-predicational proposition is contingent; thus, if, as is almost certainly the case, it is false that the property of being interesting to every physicist is interesting to every physicist, that is a contingent truth about the interests of physicists, not a necessary truth. Some attributes, again, are predicable of other attributes, the truth or falsity of the predication being contingent, while their self-predication is necessarily false or unintelligible (I am not concerned to demarcate the disputed boundary between the latter two concepts); thus while beauty may be bestowed by the gods, being bestowed by the gods cannot be said to be bestowed by the gods, nor beauty to be beautiful. The necessary or contingent truth or falsity of any self-predicational proposition must be examined in the particular case. As regards the examples here, justice as an attribute of persons cannot be said to be just whether we take 'just' as 'disposed to behave fairly' or as 'having the correct relation between the parts of one's soul'. It is likely that 'Holiness is holy' involves an equivocation between the sense of the term as applied to things and its sense as applied to persons: see n. on 325a1, pp.96–7 above. Hence it is not, strictly, a genuine example of self-predication.

330c5 The presentation here and at d6 of the pairs 'just–unjust' and 'holy–unholy' as apparently exhaustive alternatives indicates that no distinction is made here between contrary and contradictory. Since 346d1–3 shows Plato aware of the distinction, we should not take him to be confusing the notions of contrary and contradictory as such, but rather to be treating these particular pairs as pairs of contradictories. On the legitimacy of that procedure see n. on 331a9–b1, pp.114–5 below.

330c7 'justice is such as to be just'. 'Such as to be F' is frequently used by Plato as equivalent to the simple 'F', as is clearly the case here and at d5–e1. (Here Socrates, having said that justice is just, immediately adds, 'So I should answer the question "Is justice just or unjust" by saying that it is such as to be just.' At d5–e1 the question 'Is holiness such as to be holy or unholy?' receives the reply, 'How could anything else be holy if holiness itself isn't?') The 'as' in 'such as to be' renders *hoion*, the word also rendered by 'like' at 330a5 etc. The point of expressing the self-predications in a form containing *hoion* may perhaps be that Plato feels that the desired conclusion emerges more clearly if the argument is in the form

x is such as (*hoion*) to be F
y is not like (*hoion*) x
∴ y is not such as (*hoion*) to be F,

than if it is in the simpler form

113

$$x \text{ is } F$$
$$y \text{ is not like } x$$
$$\therefore y \text{ is not } F$$

Whether the former schema has any heuristic advantage is a matter of doubt; logically the two are equivalent.

330d6 Cf. c5, with n. p.113 above.

330d7 'watch what you say': lit. 'do not say anything blasphemous or ill-omened'.

331a9 The point of the transition from 10 'Justice is not such as to be holy' to 11 'Justice is such as to be not-holy' is presumably to facilitate the clinching move to 14 'Justice is such as to be unholy.'

331a9–b1 As was remarked on 330c5, for the purposes of this argument 'just' and 'unjust' and 'holy' and 'unholy' are treated as pairs of contradictories rather than as contraries. In general, both pairs must be regarded as pairs of contraries, since failing a special context most things are neither just nor unjust and neither holy nor unholy. In some restricted contexts, e.g. those of games or judicial proceedings, 'just' (or 'fair') and 'unjust' (or 'unfair') are indeed contradictories, e.g. every chess move which is not fair is unfair and vice versa, and every judicial decision which is not just is unjust and vice versa. But where, as the context here requires, the terms are applied in virtue of settled dispositions of character, they must be contraries, not contradictories. Thus if 'just' as applied to persons means 'having a settled disposition to respect the rights of others' and as applied to actions 'appropriate to someone with a settled disposition to respect the rights of others', then 'unjust' must mean 'having or appropriate to someone having a settled disposition not to respect the rights of others', i.e. it must be the contrary, not the contradictory. For if we render 'unjust' as the contradictory, i.e. 'not having or not appropriate to someone having a settled disposition to respect the rights of others', we reach absurdities, e.g. that children are unjust in so far as they do not have any settled dispositions at all, and that acts which manifest no disposition with regard to others, e.g. blowing one's nose, are unjust acts. The case of holiness gives similar results. The treatment of these pairs as contradictory pairs is thus fallacious.

In fact, Socrates' argument does not require this additional stage. The essence of the argument is that 3, together with 5 and 8, commits Protagoras to denying that holiness is just and justice holy, which is unacceptable (331b1—3). Therefore, since 5 and 8 are true, 3 has to be rejected. The crucial denials are elicited at 9 and 10 respectively. The function of the steps from 9 to 13 via 12 and from 10 to 14 via 11 is to highlight the unacceptability of the conclusions thus reached by putting them in the shocking form 'Holiness is unjust' and 'Justice is unholy'. Eristically this may be effective, but the logical work is complete by 9 and 10.

331b3—6 Adam and Adam (p.134) take 'the same answer' to be that just given by Socrates, viz. that justice is holy and holiness just. They point out (i) that what immediately follows, viz. that justice is either the same as holiness or similar etc., is not literally the same answer as Socrates has just given, and (ii) that at c1—2 Protagoras refers to the admission that justice is holy and holiness just, not to the admission that justice and holiness are like one another. Consequently they render b4 as '*because* justice is either the same thing as holiness . . .'; *hoti* may mean either 'because' or 'that'. On this interpretation the conclusion of the argument is 'Justice is holy and holiness just', while 'Justice and holiness are like one another' is a premiss or intermediate stage from which that conclusion is derived. But (a) it is clear from 330a—b that the thesis under examination is Protagoras' assumption that none of the virtues is *hoion* any other; consequently we should expect the argument to conclude with the negation of that thesis. (b) That expectation is fulfilled at 333b5—6, where Socrates says that it has been shown that justice and holiness are practically identical. Hence we must reject this interpretation. Both the Adams' grounds are met by the same reply, viz. that since, given the preceding steps of the argument, the conclusion that justice and holiness are like one another follows directly from the admission that justice is holy and holiness just, that step which leads directly to the conclusion is treated (loosely) as just the same answer as the conclusion itself; cf. Gallop op. cit. pp.92—3.

Socrates' three alternative formulations of the conclusion correspond roughly to the different senses of 'like' identified in the note on 330a6—7, pp.110—11 above. 'Justice is the same thing as holiness' is sense (i), 'justice is very similar (to holiness)' covers a spread from sense (ii) upwards to sense (i), while 'justice is like holiness' covers senses (ii)—(iv). It was pointed out in that note that while Protagoras' original position involved sense (i) and perhaps sense (ii), the argument required a shift to senses (iii) and (iv). While one might at first suspect that it is a sense of this shift which makes Socrates give most emphatic expression to the weakest formulation 'Justice

is like holiness and holiness like justice', this can hardly be so, for at
333b5–6 the conclusion is stated in terms of the stronger
formulation 'Justice and holiness are virtually identical', indicating
that Socrates feels himself as entitled to the stronger as to the
weaker formulation.

331b4–5 'justness'. This form, occasionally found in Plato and
other authors as a variant for 'justice', is presumably used for the
sake of the identity of termination with 'holiness', which is
particularly appropriate in an assertion of identity between the
virtues for which the names stand.

The foregoing account of the argument takes the self-predicational
propositions in the simple sense 'Justice is an attribute of justice'
and 'Holiness is an attribute of holiness.' It might, however, be
objected that this does less than justice to the special nature of
self-predication, which indicates not merely an attribute of the
subject, but at least an essential attribute and perhaps even the
sole essential attribute. (F is an essential attribute of x if and only
if, if x exists, it follows that x is F.) If 5 is accordingly rephrased as
    5a it is an essential feature of justice that it is just,
and 3 is interpreted in terms of essential features, giving (to take the
simplest interpretation)
    3a No virtue has any essential feature in common with any other,
        either in itself or with respect to its power,
then we may validly derive
    9a It is not an essential feature of holiness that it is just.
But from this we cannot proceed as the argument requires to
    12a It is a feature of holiness that it is not just,
since though being just cannot (by 9a) be an essential feature of holiness it might be a non-essential feature. Cf. the parallel inference
from 'It is not an essential feature of all triangles that they are equiangular' (true) to 'It is a feature of all triangles that they are not
equiangular' (false). In order that 12 should be validly derived, 3a
would have to be further strengthened, to become
    3a′ No virtue possesses, either essentially or non-essentially, any
        attribute which is an essential feature of any other virtue,
        either in itself or with respect to its power.
It is clear that the thesis which Protagoras commits himself to at
330a4–b6, represented by 3 in the original formulation of the
argument, cannot be understood in the sense of either 3a or 3a′.
Both have the immediate consequence that, since a virtue is essentially a good state of character, there cannot be more than one
virtue. According to 3a, if goodness is an essential feature of x it
cannot be an essential feature of y, unless x is identical with y,

116

i.e. unless *y* is identical with *x* it cannot be a virtue. According to 3a′, if goodness is an essential feature of *x* then no virtue other than *x* can be good either essentially or non-essentially, i.e. once again no virtue other than *x* can exist. Since Protagoras' intention is to insist on the plurality of the virtues, his words should not be interpreted, provided a reasonable alternative interpretation is available, in a sense which immediately commits him to the denial of that thesis.

Savan *Phron* 64 attempts to present the argument in such a way that self-predication is not involved. He interprets 330c7 'Justice is such as to be just' as 'The *dunamis* of justice is just action' and d5 'Holiness is such as to be holy' as 'The *dunamis* of holiness is holy action.' By the analogy of the parts of the face, each with its own function, these are parallel to 'The *dunamis* of the eye is sight' and 'The *dunamis* of the ear is hearing.' He sees the remainder of the argument as relying on a parallelism between what is actually said about the virtues and an implicit argument about the objects of the senses. The latter runs:

> Sight is necessarily a seeing of colours.
> Hearing is not coloured.
> ∴ Hearing is invisible.

Hence, by the analogy, justice is unholy and holiness is unjust. Since the conclusion is unacceptable, the analogy must be rejected.

Savan is indeed correct in saying that Socrates is in fact represented as holding that, on the analogy with the power of the eye or the ear, the power of justice, conceived as a permanent state of the person, is to promote just action, and that of holiness to promote holy action (see n. on 330a4, p.110 above). But it is quite impossible that the Greek of 330c7 should *mean* 'The power of justice is (to promote) just action.' For that sentence follows directly from c1–2 'Justice is something' and c3–6 'That thing is just', and is given as the answer to the question 'Is justice just or unjust?' (see p.113 above). Again, Savan's interpretation does not give a good sense to 330d8–9 'How could anything else be holy, if holiness itself is not to be holy?' The first occurrence of 'be holy' in that sentence is clearly an ordinary predication; it is very hard to see the second as something altogether different.

Secondly, the analogy between the virtues (with their powers) and the parts of the face (with theirs) does not appear in the text from 330b2 to the end of the argument. Moreover the crucial point of Savan's interpretation, that whatever is seen must be coloured, whatever is heard must make a sound etc., does not appear at all. In short, the argument which Savan ascribes to Socrates is not in the text.

117

Thirdly, as presented by Savan, that argument is incoherent. The analogy on which it depends breaks down, since in the case of the virtues nothing corresponds to the objects of sense. This becomes clear when we attempt to set out the analogy in tabular form.

	Senses			Virtues	
Organ	Power	Object	State	Power	?
eye	sight	colour	justice	just action	?
ear	hearing	sound	holiness	holy action	?

It is therefore impossible to construct for the virtues an argument parallel to that which Savan supplies for the sense-organs:

Sight is necessarily a seeing of   Just action is necessarily ?
colours.
Hearing is not coloured.   Holy action is not ?
∴ Hearing is invisible.   ∴ Holy action is ?

In fact Savan falls into confusion even over his own analogy. Justice corresponds to the eye and just action to sight. Holiness corresponds to the ear and holy action to hearing. Hence the proper parallel to 'Holiness is unjust' is not 'Hearing is invisible' but 'The ear is invisible', which is false. In order to reach the desired conclusion by way of the true proposition 'Hearing is invisible' Savan has to treat holiness as what corresponds to hearing, thus destroying the analogy. He blurs this crucial distinction by referring (p.133) to 'justice (understood as *dunamis*)' and to 'holiness (understood as *dunamis*)'.

I conclude that Savan's interpretation is to be rejected, on the following grounds:
(i)   it falsifies the natural meaning of the Greek,
(ii)   it presents an argument not found in the text,
(iii)   the argument which it presents is incoherent.
(i) and (ii) are grounds for rejecting the interpretation as an account of what Plato meant. (iii) is not directly a ground, since Plato might himself have put forward an incoherent argument. But the only plausible ground for assuming that Plato must have meant something different from what he explicitly says is that his own words are vitiated by obvious flaws from which the interpretation is free (cf. the discussion of Vlastos which follows). If the interpretation itself is incoherent, as Savan's is, then nothing is gained by positing it.

Yet another account of the self-predication in this argument is given by Vlastos op. cit. According to this view all the instances in the dialogue where a virtue-character is predicated of a virtue (e.g. 'Justice is holy'), including the instances of self-predication, are cases of 'Pauline predication' (so called from the example

'Charity suffereth long etc.' in St. Paul's First Epistle to the Corinthians). Pauline predication is the grammatical ascription of a predicate to a universal, when in fact the predicate properly belongs (and is (?) implicitly understood by the speaker to belong) to the instances of the universal, and belongs to them necessarily: thus 'Justice is holy' is to be understood as 'Justice is such that whatever is just is, necessarily, holy', and 'Justice is just' as 'Justice is such that anything which is just is, necessarily, just.' (See Vlastos op. cit., *PS* ch. 11, and *Phron* 74; also Peterson *PR* 73.) On Vlastos's account of the dialogue as a whole (see p.104 above) Socrates' thesis is that the names of the virtues are names of one and the same thing, in the sense that these names are inter-predicable *as Pauline predications.* Thus the thesis that e.g. 'holiness' and 'justice' name the same thing (i.e. the thesis that holiness is justice) is equivalent to the conjunction of 'Holiness is just' and 'Justice is holy' understood as Pauline predications, i.e. to 'Justice and holiness are such that, necessarily, anything is just if and only if it is holy.'

The grounds for Vlastos's reinterpretation are discussed above (pp.104–8). In general, it invites the objection that it requires the reader to read an enormous amount into the text without any guidance: e.g. Vlastos nowhere explains how the reader might be expected to understand 'Holiness is justice' in the sense given above, in advance of the painstaking step-by-step explanation which he himself gives (pp.224–42). This highlights the difficulty in Vlastos's view that Plato used Pauline predication without knowing that he was doing so (pp.263–5). If a meaning imputed to an author is apparent neither to the author himself nor to an intelligent and linguistically competent reader, the sense in which the author actually had that meaning remains obscure. On this argument in particular, Vlastos's reinterpretation (i) fails to account for the emphasis on the attribution of the qualities to the things (*pragmata,* i.e. the virtues) themselves (330c–d), and (ii) like Savan's interpretation, does not deal adequately with 330d8–9 (see p.117 above). Vlastos does not consider (ii), while on (i) he merely asserts without argument (p.252) that 'We know . . . that Socrates thinks of "Justice" as the name of a universal and that he does *not* think of universals as persons, nor yet as ontological dependencies of persons . . . This being the case, to say of any universal that it is just or unjust . . . would be sheer nonsense.' Against this, it is clear that Socrates is represented in this dialogue as thinking of the virtues as things (characters or perhaps forces) in people which account for their acting in certain ways, but quite unclear what, if anything, Socrates might have been supposed to think about the ontological status of those entities. If justice is seen as a force in a man causing him to act justly, it is by no means *obviously nonsensical* to describe it as holy, or for that matter as just. (For evidence from dialogues other than the *Protagoras* that the virtues are regarded primarily as properties of persons see Penner *PR* 73 p.48 n.17; cf. Santas in *EA* pp.110–11.) See also Devereux *Apeiron* 77.

Vlastos claims confirmation for his interpretation on the ground that given that interpretation the Biconditionality Thesis follows from the Similarity Thesis, as it is required to do e.g. at 349d. On that passage see pp.148–9 below. It is certainly true that his interpretation has that consequence, since on that interpretation the Similarity and Biconditionality Theses are in fact identical. He claims, however, that if the predications in this argument are ordinary, non-Pauline predications, then the Biconditionality Thesis does not follow. All that Socrates could show would be that justice and holiness resembled each other in being just and holy, and *'from the fact that a universal has certain properties nothing follows to the effect that its instances have those properties'* (pp.255–6; author's italics). The quoted assertion is true, but misses the point. As has been shown (pp.108–9, 115–6 above), what Socrates is claiming to show is that the two virtues resemble one another in every respect, i.e. are identical. Hence whoever has one, has the other, i.e. the Biconditionality Thesis is true. Vlastos's interpretation therefore lacks the support which he claims to be given by this argument. See also Weiss *Phoenix* 85, McKirahan ibid., Wakefield *Phron* 87.

331b8–332a4 *Protagoras objects to Socrates' argument; the discussion ends inconclusively.*

331d1–e4 Protagoras comes very near to identifying the central flaw in Socrates' argument, the shift in the force of 'like' which it requires. He agrees that the virtues, like the parts of the face and indeed anything whatever, are like one another in sense (iv), i.e. they have some characteristic(s) in common, but maintains, rightly, that that minimal sense of 'like' is not sufficient to warrant the description of things which are thus alike as similar in the ordinary sense, i.e. sense (ii) of 'like'. He implies that his original thesis commits him to no more than that the virtues are dissimilar in that sense, and that that thesis has not been touched by Socrates' argument. In both implied contentions he is correct.

331d1-5 Protagoras states a necessary truth, viz. that given any two things x and y, there is some predicate F such that Fx and Fy. A modern writer would make this clear by giving F the sense 'belonging to the class consisting of x and y'; Protagoras is more probably represented as having in mind the fact that everything whatever is something, one thing, something which is etc. (cf. *Theaet.* 188e−189a). Though his examples are both of opposites which merge into one another in an intermediate area, he can hardly be thought of as making the obviously false assertion that any two things whatever shade into one another. Rather the point of choosing opposites is presumably that if the universal thesis is true for things which are 'completely opposite', i.e. completely unlike, it will be true *a fortiori* for things which are less completely unlike. In that case the examples are ill-chosen, since opposites must be of the same kind as one another, hence not completely unlike.

331e5−332a1 Protagoras is as imprecise in his statement of his position as Socrates was in drawing his conclusion (b4−6). He presumably feels that the actual degree of resemblance between the virtues is somewhere between genuine similarity (sense (ii)) and minimal likeness (sense (iv)), i.e. in the area occupied by sense (iii). Clarity is impossible in the absence of any attempt at a precise demarcation of these senses.

331e6 'Not exactly'. The phrase translates *ou panu*, lit. 'not' + the intensive adverb, similar in sense to 'very'. Examination of the usage of this phrase suggests that it may be taken either as 'not very much, not altogether' or as 'very much not', i.e. 'not at all'. Some contexts fit the former better, some the latter, while many, like the present, could fit either. Guthrie (Penguin) renders as here, 'Not quite that', Jowett[4] ('Certainly not') and Croiset (Budé: 'Nullement') in the other sense.

332a2−4 The discussion of the relation between justice and holiness is broken off at this point without an agreed conclusion, and is not resumed. Protagoras, though in a somewhat undecided state of mind (see above on 331e5−332a1) has not accepted Socrates' conclusion, and has indeed indicated a major weakness in his argument (see n. on 331d1--e4, p.120 above). Since it was a cardinal rule of Socratic dialectic that both parties to the discussion must agree on any step before it could count as established (for refs. see Robinson pp.15−17), it is particularly surprising that Socrates should claim at 333b5−6 that the virtual identity of justice and holiness has been shown, and even more surprising that Protagoras should let the claim go unchallenged. Cf. n. on 349d2−5, pp.148−9 below.

332a4−333b6 *Socrates argues that wisdom is identical*

with soundness of mind (sōphrosunē).

The structure of the argument is as follows:
1. Wisdom is the opposite of folly (332a4−6; agreed without argument).
2. Soundness of mind is the opposite of folly (e4−5; established by an argument in three stages, (i) a6−b4, (ii) b4−c2, (iii) d1−e5).
3. Each thing which is an opposite has only one opposite (c7−8; established by induction in c3−7).
4. Therefore, wisdom and soundness of mind are identical (333b4−5).

An argument of the same structure is used at *Alc. II* 138c−139c; there Socrates argues that madness and folly must be identical, as they are both opposites of intelligence (*phronēsis*).

332a4 'folly'. The sense of the Greek *aphrosunē* is close to that of its English rendering, viz. failure, often of a gross kind, to take proper account of the considerations which should guide one's actions. It is thus the opposite of wisdom when the latter is understood as prudence, which is one of several senses of the Greek *sophia*. The latter term was used to designate either intellectual excellence in general or particular aspects thereof, and hence may in context require to be rendered 'wisdom', 'knowledge', 'learning', 'cleverness', or 'intelligence', as well as 'prudence'. Socrates' ignoring of the wider aspects of *sophia* represents a major flaw in the argument, since it is clear that Protagoras intends the term, not in the narrower sense of 'prudence', but in the wider sense of 'intellectual distinction'; see 349d, where he gives the opposite of 'wise' not as 'foolish' (i.e. imprudent, *aphrōn*) but as 'stupid, ignorant' (*amathēs*). (Cf. 337a where Prodicus contrasts the (intellectually) abler man (*sophōteros*) with the less able (*amathesteros*).) On the sense of 'opposite', see below, pp.127−8.

332a7 'act sensibly'. The context requires that the noun *sōphrosunē* and its cognates (including the verb *sōphronein*, which occurs here) be understood in the basic sense of 'soundness of mind, good sense' rather than in the derived sense of 'self-control, mastery of the bodily appetites', which predominates elsewhere in Plato (e.g. *Gorg.* 491d etc., *Rep.* IV, 430e etc.) and which is taken by Aristotle (*EN* III.10) as the central sense. Stage i of the argument for step 2 depends on two premisses 'If anyone acts rightly he *sōphronei*' and 'If anyone acts wrongly he does not *sōphronei*' (see below pp.124−5). While these premisses are at least reasonably plausible if *sōphronei* is taken as 'acts sensibly, shows good sense', they seem plainly false if the verb is read as 'shows self-control', since in some cases of right and wrong action the bodily appetites or similar impulses (e.g. anger) are not involved. In addition to this basic use of the term *sōphrosunē*, which is regular from its earliest occurrences in Homer to the fourth century B.C. and later, the word comes to stand for specific manifestations of soundness of mind, especially proper consciousness of one's own position relative to the claims of others, and hence respect or reverence (whether towards gods or men), self-abnegation, moderation, and modesty, and also mastery of one's desires, especially the bodily desires (see North). The contexts in which the term has previously occurred in this dialogue seem more appropriate to other aspects of soundness of mind than the control of appetite. In the myth, where *sōphrosunē* appears to be synonymous with *aidōs* and to be intimately associated with *dikaiosunē* as a central constituent of good citizenship (a traditional association, see North), the sense is that soundness of mind which makes a man accept his proper role in society and pay due regard to the rights of others (cf. n. on 322c2, pp.85–6), in which sense *sōphrōn* became a standard term of praise in the vocabulary of conservative political writers of the fourth century. At 323b4 it is used in the sense of soundness of mind as opposed to madness, another regular usage, especially frequent in Herodotus, while at 326a4 it occurs in the context of Protagoras' description of traditional Athenian education, with the sense of 'good behaviour', carrying implications of modesty, decorum, and respect for elders (as in the Right Argument's encomium of the old education, Arist. *Clouds* 961ff.). It is noteworthy that in the *Charmides*, an early dialogue devoted to the subject of *sōphrosunē*, mastery of appetite does not figure among the suggested accounts of the virtue; instead, the accounts offered are decorum, modesty (*aidōs*), performance of one's proper role (cf. the political sense mentioned above), the doing of good things, and self-knowledge, while Socrates hints, without asserting, that the correct account is the knowledge of good and bad (esp. 171d–176a), an account which, like the similar account of courage in the *Laches* (199c–e), would assimilate the specific virtue to *aretē* as a whole (see pp.153-4 below). It seems clear that the main purpose of the *Charmides* is to explore various aspects and possible developments of the traditional conception of *sōphrosunē* as soundness of mind, in which the term is virtually synonymous with one kind of *sophia*. In view of the statement of Xenophon (*Mem.* III.ix.4) that 'Socrates made no distinction between *sophia* and *sōphrosunē*, but used to say that the man who could recognize and make use of fine and good things and recognize

123

and avoid shameful things (cf. *Charm.*) was *sophos* and *sōphrōn*', it is possible that the view of *sōphrosunē* which predominates in the *Charmides* and *Protagoras* is closer to Socrates' own than the greater emphasis on self-control as the primary manifestation of soundness of mind which we find in the *Gorgias, Republic,* and elsewhere, which may represent a specifically Platonic development. This hypothesis receives some support from the fact that at *Laws* IV, 710a Plato defines 'everyday' *sōphrosunē* as self-control and describes the identification of *sōphrosunē* with *phronēsis* as a forced and exaggerated use of language. On the *Charmides* see Santas in *EA*.

332b1–2 'acts wrongly'. This renders *mē orthōs prattontes*, lit. 'acting not rightly' or 'not acting rightly'. 'Act rightly' and 'act wrongly' are contradictories, corresponding to the Greek *orthōs prattein* and *mē orthōs prattein.* Hence where '*R*' stands for '. . . acts rightly', '. . . acts wrongly' may be formalized as '–*R*'.

332a6–b4 Argument for premiss 2. Stage i. Using '*R*' to stand for '. . . acts rightly', '*S*' for '. . . acts sensibly', and '*F*' for '. . . acts foolishly', the first premiss (a6–7) of this stage may be formalized as

$$\text{(i) } (x) (Rx \to Sx),$$

i.e. 'If anyone acts rightly, he acts sensibly.' (This is to be understood as 'If anyone acts rightly, on every occasion of acting rightly he acts sensibly', not merely as 'If anyone acts rightly, he (sometimes) acts sensibly'. The stronger interpretation is indicated by the presence of 'in so acting' (a7).) I assume that 'and usefully' may be omitted from the formalization, on the ground that it is taken for granted here (as generally in Greek thought) that usefulness is not an extra condition which a case of acting rightly has to satisfy in order to qualify as sensible, but is a necessary feature of all right action, i.e. 'rightly and usefully' is truth-functionally equivalent to 'rightly'. There is no indication that 'rightly' has any specifically moral connotations here; rather it should be taken in the widest sense of 'doing the right thing'.

The second premiss (b1–3) may be taken in either of two ways, depending on the reference of the phrase 'in so acting'. That phrase may be taken as referring either to acting wrongly or to not acting sensibly. If it is taken in the former way, parallel to the use of the same phrase in a6–7, then the second premiss asserts that if anyone acts wrongly he has the two further characteristics of acting foolishly and not acting sensibly, i.e.

$$(x) (-Rx \to (Fx \,\&\, -Sx)).$$

If it is taken in the latter way, the implication of the sentence is that if anyone acts wrongly he acts foolishly and *therefore* (in so far as or because he acts foolishly) not sensibly. That implication is best captured by the formulation

$$(x)\,((-Rx \to Fx)\,\&\,(Fx \to -Sx)).$$

We thus have two possible pairs of premisses
    (a) i $(x)\,(Rx \to Sx)$
       iia $(x)\,(-Rx \to (Fx\,\&\,-Sx))$;
    (b) i $(x)\,(Rx \to Sx)$
       iib $(x)\,((-Rx \to Fx)\,\&\,(Fx \to -Sx)).$
From premiss–set (b) we may validly derive
       $(x)\,(Fx \leftrightarrow -Sx),$
as follows:

1. $(x)\,(Fx \to -Sx)$ from iib
2. $(x)\,(-Sx \to -Rx)$ from i, by contraposition
3. $(x)\,(-Rx \to Fx)$ from iib
4. $(x)\,(-Sx \to Fx)$ from 2 and 3, by syllogism
5. $(x)\,(Fx \to -Sx)\,\&\,(x)\,(-Sx \to Fx)$ from 1 and 4, by conjunction
6. $(x)\,(Fx \leftrightarrow -Sx)$ from 5, by def. of '$\leftrightarrow$'.

We have thus proved that acting foolishly is the *contradictory* of acting sensibly, which is one sense of 'opposite'.

    Premiss-set (a) does not, however, entail as it stands the conclusion that acting foolishly is the opposite of acting sensibly, in any sense of 'opposite'. Opposites are incompatible, but from i and iia we may not deduce

$$(x)\,-(Fx\,\&\,Sx),$$

since given i and iia there may be something which is both F and S, provided that it is also R. It is, however, possible that Plato assumes the incompatibility of F and S throughout, on the basis of the ordinary meaning of the terms. iia thus states explicitly a condition presupposed by i, viz. that F and S do not apply together to the same thing. On that reading i may be re-formulated as

$$\text{ia}\ (x)\,(Rx \to (Sx\,\&\,-Fx)),$$

from which, together with iia, we can once again reach the conclusion

$$(x)\,(Fx \leftrightarrow -Sx).$$

(The proof is left to the reader.) Thus, given a reasonably plausible assumption, either reading of premiss ii enables Socrates to reach (validly) a conclusion to the effect that acting foolishly is the opposite of acting sensibly. There seems little point in speculation as to which reading of the premiss is closer to Plato's intentions.

COMMENTARY 332b4

332b4–c2   Stage ii. Socrates establishes the premisses which will
be used in stage iii to reach the conclusion that folly is the opposite
of soundness of mind. The premisses are:
i.   Acting foolishly is the opposite of acting sensibly (b3–4).
ii.   Foolish acts are done from folly, sensible acts from good sense
      (b4–6).
iii. If x is done oppositely (to y), then x is done from the opposite
      (of that from which y is done) (c1–2).
The parentheses in iii are necessary to complete the sense. iii is
supported by a number of examples, evidently designed to establish
the (unstated) generalization

(x) if x is done F-ly, then x is done from F-ness.

In giving his examples Socrates slips back and forward between
examples satisfying that formula and examples satisfying its converse;
only the former has any role in the argument.
    The sense of 'from' in the above generalization is problematic.
At a8–b1 it is taken as an immediate consequence of 'A acts
sensibly' that it is with good sense that A acts sensibly. It is an
immediate (and trivial) consequence if 'acts with good sense' is
equivalent to 'acts sensibly', but not if 'acts with good sense'
means 'acts as a result of the possession of a specific state of
character called "good sense" '. The construction translated 'with'
(the dative case of the noun) is capable of being taken in either way.
The same construction, generating the same ambiguity, is employed
in the next three instances, folly, strength, and weakness (b4–7),
while the instances of speed and slowness (b8–c1), where the
sentence employs the preposition 'with' (*meta* + genitive case),
normally indicating accompaniment rather than cause, suggest that
the inference is rather of the trivial than of the substantive, causal
type. Yet in the next sentence the construction shifts to the
preposition 'from' (*hupo* + genitive), whose main use is causal,
and which is regularly used of the causation of action by mental
states; this construction is maintained throughout the rest of the
argument. In view of the emphasis placed on the powers of the
virtues (330a, 333a; see n. on 330a4, p.110 above), and in view
of the undeniably causal account of the relation between wisdom
and courageous action (360a–c, see below p.211), it is likely that
Plato intends his conclusion, at least as applied to good sense and
folly, in the sense that it is the presence of these internal states
which accounts for the doing of the corresponding actions, and not
merely that the actions may be described as actions displaying those
characteristics, where the description is purely classificatory, without
any explanatory force. Yet some of the instances which support his

conclusion suggest the latter model or at least allow it as well as the former. It is likely that Plato is unaware of the ambiguity in his instances, which may reflect a failure to grasp with sufficient clarity the distinction between the application of predicates such as 'sensible' or 'just' to persons and their application to actions. In so far as 'sensible' or 'just' signify attributes of actions, then acting sensibly or justly is acting with good sense or justice; in so far as they signify attributes of persons, viz. the possession by those persons of states of character which account for actions, then acting sensibly or justly is not necessarily acting *from* good sense or justice, but the connection between action and internal state needs to be established. At *Rep.* IV, 444c Plato shows himself more clearly aware of the distinction between the application of these terms to persons and their application to actions. (I am indebted for this point to Mr. M. J. Woods.)

332c1–2 The translation, which follows the Greek closely, is to be read as 'If x is done in the same way (as y), then x is done from the same (as that from which y is done), and if x is done in the opposite way (to y), then x is done from the opposite (of that from which y is done).' d3–4 and e1–2 are to be read similarly. The Greek, unlike the English, is idiomatic.

332c3 'is there such a thing as the beautiful?': lit. 'is anything beautiful?' This (and the similar constructions in c5 and 6–7) might be taken merely as the minimal question whether there are any beautiful things. But the fact that 'the beautiful' is treated as something singular (c3–4), which has *one* opposite, not many (c8–9), makes it clear that the expression 'the beautiful' refers to that single character common to all beautiful things, which has a single opposite character, viz. the ugly; see n. on 330c2–7, pp.112–3 above. The grammatical construction of the sentence is probably 'Is anything (the) beautiful?', where the 'is' is the 'is' of identity, and the definite article is omitted, as is ordinarily the case, from the grammatical complement. The ontological status of characters such as the beautiful is not discussed in this dialogue.

332c3–9 The argument for premiss 2 is interrupted by the induction to establish premiss 3, viz.
    Each thing which is an opposite has only one opposite. The examples, fine or beautiful (*kalon*) and shameful or ugly (*aischron*), good and bad and high- and low-pitched, are examples not of contradictories nor of simple incompatibles but of polar opposites, i.e. of qualities at either end of a continuous scale. *Kalon*

127

and *aischron* are treated as polar opposites rather than contradictories at 346d1–3, and good and bad similarly at 351d6–7; the intermediate pitch between high and low is mentioned at *Phil.* 17c4–5. While Plato's usage of the term 'opposite' (*enantion*) covers cases both of polar opposites and of contradictories, together with a number of undifferentiated cases, clear examples of polar opposites are more frequent than clear examples of contradictories; further, the definition of 'opposition' given in the Platonic *Definitions* (a collection probably compiled in the Academy), amounts to a definition of polar opposition, viz. 'the greatest distance according to any differentia of things falling under a single genus' (416, 24–5). The most likely rendering of premiss 3, therefore, is not 'Each thing has only one contradictory' but 'To any quality at one end of a scale there is opposed only one quality at the other end of that scale', which is analytically true. It is also likely that this is the sense of 'opposite' required in premiss 1, not merely because the phrase 'the very opposite' (*pan tounantion*) is used by Plato more frequently of polar opposites than of contradictories, but also because one would suppose that many people and actions display neither wisdom nor folly. Premisses 1 and 3, then, should be read as

1. Wisdom is a polar opposite of folly

and

3. Any quality that is a polar opposite has only one polar opposite. Hence if the argument were to be valid, premiss 2 would have to be read as

Good sense is a polar opposite of folly.

The deduction from those premisses of the conclusion

Wisdom is identical with good sense

would amount to a demonstration of the synonymy of the terms 'wisdom' and 'good sense', since properties are normally thought of as grouped in scales in virtue of the meaning of the terms which designate them, e.g. we think of 'hot' and 'cold' and '100°C' and 'O°C' as lying on different scales. A valid instance of this argument form would be:

'Torrid' and 'freezing' are polar opposites. In virtue of the mean-
'Torrid' and 'icy' are polar opposites.   ing of the terms.
Any polar opposite has only one opposite.
∴ 'Freezing' and 'icy' designate one and the same property (in virtue of the meaning of the terms).

It would be possible, but more far-fetched, to construct a similar argument which does not rely wholly on considerations of meaning, as follows:

'Torrid' and 'freezing' are polar opposites (as above).
'Torrid' and 'below O°C' are polar opposites (established by

observation of the continuous progression of temperatures from below O°C to a level which we should call 'torrid').
Any polar opposite has only one polar opposite.
∴ 'Freezing' and 'below O°C' designate one and the same property (in virtue of the meaning of the terms and of the observed facts).
But the actual argument requires us to take premiss 2 as
Good sense is the contradictory of folly
(see n. on 332a6–b4, pp.124–5 above). Hence 'opposite' is used in two different senses, and consequently the argument is invalid through the fallacy of equivocation.

In the case of any range of qualities one of whose extremes is designated by the term '*P*', the contradictory term 'not-*P*' will designate all the rest of the range, including the opposite extreme (which may be designed by '*O*'); hence the quality *O* will be a member of a set of qualities designated by 'not-*P*', and the set of things characterized by *O* will be a sub-set of the set of things characterized by not-*P*. This relation is satisfied by Plato's examples. If 'good sense' means that soundness of judgement which one displays on *every* occasion (no matter how trivial) on which one does the right thing, then 'wisdom' must surely stand for a higher degree of soundness, something more than minimal common sense. Plato's argument leads to the unremarkable conclusion that wisdom, in the sense of a noteworthy degree of practical intelligence, is an instance or kind of soundness of mind, but fails to show that the terms 'wisdom' and 'soundness of mind' are synonymous, or even that they designate one and the same state of character. It is probable that Plato was attempting to give a rigorous demonstration of the synonymy between *sophia* and *sōphrosunē* which emerges (given the appropriate senses of the terms) from ordinary usage (see n. on 332a7, pp.122–4 above), but that he failed to notice that his argument involved a slip between senses of 'opposite'.

This flaw in the argument also invalidates Vlastos's claim (op. cit. pp.243–6) that the structure of this argument provides clear support for his interpretation of the unity of the virtues in terms of the Biconditionality Thesis: 'The argument for their "unity", if sound, has established that they are "one and the same" in just the sense required by the Biconditionality Thesis: they are attributes necessarily instantiated *in one and the same class of persons*' (p.246; author's italics). It is indeed true that the argument which establishes premiss 2 shows that that premiss has to be taken as asserting that folly and soundness of mind are opposite attributes, in the sense that the classes of those who possess them are mutually exclusive and exhaustive. Hence if the whole argument were to be

129

valid, it would require premiss 1 to say that wisdom and folly are opposite in the same sense of 'opposite', and premiss 3 to say that each thing has only one opposite, again in the same sense of 'opposite'. From those premisses it would follow that the class of the wise was identical with that of the sound in mind, i.e. the conclusion would be the Biconditionality Thesis, with respect to wisdom and soundness of mind. But we have seen that in premisses 1 and 3 Plato shifts, apparently unconsciously, to a different sense of 'opposite', (viz. polar opposite), which would more naturally be used in arguments in support of a thesis to the effect that different terms designating opposites are synonymous (though it could, at a stretch, be used to support a thesis that different terms have the same reference (pp.128–9 above). Hence it cannot be maintained that Plato's intention in this argument is clearly to establish the Biconditionality Thesis only.

332d1–e5 Argument for premiss 2. Stage iii. Socrates resumes the argument interrupted at c3. d2–3 repeats premiss 3, and d3–7 recapitulates premisses i–iii of stage ii of the argument for premiss 2. (The order of the recapitulation is iii, i, ii.) e1–3 adds the required steps that, since sensible action, being done oppositely to foolish action (by i), is done from the opposite of that by which foolish action is done (by iii), and since sensible action is done from good sense and foolish action from folly (by ii), therefore folly is the opposite of good sense. The argument is invalid, since x could be done oppositely from y, and x be done from F-ness and y be done from G-ness and F-ness still not be the opposite of G-ness, in the case where x is done both from F-ness and H-ness, when H-ness is not identical with F-ness and H-ness is the opposite of G-ness; e.g. an action done from thoughtlessness and boredom would be done oppositely to an action done from good sense, but it is thoughtlessness, and not boredom, which is the opposite (i.e. contradictory) of good sense (cf. Penner *PR* 73 p.53, n.25). As it stands the argument justifies the conclusion that sensible action is done from the opposite of folly; in order to reach the conclusion that good sense is the opposite of folly it requires in addition specification of the sense of 'from', such that if x is done from F-ness, then it cannot be the case that x is also done from anything other than F-ness. Any such specification would involve substantial recasting of the argument, since it would require the rejection of the implicit generalization on which premiss iii depends (see n. on b4–c2, pp.126–7 above):

(x) If x is done F-ly, then x is done from F-ness.

For if that generalization is retained, together with the new requirement that if *x* is done from *F*-ness it is not done from anything other than *F*-ness, it follows that if *x* is done *F*-ly it cannot be done in any way other than *F*-ly, i.e. no action may be modified in more than one way, which is absurd. If Plato were to avoid these difficulties he would have to distinguish more clearly than is done in the actual argument between the force of 'from *F*-ness' as a causal account of action and 'by or with *F*-ness' as a description.

333a1–b6 Having reached a conclusion which is incompatible with Protagoras' original thesis of the non-identity of *sophia* and *sōphrosunē*, Socrates offers him the choice of abandoning that thesis or giving up premiss 3, 'Each thing which is an opposite has only one opposite.' He assumes without justification that premisses 1 and 2 are not open to question.

333a2–5 The theses of the non-identity of the parts of excellence, and of their unlikeness and that of their powers (i.e. Protagoras' original theses 1, 2, and 4, see p.109 above) are referred to as a single *logos*. This provides some indirect support for the suggestion made above (p.109) that in the first argument Socrates is concerned to criticize all three, not just thesis 2.

333b5–6 See notes on 331b3–6 (pp.115–6 above) and on 332a2–4 (p.121 above).

333b7–334a2 *Socrates begins an argument to prove the identity of justice with sōphrosunē.*

333c1 The context requires that *sōphronein* have the same sense here as in the previous argument. While it might be argued that on a particular occasion a man might show self-control in the course of acting unjustly (e.g. a robber waiting in ambush for hours in the heat of the day), the common opinion (c2–3) cannot be that some men show self-control *because* or *in so far as* they act unjustly, since unjust conduct was generally associated in ordinary opinion with lack of self-control (see e.g. 322c–323a). Rather the common opinion is that some men are sensible to act unjustly (i.e. those who can get away with it); cf. *Rep.* II, 366b.

333c6–9 In order that a thesis should be open to examination by Socrates' method of questioning, it has to be verbally maintained by someone, irrespective of whether the person defending it actually believes it. If he does not believe it, it turns out to be a test for him presumably in the sense of a test of his ability to defend a thesis. There does not seem to be any inconsistency with 331c5–d1; in that passage the demand is not so much that Protagoras should state his personal opinion as that he should state his thesis in an unconditional form. Contrast *Gorg.* 495a, where Socrates warns Callicles against preserving consistency by answering contrary to his real opinion. The rule of the game was presumably that anyone defending a thesis *of his own* must give only what he believed to be true answers, while anyone answering on behalf of someone else could give whatever answers he took to express the belief of the person whose views he was defending.

333d5–6 'mean'. The Greek is literally 'to be sensible you say (*legeis*) (is) to show good sense'. *Legein A B* can mean either 'to call *A B*', e.g. 342b 'those whom Protagoras called "the Sophists"' or 'those whom Protagoras called sophists', or 'to mean *B* by *A*', e.g. 341b–c, ' "What did Simonides mean by *chalepon*?" (*ti elegen to "chalepon"*;). "He meant 'bad'." ' While either sense is possible here, the phrases rendered 'show good sense' and 'plan well', *eu phronein* and *eu bouleuesthai*, are pretty clearly synonymous, and it is most natural to suppose that *legein* is used to pick out this synonymy; if so, it must have the same sense in linking 'be sensible' and 'show good sense', since the verb actually occurs only once, at d5, being understood (naturally with the same sense) at d6.

While any reconstruction of the unfinished argument must be conjectural, the early introduction by Socrates of the theses that a man shows good sense when he acts well (i.e. successfully, d7) and that things that benefit men are good (d8–e1) suggest that Plato might have had in mind an argument on the lines of *Gorg.* 469a–479d, to the effect that someone acts in such a way as to benefit himself, i.e. acts in such a way as to gain the possession of good things, i.e. acts well, i.e. shows good sense, if and only if he acts justly, cf. Sprague *Apeiron* 67 and McKirahan *Apeiron* 84. Such an argument might terminate with the demonstration of the biconditional relation, or it might proceed to the conclusion that, since it is through or in acting justly that one acts with good sense (*sōphronōs*), and since *sōphrosunē* is (by definition) that by which one acts *sōphronōs*, then justice proves to be the same state of character as *sōphrosunē*. At 360b–d Socrates uses a similar argument concerning courage and wisdom; see pp.210–12 below.

334a3–c6 *Protagoras interrupts the argument with a short speech on the complexity and relational nature of goodness.*

In reply to Socrates' questions (a) whether those things are good which are beneficial to men (which is how Protagoras takes d8–e1, though the Greek could also mean 'whether good things are those which are beneficial to men', which may be how Plato represented Socrates as intending the question), and (b) whether there are some good things which are not in any way beneficial, Protagoras makes or implies three points about goodness:

i. Everything good is in some way beneficial (a3).
ii. The notion 'good for' is relational, i.e. it requires to be completed by a subject expression, to give 'good for x', 'good for y', etc.
iii. The same thing may be good for x and bad for, or not good for y. (ii is implied throughout, and iii is asserted with examples from a7 to c2.)

The central point here is that 'good for' is a relational expression, like 'taller than', 'half of', 'father of', etc. Hence there is no single answer to the question 'Is x good?', any more than there is a single answer to the question 'Is x the half?' or 'Is x to the right?' In all cases the question must first be completed by specification of that to which the relation is held, and in all cases we must expect the answer that x has the relation to one thing but does not have it to something else. By describing goodness as 'varied and many-sided' (b6–7) Protagoras may be represented as alluding to just this feature. Plato may, however, have in mind another thesis, viz. that there is no single set of characteristics or single relation common to all good things, which is the contradictory of Plato's own view that there is a single nature called goodness which all good things share. The former thesis was maintained by Aristotle (*EN* I.6) and is maintained by many modern writers, e.g. Hare *Language of Morals* ch. 6. It does not, however, follow from what Protagoras says, since all the different things which he cites as good for some kinds of things and not good for others might be good or not in virtue of possessing or lacking one and the same set of highly general characteristics or one and the same relation to something, as all the numbers are halves in virtue of possessing the same characteristic, viz. that when added to themselves they form their double.

Equally, Protagoras' speech does not imply that if anyone believes that something is good, then that thing is good (for him), i.e. the application of goodness of the general thesis of Protagorean subjectivism. The observation that manure is good for roots but bad for leaves neither entails nor follows from the thesis that whatever anyone believes to be good is good (for the person who believes it). The conjunction of Protagoras' theses ii and iii (which we might call the Relational Thesis), is not only true, but also logically independent of subjectivism. The view of commentators (e.g. Adam and Adam p.138) that in this passage we have an instance of the latter is sheer confusion. It is worth noting that Xenophon represents Socrates as also defending the Relational Thesis (*Mem.* III.viii, esp. sects. 3 and 7; cf. IV. vi.8). While it is of course possible that Plato may have suffered from that very confusion in giving this speech to Protagoras, nothing obliges us to think that he was. Plato was indeed worried by relational concepts (e.g. *Ph.* 102b–d, *Theaet.* 154c–155c), but by the time of writing the *Phaedo* he was clear that the recognition of those concepts does not commit one to subjectivism (loc. cit.), and in default of evidence it is gratuitous to suppose him guilty of this confusion at an earlier time.

Thirdly, Protagoras does not here espouse any version of evaluative relativism, i.e. the doctrine that the standards by which things are judged good or bad vary in different circumstances (e.g. in different cultures, at different historical epochs, according to the different interests of different individuals) and that there is no second-order criterion by which it is possible to judge any standard more correct than any other. Protagoras' examples, which are all of facts of nature, e.g. that oil is bad for plants, do indeed presuppose agreed standards of what counts as a good state for plants and animals, but there is no reason to suppose that Plato represents him as looking on these as culture-relative, nor is it clear that they are in fact. The logical point which is the kernel of Protagoras' speech, viz. that 'good for' is a relational concept, is quite independent of any question of the status of the standards by which we judge things good. Plato argues at *Rep.* V, 479a–c that, since any instance of justice, beauty, etc. may equally be regarded as an instance of injustice, ugliness, etc., the only things which are just, beautiful, etc. without qualification are justice, beauty, etc. themselves. This may indicate his acceptance of a relativistic account of standards of evaluative judgement, combined with an 'absolutist' theory of the nature of evaluative concepts themselves; i.e. what beauty is is in itself something unitary and independent of human convention, but any instance may with equal legitimacy be judged beautiful or not, more or less beautiful etc. according to different standards.

Objections might be raised to Protagoras' thesis i 'Everything good is in some way beneficial' on the following grounds: (a) There are many aspects of goodness which it does not cover, such as moral, aesthetic, and technical goodness (e.g. being good at tennis); (b) it creates an infinite regress, since 'beneficial' means 'instrumental in bringing about a good state'. Hence Protagoras would appear to be committed to the view that nothing is good in itself, but anything good is so in so far as it brings about something else, which is absurd (cf. Ar. *EN* I.2, 1094a18–22). As regards (a), while it might indeed be argued that some of the things which are called good in these various ways are beneficial to someone, that is unnecessary, since it is clear that Protagoras is not putting forward a thesis which is meant to cover every application of the term 'good', but rather making an assertion about the things we call 'goods', i.e. things worth having. On (b), it is likely that 'beneficial' covers both things which are instrumental in bringing about good states and the good states themselves which *are* benefits to the person who has them. Cf. *Rep.* II, 358b–367e, where it is clear that showing justice to be something valuable in itself is one and the same with showing that it benefits the man who has it (see also 368c4–7, and on the whole passage Kirwan *Phron* 65).

Modern studies which emphasize the complexity of goodness include von Wright *The Varieties of Goodness*, Ziff *Semantic Analysis* ch. 6, Vendler *PR* 63, Patton and Ziff *PR* 64, Urmson *The Emotive Theory of Ethics* chs. 8–11.

334c7–335c7 *Socrates protests at the length of Protagoras' speech and makes as if to break off the discussion.*

335a4–8 This is one of the pieces of evidence which indicate that debating contests conducted according to agreed rules were part of the characteristic activity of sophists. Other relevant passages are 338a7–b1, where Hippias suggests the appointment of an umpire for the present discussion, and *Hipp. Min.* 363c–364a, where Hippias describes how he goes regularly to the Olympic Games to take part in contests (*agōnizesthai*, the regular word for athletic and similar competition) of question and answer and has never yet been beaten. According to Diogenes Laertius, Protagoras was the first to institute such contests (IX.52). See Ryle in Bambrough ed. (revised version in *Plato's Progress* ch. 4).

335c8–338e5 *Argument as to how the discussion should be continued. It is agreed to proceed by question and answer, with Protagoras questioning first.*

335e1 'I praise and love'. See n. on 346d8–e2, pp.147–8 below.

335e3 Crison from Himera in Sicily won the sprint at three successive Olympic Games, in 448, 444 and 440 (Diod. XII.5; 23; 29).

335e4 'couriers': not athletes, but messengers, such as Pheidippides who ran from Athens to summon help from Sparta on the occasion of the campaign of Marathon in 490 (Hdt. VI.105.1).

336b6 'and for you to speak as you like'. The reading here translated is that of two of the three main manuscripts (and of a corrector in the third), which is followed by Croiset (Budé). The reading of the third MS., adopted by Adam and Adam and by Burnet (OCT) is 'and you as you like'. This elliptical expression may be supplemented in either of two ways; (i) 'and you (seem right in asking to be allowed to speak) as you like' or (ii) 'and you (seem right in asking that he speak) as you like'. Neither way of understanding this gives a satisfactory sense. (i) seems unlikely, since Socrates claims not merely to be allowed to speak as he likes (which Protagoras has not disputed) but to dictate how Protagoras shall speak. (ii) (the interpretation favoured by Adam and Adam p.143) does indeed represent what Socrates really claims, but its total impartiality is inconsistent with Alcibiades' objection on behalf of Socrates and with Critias' remark (d7–e1) that Callias is very much on the side of Protagoras. Against the reading adopted here Adam and Adam say '*Protagoras* has nowhere asked that Socrates should be permitted to converse as he likes; quite the contrary' (their italics). But Protagoras has not objected to Socrates' *speaking* as he likes, i.e. putting questions; he implies (334d–335a) that he is willing to be questioned, provided that he is allowed to answer at the length he sees fit.

336b8–d5   Cf. 309b6.

337a1–c4   This is the most important single piece of evidence for the semantic distinctions in which Prodicus specialized. Other instances of distinctions which are said to be in the style of Prodicus occur at 340a (between 'wish' and 'desire'), 340c ('be' and 'become'), 358a ('pleasant', 'delightful', and 'enjoyable'), 358d ('fear' and 'apprehension'), *Meno* 75e ('end' and 'limit'), *Lach.* 197b–d ('fearless' and 'courageous'), *Charm.* 163b–d ('do' and 'make' or 'work') and *Euthyd.* 277e–278a ('learn' and 'understand', both represented by the verb *manthanein*). This passage contains four distinctions.

   (i) Between 'impartial' and 'undiscriminating'. The words so rendered, which have the respective basic senses 'common' and 'equal', may both be used to mean 'impartial', and are sometimes coupled as synonymous terms in that sense (LSJ s.v. *isos* II.3). While it does not appear that 'equal' (*isos*) had 'undiscriminating' as a regular sense, Prodicus shows that the ordinary notion of giving equal shares can be extended to 'making no distinction'. Thus while he appears to be suggesting an innovation rather than faithfully reflecting current usage, his procedure is unobjectionable, since (a) the distinction itself is a useful one and (b) it can be reached by a readily acceptable extension of current usage.

(ii) Between 'argue' and 'wrangle'. Unlike (i), this is a distinction current in ordinary speech. While 'argue' can indeed convey the notion of ill-will between the parties, it frequently occurs without that implication, which is, however, always present in 'wrangle' (*erizein*, from *eris*, 'quarrel, strife', whence 'eristic'). At *Rep.* V, 454a Plato makes a similar distinction between 'wrangle' and 'discuss scientifically' (*dialegesthai*, whence 'dialectic').

(iii) Between 'esteem' and 'praise'. Prodicus points out correctly that it is possible to praise someone insincerely, but impossible to esteem him insincerely; a modern writer would say that 'praise' (noun or verb) names a speech act, while 'esteem' (noun or verb) names a pro-attitude. As the usage of the Greek words corresponds fairly closely to that of the English, this distinction too has a firm basis in Greek usage.

(iv) Between 'derive enjoyment' (*euphrainesthai*) and 'derive pleasure' (*hēdesthai*). This is the most problematic of the four distinctions.

(a) The renderings adopted here are purely conventional, since the distinction which Prodicus is making does not correspond to any distinction marked by a pair of English verbs. But since that is true of the Greek terms also (see below), the artificial use of the expressions 'derive enjoyment' and 'derive pleasure' is in fact true to the text.

(b) Prodicus' distinction is between physical and mental pleasures, or more strictly between the enjoyment of physical activities such as eating and of mental activities such as learning. These are indeed importantly different kinds of enjoyment, as Plato emphasizes (e.g. *Rep.* IX, 580d ff.). But firstly, Prodicus' presentation of the distinction is misleading to the extent that it suggests that mental pleasure is something 'purely' mental and bodily pleasure something 'purely' physical, as though the two kinds of pleasures had nothing in common. In fact, as Aristotle and modern writers have emphasized, enjoyment of anything, physical or mental, is a kind of effortless concentration on the thing enjoyed (see e.g. Urmson in Moravcsik ed.). The different kinds of things thus enjoyed may be classed as more or less mental or physical according to the relative prominence of short-term physiologically-based appetites, bodily sensation, and physical activity and of such faculties as discrimination and imagination. The distinction is rather one of degree than of kind, and, like all such distinctions, admits many cases which resist classification;

thus while enjoying mathematics may stand for a paradigm of mental pleasure and enjoying a hot bath for a paradigm of physical pleasure, there are no clear criteria for the classification of the enjoyment of e.g. gardening, country walks, or fine food and drink. Secondly, the distinction between physical and mental pleasures is not picked out by any pair of terms in fourth-century Greek usage. The verbs which Prodicus presses into service are both used in contexts which require renderings such as 'be pleased that' as well as contexts referring directly to enjoyment, and in the latter case they cover a wide range of enjoyments falling into both of Prodicus' categories; no distinction of sense is apparent, though *hēdesthai* is much the more frequent. (It is amusing to note that Xenophon's paraphrase of Prodicus' fable of the choice of Heracles (see Biographical Notes, p.62 above) contains a counter-example in its use of *euphrainesthai* of sexual enjoyment, *Mem.* II.i.24.). It appears, then, that while here as above there is a worth-while distinction to be made, in this case as distinct from the others the means of marking the distinction which Plato attributes to Prodicus is supported neither by actual idiom nor by any natural extension of it, but rather conflicts with standard usage. The method exemplified in this section, then, is a mixture of classification of actual usage and prescription for linguistic reform (contrast the painstakingly empirical character of the superficially similar work of Austin, e.g. 'A Plea for Excuses'; see also Urmson *JPhil* 65). It is possible that, as Adam and Adam suggest (p.145), the proposed restriction in the sense of *euphrainesthai* is intended to be justified by a supposed etymological connection with 'intelligence' (*phronēsis*), since we have some evidence that the historical Prodicus attached some weight to etymology; Galen (second century A.D.) reports his proposals for certain changes in medical terminology on etymological grounds (DK 84 B 4). (Plato's *Cratylus* contains lengthy parodies of etymological methods of semantic analysis.)

(c) Aristotle (*Top.* II.6, 112b22–4; DK 84 A 19) and a scholiast (i.e. ancient commentator) on Plato's *Phaedrus* (see Guthrie III, p.222, n.3) report that Prodicus distinguished terms concerning pleasure in a way different from that in the text. Both say that he treated *hēdonē* (the cognate noun to *hēdesthai*, whence 'hedonism') as the generic term and distinguished three kinds, to one of which (defined by the scholiast but not by Aristotle as 'pleasure through the eyes') he gave the name *euphrosunē* (the cognate noun to *euphrainesthai*) and to another the name *chara* (lit. 'joy'), the latter being, according to the scholiast 'pleasure of the mind'. Aristotle's testimony makes it probable that the distinction itself was made by Prodicus, but the scholiast's interpretation may well derive from later sources; Alexander (third century A.D.) commenting on Aristotle's remark (DK ibid.) refers to a similar distinction made by the Stoics. The distinction mentioned at 358a between 'pleasant', 'delightful' and 'enjoyable' employs the adjectives cognate to three of the four nouns mentioned by Aristotle, indicating that that distinction was probably made by Prodicus.

The above passages apart, all our detailed evidence on Prodicus' distinctions comes from Plato. We have no means of knowing whether any of the distinctions (apart from that in 358a, see above) put into the mouth of Prodicus in this dialogue was actually made by him, while in the passages from other dialogues referred to above it is said merely that these are the kinds of distinction Prodicus made. Allowing for the element of parody apparent in this dialogue, it is reasonable to conclude that Plato gives what he takes to be typical examples; he does not, however, indicate whether Prodicus had any general presuppositions or systematic method of making distinctions. On this point Aristotle (loc. cit.) says that Prodicus based his distinction of kinds of pleasure on the fact that the names are different. If that is correct, it may indicate that Prodicus held that every word has its own distinct signification, which it is the business of the investigator of language to separate from every other. General theories of the nature of language and its relation to reality were much in the air in the fifth and fourth centuries; e.g. Cratylus, who is said by Aristotle (*Met.* A6, 987a32) to have influenced Plato, has attributed to him by Plato the theory that each thing has its own proper name, which expresses (through its etymology) the nature of the thing it names, and which has significance only when correctly applied, but is otherwise a mere noise. Hence there can be no misapplication of a name (since a misapplied name is not a name, but just a noise), and hence no such thing as a false statement, since (it is assumed) every false statement involves misapplication of some name (*Crat.* 429b–430a). The thought is presumably that to make a false statement, e.g. 'Socrates is foolish' is to apply the name 'Socrates', which is properly the name of a wise man, to someone who is not wise, i.e. to someone other than the real bearer of the name. Similarly Antisthenes, a pupil of Socrates, held that each thing has its own proper definition or description, which cannot be applied to anything else, from which again the impossibility of falsehood follows (Ar. *Met.* Δ 29, 1024b32–4), while at *Soph.* 251b–c Plato refers to a theory held by some young men and old men who come to learning late in life, to the effect that each thing may be called only by its own name, e.g. man may be called only 'man' and not e.g. 'good'. On these and other theories see Guthrie III, ch. 8, sect. 5. Aristotle's testimony is inexplicit as to the precise view which Prodicus held of the relations between a term such as 'pleasure', the definition which gives the meaning of that term and the element of reality for which the term stands, but it is at least possible that he held that each element of language stands in a one-to-one relation with some element of reality which is described in the definition, i.e. that his position was an extreme form of Cratylus' view, from which an extreme form of Antisthenes' view would follow. Again, a failure to distinguish predication from naming or defining could lead from that view to the late-learners' position. While the details of the above are conjectural, it seems probable that Prodicus had some interest in general questions about the nature of language and its relation to reality, and was not interested in distinctions *merely* for their own sake or as rhetorical devices.

337d1–3 The distinction between nature and convention to which Hippias refers was of considerable importance in fifth-century thought. There are in fact two contrasts. On the one hand there is what is the case in reality or in the nature of things (*phusei*), i.e. independently of human choice or convention. Opposed to that we have two categories, shading into one another yet distinguishable, both of which the Greeks called 'things which are (the case) by convention' (*nomōi*). These are:

   (a) things which are in fact F, but are so only because men have decided that they should be regarded as being F.

   (b) things which are not in fact F, but are merely called F. In so far as it is disputable how far anything actually becomes F by being generally regarded as, or generally said to be F, these two categories and hence the two distinctions shade into one another. In different contexts one or other contrast predominates. In one of the earliest examples, from Empedocles (DK 31 B 9) we have a clear case of (b); when the elements mingle to form an animal or some other creature, men call that coming-into-being, and when they separate, destruction; 'they do not call it what they ought, but I too comply with their usage' (*nomos*). Here what is conventionally called coming-into-being is not so in reality. Similarly, at *Laws* X, 889e Plato attacks the view that the gods exist 'not in reality but according to certain conventions', i.e. the view that there aren't really any gods, but people have agreed to say that there are, which is clearly sense (b), but in the same passage we find him shifting to a sense nearer to (a), referring to the view that what is right (*ta dikaia*) has no existence at all in reality, but whatever enactments men lay down are valid, so long as they remain in force. Here we have a borderline case, as suggested above. In the present instance, sense (a)

140

seems to be more clearly indicated; Hippias is not saying that the artificial political divisions between the various Greek states do not exist at all, but rather that while they do indeed exist and have undoubted force ('convention (is) a tyrant . . . (which) ordains many things by force'), they exist only because men have decided that they should. (Cf. Hdt. IV.39.1 on an artificial geographical boundary.) In this passage, as in most other instances, we find a devaluation of the conventional in favour of the real or natural; this is most marked in moral contexts, where the contrast is used to devalue conventional morality in favour of some supposedly more natural (i.e. higher) morality, frequently a 'morality' of unrestricted self-indulgence and self-aggrandisement, as in the most notorious instances, the speech of Callicles in the *Gorgias* (482c—486c, esp. 482c—484c) and a papyrus fragment of the sophist Antiphon (DK 87 B 44), but sometimes a more enlightened humanitarianism, e.g. Ar. *Pol.* I.3, 1253b20—3: 'Others affirm that the rule of a master over slaves is contrary to nature, and that the distinction between slave and free man exists by convention only, and not by nature; and being an interference with nature is therefore unjust.' It was one of Plato's main concerns to show that in the area of morality the contrast does not exist, in that the demands of conventional morality, especially justice and *sōphrosunē*, arise naturally from the conditions of human life. As was seen above (pp.80 ff.) Protagoras maintains the same position in this dialogue; see Loenen pp.58, 80, 107—8. Similarly, Xenophon represents Hippias (*Mem.* IV.iv.14—25) as accepting Socrates' thesis that certain fundamental moral rules (e.g. that one should honour one's parents) are 'unwritten laws' laid down by the gods. These universal laws, which are independent of convention, could readily be seen as arising from human nature. For a full discussion of the contrast and the ancient sources see Guthrie III, ch. 4. See also Kerferd ch. 10, Rankin ch. 4.

338e6—347a5 *The discussion is continued by means of the criticism of a poem of Simonides, first by Protagoras and then by Socrates.*

338e6—339a3 In view of Protagoras' general educational programme, and in view of his comments on the poem, it seems likely that he saw the importance of literary criticism rather in developing the critical faculty and the exact use of language than in promoting the understanding and appreciation of poetry as an end in itself.

Simonides (*c.*556—468) was one of the most celebrated lyric poets. The poem quoted here was probably written when he was living in Thessaly (in northern Greece) as the guest of one of the aristocratic families of the region, the Scopads, one of whom, Scopas son of Creon, is mentioned at 339a7. It survives only in the quotations given here, which are, however, fairly complete (344b3-4, cf. 343c4-5, 345d1-6). Critical discussion (of which a bibliography is given by Donlan *TAPA* 69) has established that it is in four stanzas of ten lines each. The first stanza begins with the three lines quoted at 339b1-3; the rest is lacking. The second, beginning with the lines quoted at 339c3-5, continues with the lines quoted in 344c-e; the last two lines are missing, but are probably paraphrased at 345c3. The third stanza is given in entirety at 345c-d, and the fourth, lacking the opening three lines, at 346c. For the text see *PMG* 542; for a translation, Adam and Adam p.200, *LG* II, pp.284-7.

339c3 Pittacus was ruler of Mytilene on the island of Lesbos, at the end of the seventh century, and was reckoned as one of the Seven Sages (see below, p.144).

339e6 'a fellow citizen'. Simonides came, like Prodicus, from Ceos.

340a4-5 *Il.* XXI. 308-9.

340d2-5 A paraphrase of *Works and Days* 289 and 291-2. In another poem Simonides himself describes excellence, in terms probably intended to recall Hesiod's description, as dwelling on top of a steep cliff, only to be achieved with much sweat (*PMG* 579, *LG* II, pp.318-21).

341a4 'through being Prodicus' pupil'. Cf. *Meno* 96d, *Crat.* 384b, *Charm.* 163d.

341a7 'terrible'. The Greek *deinos* can be used with a favourable nuance as equivalent to 'marvellous' (cf. the French 'formidable'), and hence acquires the specific sense 'clever, skilful', used especially of persons. The phrase rendered 'terribly wise' (lit. 'clever and wise') does not have as much intensive force as the English.

341b5 'hard'. The basic sense of the Greek *chalepos* is 'hard to bear', from which 'difficult' is a derivative sense. In the basic sense, when used of such things as war or famine, it is close in sense to 'bad' (*kakos*). But, as is clear from 341d-e, there is no question of its having that sense in the passage under discussion. The reference to Cean dialect and the suggestion that Pittacus, coming from

Lesbos, could not speak proper Greek are all part of the joke.

Attempts to resolve the contradiction adduced by Protagoras between the opening lines of the first stanza and those of the second are hindered by the lack of the rest of the first stanza. The following suggestions have been offered:

(a) The opening lines do not state Simonides' own view, but present the traditional saying of Pittacus, which Simonides proceeds to criticize.

(b) Both passages do represent Simonides' view, but, as Socrates suggests, the poet intends to make a distinction between being and becoming good, which is sufficient to resolve the contradiction.

(c) Again, while both passages represent Simonides' view, there is an important difference of sense between the word rendered by 'good', viz. *agathos*, in the first passage and that rendered by 'noble', viz. *esthlos*, in the second.

Against (a), if it were clear from the text of the poem that the opening words represented the view of Pittacus, not of the poet himself, then the misrepresentation would be too crass to pass for an exhibition of sophistic cleverness which Socrates admits to be plausible (339c8–9), which has him in difficulties (e1–5) and which evokes the applause of the audience (d10–e1); it would be hard, too, to explain the emphatic assertions by Protagoras (d2) and Socrates (340b6–7) that Simonides begins the poem with his own view. It seems much more reasonable to assume, as in (b) and (c), that in both passages Simonides is speaking in his own person. Of the latter interpretations, (c) has little plausibility in view of the fact that in early Greek the two terms are generally used interchangeably; moreover the description of the *agathos* in the opening lines as the man of all-round excellence, possessing martial and athletic prowess (and perhaps even manual skill as well) together with moral and intellectual qualities, gives the traditional Homeric picture of the complete man, for whom *esthlos* was the standard term of commendation. Despite the generally perverse character of Socrates' interpretation (see below, pp.145–6), the distinction suggested in (b) is not impossible. The verb in the opening line, rendered above 'to become', is in fact the past infinitive, which could have the sense either 'to have become' or 'to become on one occasion' (as opposed to acquiring a lasting disposition), while there is some evidence in early Greek of a distinction between becoming F in the sense of manifesting F-ness for a limited time and being F permanently (e.g. Pind. *Pyth.* x.21–4). Simonides may, then, have said, as Socrates asserts at 344b6–c7, that while it is hard to manifest complete excellence for even a short time, to do so permanently is something utterly impossible for men, a privilege reserved to the

143

gods alone. Another possibility is that the opening statement was qualified in the intervening lines, and then withdrawn in favour of the more emphatic opening of the second stanza, giving the train of thought, 'It is hard to be good . . . or, to be more precise, impossible.' In the absence of the complete text it is not possible to reach any definite solution.

341e7 'never a Cean'. The Ceans had a reputation for uprightness. see Adam and Adam's note, p.156.

342a7–b1 While Socrates' references to philosophy in Crete and Sparta are of course ironical (for Spartan attitudes to intellectual matters see e.g. *Hipp. Maj.* 285b–e), admiration for the institutions and particularly for the educational systems of the two states was shared by many Greeks, including Plato. See *Rep.* VIII, 544c, *Hipp. Maj.* 283e–284b, *Laws passim*, e.g. I, 631b, 636e; cf. Ar. *EN* I.13, 1102a7–11.

342b1 'wise men': lit. 'sophists'. Cf. n. on 311e4, p.66 above.

342b3–4 'those whom Protagoras described as sophists': 316d–e. Cf. n. on 333d5–6, p.132 above.

343a1–b3 The Greeks traditionally recognized a list of seven wise men, mostly historical persons of the seventh and sixth centuries, to which this is the earliest surviving reference. While there was some variation in the list (see D.L. I.13 and 40–2 (the latter passage in DK 10.1)), they were always seven in number. They were renowned chiefly as lawgivers and founts of practical wisdom, expressed in a number of maxims, of which the most famous were the two quoted here. A collection of these maxims was made by the fourth-century writer Demetrius of Phaleron (DK 10.3). See *RE* s.v. 'Sieben Weise'. On Thales, Solon, Pittacus, and Chilon see OCD^2; on Myson of Chen or Chenae see Adam and Adam p.159; on Bias see How and Wells I, pp.65–6. The lives in D.L. I contain a mixture of legend and historical information.

343b5 'Laconian': i.e. Spartan. Laconia was the district surrounding the city of Sparta. 'Laconic' is derived from the name.

343d1 'rather'. This renders the Greek *men*, whose function is to mark the first leg of a contrast or opposition, the second leg being marked by *de*; the Greek for 'poor but honest' would be *penēs men, dikaios de*. Its use in the first sentence of the poem shows that that sentence was contrasted with something that followed, possibly the opening lines of the second stanza, which contain *de* and could make a contrast with the opening, but more probably with something in the missing lines, which may have served to tone down or retract the first assertion (as suggested above, p.144). Socrates reads the lines in the former way, as 'it is rather (*men*) becoming good which is difficult, not (*de*) being good'. While, as has been argued, that interpretation is not impossible, no particular weight should be placed on Socrates' insistence on it here, since his treatment of the word 'truly' is altogether far-fetched, presumably in parody of sophistic methods of interpretation, which Plato must have held guilty of similar perversions of the sense. The word order requires 'It is hard to become truly good' and excludes 'It is truly hard to become good'; moreover, the phrase 'truly good' is expanded in the next line 'foursquare in hand and foot etc.' It is possible, though not certain, that his treatment of *men* is intended to be seen as equally strained.

344b6–345c3 Socrates now proceeds to the second stanza, whose sequence of thought, whatever its precise connection with the first stanza, is reasonably clear. The gods alone are perfectly good; men cannot help being bad when they are the victims of irresistible misfortune, for every man is good when he is faring well and bad when he is faring ill. (It is clear that 'does well' and 'does ill' at 344e7–8 should have this sense, since these lines state the connection between misfortune and badness.) The best are those whom the gods love. The main problem is how to take the statement that the victim of misfortune cannot help being bad. The poet might be saying that misfortune makes a man poor, hungry, weak in body, lacking in reputation etc., i.e. *kakos* (inferior) according to the traditional success conception of *aretē*, or (alternatively or additionally) that the man in that situation has no choice but to act in shameful ways, e.g. begging or even stealing, to keep body and soul together. Both conceptions occur in the poems ascribed to the sixth-century poet Theognis, the former in lines 53–8 and 1109–13, the latter in 373–92 and (probably) 649–52. The end of the third stanza (345d3–5) may suggest that Simonides has the latter in mind: the poet is content with the man who does nothing shameful of his own free will, but against necessity not even the gods fight, i.e. in necessity a man will have to do some shameful things. It is simplest to suppose that no distinction is made among the sorts of shameful acts that a man may be forced to between acts which we should consider morally disgraceful, e.g. stealing, and those which would merely bring some social stigma, e.g. begging. Socrates' interpretation of these lines in terms of his own thesis that goodness

145

consists in knowledge is clearly anachronistic and whimsical.

344c5 'helpless disaster'. The Greek *amēchanos* (from *mēchanē*, 'contrivance', hence 'machine') may mean either 'lacking in resource or means' or 'such as not to be dealt with by any resource or means'. It is used in the latter sense in this line and the next and in d1, and in the former in d1–4. 'Helpless' is used here in the archaic sense 'such that it cannot be helped' in order to cover the same range of senses.

344d7 The authorship of the line is unknown; see Adam and Adam p.164.

345c8–346b7 Third stanza. An utterly faultless man is not to be found. One must be content with the man who does nothing shameful of his own free will. (Yet anyone may on occasion be forced to act shamefully) for not even the gods fight against necessity.

345d4 'Freely' translates '*hekōn*', also rendered 'of one's own free will' (d8). One acts *hekōn* if one's action is not done (a) under constraint or (b) through ignorance of some material circumstances. See Ar. *EN* III.1 and V.8. Here the contrast is with constraint, as is clear from the occurrence of 'necessity' in the next line. The kind of constraint is not specified. In another lyric poem on the same topic, of which some lines survive in a papyrus fragment (*PMG* 541; see Donlan), the poet, who may be Simonides, speaks of someone's being forced against his will by irresistible gain or the powerful sting of crafty Aphrodite (i.e. sexual passion); he thus treats at least some cases of giving in to temptation as cases of acting under compulsion. While such a view might be pressed into assimilating all cases of wrongdoing to acting under compulsion, that would in effect require the abandonment of the distinction between free and constrained action (cf. Ar. *EN* III.1, 1110b9–15). Since Simonides used the distinction in this poem, it is simplest to credit him, not with the view that all wrong actions are done under compulsion, but with the common-sense view that sometimes a man cannot help doing wrong, either because he is subject to irresistible temptation, or because he is forced to adopt dishonest means to keep alive (contrast Aristotle's 'rigorist' treatment of constraint in *EN* III.1). In the Socratic thesis that no one does wrong *hekōn* the contrast is with ignorance (see below, p.173). Once again, Socrates' assimilation of the poet's thought to one of his own theses involves a blatant perversion of the plain sense of the poem.

345d9—e4   Socrates' claim that his thesis is universally accepted by the wise is ironical, as it was generally regarded as outrageously implausible (e.g. *Gorg.* 475e, Ar. *EN* VII.2, 1145b25—8).

346b8—347a5   Fourth stanza. ... It is enough that a man should be not bad nor altogether wicked, but a sound man with a sense of justice. He is not to be found fault with. Everything is good which has no taint of shamefulness.

346c4   'wicked'. The Greek word, whose literal meaning is 'handless' may also mean 'helpless'. Either sense is possible, but 'wicked' is more common in lyric poetry and fits the context better, esp. the contrast with justice.

'Sound': lit. 'healthy'. This is the earliest instance of the use of the word in the transferred sense 'sound in mind' (= *sōphrōn*, see above pp.122—4), though the word occurs once in Homer in the expression 'sound speech' (*Il.* VIII.524). The transferred use is common in the fifth century and frequent in Plato, reflecting his view of goodness as spiritual health (see Kenny *PBA* 69).

'Justice that benefits the city': cf. Theognis 43—52 (and above 324e and 327b).

346d1—3   See n. on 332c3—9, pp.127—8 above. While Socrates treats *kalon* and *aischron* as polar opposites, not contradictories, there seems insufficient reason to suppose Simonides to mean anything other than what he says, viz. that he counts all actions as worthy or creditable which are not positively discreditable. Many such actions will indeed be intermediate between good or excellent (*agathon*) and bad (*kakon*), but not, as Socrates takes it, intermediate between creditable (*kalon*) and discreditable (*aischron*).

346d8—e2   The verb 'praise' is in the form used in the Aeolic Greek dialect spoken in Lesbos and north-west Asia Minor. Since words in this dialect occur frequently in lyric, the use of an Aeolic word here gives no reason to suppose that Simonides intends any reference to Pittacus at this point in the poem. On Socrates' treatment of 'freely' see above, p.146. There is a 'pre-echo' of the phrase 'I praise and love' at 335e1; this is presumably intentional, as this was a well-known poem, from which many phrases became proverbial, e.g. 'Not even gods fight against necessity'. See refs. in *PMG*, p.283.

The poem deals with a number of themes which were current in the poetry of the sixth and fifth centuries, such as the impossibility of perfection, the unbridgeable gulf between gods and men, the ineluctable vicissitudes of human life and the necessity for moderation in everything. See Parry *TAPA* 65. In representing Socrates as wrenching the poem from this historical context in order to interpret it in the light of his own, quite different, interests, Plato presumably intends to point out a fault in the methods of interpretation which he judged characteristic of the sophists. We have no means of estimating the extent to which this implied criticism was justified.

*

347a6–348c4 *It is agreed to abandon criticism of poetry and to resume the original discussion.*

347c3–e7 It is to be assumed that Plato intends the interpretation which Socrates has just given to show in an exemplary fashion what he regards as the cardinal fault in literary interpretation, viz. the impossibility of definitively establishing the writer's meaning, with its consequent licence to factitious 'interpretations'. While Plato may perhaps have thought that this was particularly true of poetry (cf. *Hipp. Min.* 365c–d), he also held that in general the written word could not impart true knowledge, since knowledge implies an ability to formulate and defend one's views which requires that they be inculcated and tested by the method of question and answer (see *Phaedr.* 274b–277a, *Ep.* vii, 341c–d).

The dinner-party depicted in Plato's *Symposium* lives up to Socrates' exacting standard; a flute-girl has been hired, but is sent away (176e), and the evening given over to conversation. In Xenophon's *Symposium*, where Callias is the host and Socrates among the guests, the entertainment includes both conversation and cabaret turns. See Guthrie III, pp.340–4.

*

348c5–349d8 *Socrates recapitulates the initial question and asks Protagoras for his present position. Protagoras answers that while wisdom, sōphrosunē, justice, and holiness are very much alike, courage is something completely different.*

348d1–4 *Il.* X.224–5. See Adam and Adam's note, p. 171.

348e4–349a4 Cf. 316c–317c, 328b–c.

349a8–c5 Cf. 329c–330b.

349d2–5 At 333b Protagoras had accepted that *sōphrosunē* and *sophia* are one thing, and that justice and holiness are virtually the same thing (see n. on 332a2—4, p.121 above). Since the argument about *sōphrosunē* and justice was left unfinished (333b—334a), Socrates has not given Protagoras any grounds for accepting the identity of the four virtues (leaving aside the inadequacy of his actual arguments, see above). Yet it seems likely that Protagoras' use here of the formula 'resemble one another fairly closely' amounts to a somewhat grudging admission that the four virtues are either identical or as nearly so as makes no difference (cf. 331b). For Socrates proceeds on the basis of his admission here to devote the rest of the argument to an attempt to show that courage is identical with wisdom, and then sums up his position (361b1—2) as 'trying to show that all of these, justice and *sōphrosunē* and courage, are knowledge'. If it is implied that the argument up to that point is structurally complete, then it follows that the identity of the virtues other than courage must have been conceded, leaving only courage to be identified with one of the four (whence its identity with the others would follow by the transitivity of identity). It might indeed be argued that Socrates does not claim that he has shown that all the virtues are knowledge, but merely that he is trying to do so, and that at 361c he says that the question requires further examination, implying that the argument is *not* complete. Yet the end of the discussion makes it quite clear that what has been reached is not merely an intermediate stage in an argument which is then broken off for some unstated reason, but the end of this particular argument. Socrates says that he is trying to show the truth of his conclusion, and refers to the necessity for further discussion, not because this particular argument can be taken any further, but because he is aware that the arguments of the first part of the discussion have been less than conclusive. Hence while Protagoras' concession here required Socrates merely to prove courage identical with one of the other virtues, the arguments which elicited that admission would have to be re-examined if the demonstration were to be more than merely *ad hominem*.

349d5—8 Protagoras maintains that one can have courage without the other virtues not as a thesis in its own right, but as evidence in support of his thesis that courage is not identical with the others. Here the Biconditionality Thesis is clearly subordinate to the Identity Thesis; hence this passage provides no support for Vlastos's theory that the former is Socrates' only concern in the dialogue. Contrast Vlastos op. cit. pp.242—3, 247—8.

349d7 'wanton'. *Akolastos* (lit. 'unchastised', hence 'unrestrained') is the regular opposite of *sōphrōn* in its various applications (see above, pp.122–4). According to the particular application of *sōphrōn* with which it is contrasted, it may indicate either self-indulgence or wanton disregard for the rights of others. 'Wanton' is intended to suggest that range of applications.

349d7–8 'ignorant', Since the verb *manthanein* may mean either 'learn' or 'understand' (*Euthyd*. 277e–278a), the adjective *amathēs* may mean either 'lacking learning' or 'lacking understanding', and hence may in different contexts have the force of 'stupid', 'uneducated', 'ignorant', or 'inexpert'. No single English word covers that range of applications.

349e1–350c5 *Socrates gives an argument designed to prove that courage is identical with wisdom.*

The argument proceeds as follows:

349e2	1. The courageous are daring.
349e3–8	2. Every part of excellence is something fine.
349e8–	
350b1	3. Knowledgeable men are more daring than those who lack knowledge.
350b1–6	4. Those who are daring but lacking in knowledge are mad, which is a shameful state.
	(5. Hence, the state of being daring but lacking in knowledge is not a part of excellence (by 2 and 4)).
350b4–5,	
c1–2	6. Hence, those who are daring but lacking in knowledge are not courageous (since courage is admitted to be a part of excellence) (by 5).
350c2–4	7. Those who are wisest are most daring (by 3), and hence most courageous (by ?).
350c4–5	8. Therefore, courage is wisdom (by ?).

This argument presents many problems. I comment on five main points.

(i) If Socrates is attempting to show that courage is the same thing as wisdom, he must at the least show that all and only the courageous are wise, since the possession of one of the virtues without the other would be sufficient to show that the two are not identical. (I say 'at least', since it unlikely that the thesis of the identity of the virtues reduces simply to the Biconditionality Thesis, either in general (see above, pp.103–4) or in this argument (see below, p.159).) i.e. where '*W*' = '... is wise' and '*C*' = '... is courageous', Socrates would have at least to prove

$$(x)\,(Cx \leftrightarrow Wx).$$

Protagoras had indeed asserted (d6−8) that some courageous people are not wise, i.e.

$$(\exists x)\,(Cx \ \& \ {-}Wx),$$

and in order to refute that it would be sufficient for Socrates to prove its negation, 'There are no courageous people who are not wise', i.e.

$$-\,(\exists x)\,(Cx \ \& \ {-}Wx),$$

which is equivalent to 'Every courageous person is wise', i.e.

$$(x)\,(Cx \rightarrow Wx).$$

Yet that would not suffice for Socrates's purpose, since it still leaves open the possibility that some wise people are not courageous, i.e.

$$(\exists x)\,(Wx \ \& \ {-}Cx),$$

which is also incompatible with the thesis of the identity of courage and wisdom.

Further, the structure of the argument suggests that Socrates is not aiming simply to negate Protagoras' assertion. Given premiss 1 'Every courageous person is daring', i.e.

$$(x)\,(Cx \rightarrow Dx)$$

(where 'D' = '... is daring'), and step 6, which we shall formulate as 'No-one who is daring but not wise is courageous', i.e.

$$(x)\,(Dx \ \& \ {-}Wx \rightarrow {-}Cx),$$

(on the derivation of this step see below, pp.154–5), the negation of Protagoras's assertion, i.e.

$$(x)\,(Cx \rightarrow Wx) \text{ (see above)},$$

may be derived. But instead of pointing this out, Socrates proceeds immediately to the further step 7, which we shall formulate either as 'Everyone who is wise is daring, and everyone who is wise and daring is courageous', i.e.

$$(x)\,(Wx \rightarrow Dx) \ \& \ (x)\,(Wx \ \& \ Dx \rightarrow Cx),$$

or as 'Everyone who is wise is daring, and everyone who is daring is courageous', i.e.

$$(x)\,(Wx \rightarrow Dx) \ \& \ (x)\,(Dx \rightarrow Cx)$$

(on the alternative renderings, see below, p.155). In either case the first member of the conjunction is the formulation of premiss 3, and in either case 7 entails 'Every wise person is courageous', i.e.

$$(x)\,(Wx \rightarrow Cx),$$

which, combined with the negation of Protagoras' assertion, gives the required conclusion 'All and only the courageous are wise', i.e.

$$(x)\,(Cx \leftrightarrow Wx).$$

Protagoras' assertion is nowhere explicitly negated, and the choice of interpretations rests between one according to which that step is ignored and one where it is assumed (see below, pp.159–61). It is therefore implausible that Socrates' main intention in this argument is precisely the negation of Protagoras' assertion.

(ii) The argument has an appearance of equivocation, since steps 3–6 contain the term 'knowledge', while steps 7 and 8 contain instead the term 'wisdom'. This appearance is illusory, since those terms are frequently interchangeable in Greek, and are clearly so used here. The knowledge in question is technical expertise, which is regularly called *sophia* (e.g. *Apol.* 22d–e). The sense of premiss 3 is that the expert is more daring than the non-expert, and the terms 'knowledge' and 'knowledgeable' are used in the corresponding senses until step 7, when 'most knowledgeable' is replaced by the equivalent term 'wisest'. Hence the conclusion is that courage is some kind of technical expertise.

(iii) Premiss 3 is supported inductively by three instances, those of men who dive into wells, cavalrymen, and light infantry. (The purpose of the first-named activity is not totally clear; as the word translated 'wells' also means 'storage tanks' it seems likely that the reference is to divers' going down under water to clean the well or tank.) A minor objection to the premiss is that while the argument requires 'Knowledgeable men are daring', i.e.

$$(x)\,(Wx \rightarrow Dx),$$

Socrates in fact states his premiss in the form 'Knowledgeable men are more daring than those who lack knowledge', which neither implies nor is implied by the non-comparative form. It is plainly not implied by it, but neither does it imply it, since just as A may be taller than B though neither is tall (cf. 'Dopey was the tallest of the Seven Dwarfs'), so A may be more daring than B though neither is daring. To this Socrates might reasonably reply that he is simply not thinking of cases where the effect of knowledge is to make its possessor less timorous than someone else, but still timorous none the less, and that his examples are all intended to show that what expertise does is to make one display in a significant degree that

positive impulse which is termed 'daring[1],' while those who lack
expertise fail to show a like degree of that impetus. Yet that reply
would invite the graver objections (a) that the generalization,
whether in the comparative or the non-comparative form, is false,
and (b) that premiss 4 implies that it is false. Socrates' examples
support the plainly true thesis that sometimes an expert is prepared,
on the strength of his expertise, to do things which the non-expert
is afraid to do. But, equally plainly, there may be cases where the
expert, on the strength of his expertise, decides that something is
too risky, and is not prepared to do it, while the non-expert is willing
to have a go, either because he is ignorant of the risks, or because he
regards them as outweighed by some other factors (e.g. a parent
dashing into a burning house to save his child, despite the warnings
of the firemen that the floor is practically certain to collapse).
In those cases the expert is less daring than the non-expert, and it is
in precisely that sort of situation that the latter is described in terms
of premiss 4 as 'too daring' (b3—4) and 'mad' (b5—6). Hence if
premiss 3 is read as 'All knowledgeable men are (always) daring' or
as 'All knowledgeable men are (always) more daring than anyone who
lacks knowledge', it is false. And if it is read in the reduced sense
'All knowledgeable men are (sometimes) daring', that supports the
conclusion

$$(x) (Wx \rightarrow Cx)$$

only in the correspondingly reduced sense 'All wise men are (sometimes) courageous', which is insufficient for the thesis that courage
and wisdom are identical.

An overlapping list of examples (infantrymen, cavalry, slingers,
archers, and well-divers) is used at *Lach.* 193a—c to support the
thesis that the non-expert or the man who knows himself to be in
a worse position (e.g. the infantryman who knows that his side is
weaker) is more courageous than the expert or the man in the
stronger position, both of whom face danger in the confidence that
they will come off unharmed. The course of the argument there is as
follows: it is suggested at 192c—d that courage should be defined as
a sort of endurance, and more specifically as intelligent endurance

---

[1] The Greek is *tharros*, whose basic meaning is a positive spirit leading to
and accompanying the undertaking of arduous or dangerous action. It may
indicate boldness or warlike spirit, which makes someone eager for combat
etc. irrespective of his expectations of the outcome, or readiness for such
action arising from confidence of a favourable outcome. The daring of
experts is clearly of the latter kind, while both kinds are mentioned at
351a7—b1. The latter notion predominates in the final argument at 359a—
360e, where it is argued that cowards and courageous men alike go for things
in which they have *tharros*, i.e. things which they think will lead to the most
favourable outcome.

(no doubt to distinguish courage, as is done explicitly at 196e–197c, from fearlessness springing from lack of appreciation of danger). Socrates secures agreement, using the above examples, to the general thesis that the non-expert is more courageous than the expert, and then points out that the endurance of non-experts is unintelligent compared with that of experts. Hence the suggested definition of courage conflicts with the assessment of the non-expert as more courageous than the expert. The dilemma is not explicitly resolved, but the argument moves on to another suggested definition of courage, viz. knowledge of good and bad, which leads to an impasse when it emerges that on that definition courage would be identical with excellence as a whole. While Socrates does not indeed explicitly say that the judgement that the non-expert is more courageous than the expert is not to be withdrawn, it is worth noting that the argument actually proceeds, not by withdrawing that judgement, but by modifying the definition which led to a contradiction with it. Aristotle too distinguishes between courage and confidence arising from expertise (*EN* III.6, 1115a35–b4; 8, 1116b3–23); the courageous man faces danger even to death because he knows that that is the best thing to do, whereas the expert faces it for as long as he can master it, but runs away when he sees that he can no longer cope. This distinction provides the answer to Socrates' dilemma in the *Laches*; while the courage of the non-expert is indeed unintelligent from the purely technical point of view of the expert who aims to come out unscathed as well as to do the job, it is not unintelligent from the point of view of the rational man who decides that e.g. his obligations to his country require him to hold out to the end against hopeless odds (for instance, the Spartans at Thermopylae). We should probably see the development of the argument in the *Laches* as implicitly making the distinction between true courage and confidence arising from technical expertise. The same development takes place in this dialogue, where the present argument, which attempts to equate courage with expertise, is abandoned, to be succeeded by another argument in which courage is equated with an altogether different kind of knowledge, viz. knowledge of what is to be pursued and what is to be avoided in life as a whole. The argument at Xen. *Mem.* IV.vi.10–11 to show that courage arises from knowledge of how to make good use of what is dangerous, and cowardice from lack of that knowledge, shows no sign of that distinction between kinds of knowledge. On the *Laches* see Festugière *BCH* 46, O'Brien *YCS* xviii, Gulley pp.157–60, Santas *RM* 69, Vlastos *PS* pp.166--9.

(iv) The derivation of step 6 is invalid. While the implied step 5 does follow from premisses 2 and 4, 6 does not follow from 5;

even if the state of being daring but lacking in knowledge is not itself any part of excellence, and *a fortiori* not courage, it does not follow that those in that state do not possess some *other* state which *is* courage. The argument would require the additional premiss that no one who is mad possesses any of the virtues. Socrates probably assumes that among the properties of courage must be the property of causing such actions as risking one's life, but that in the case of 'madmen' such acts are wholly accounted for by their possession of a state other than courage. It would, then, follow that such persons do not possess courage, but that is a different argument from that in the text, which does not mention the causation of action.

The availability of the interpretation given above disproves Vlastos's claim (op. cit. p.257, n.95) that 'Virtue is noble' and 'Courage is noble' must be taken as Pauline predications. It is indeed possible that they are, but unlikely. Cf. the similar argument at *Lach.* 192c–d 'Courage is something noble, unintelligent endurance is something bad and harmful, hence unintelligent endurance is not the same as courage.' It is clear that in that argument the predications are non-Pauline (particularly obvious in the case of the second premiss), and hence likely that the similar predications in the *Protagoras* should be taken similarly. (Cf. also *Charm.* 159c–d.)

(v) The derivation of step 7 presents most problems. This step may be regarded as a conjunctive proposition

> 7a 'These people (i.e. the experts just mentioned) who are wisest are most daring'

and

> 7b 'Being most daring they are most courageous.'

7a is comparatively unproblematic, being merely a statement in the superlative of the principle enunciated in the comparative in premiss 3. Strictly speaking, the introduction of the superlative requires to be justified by the principle 'The degree of daring which a man possesses is directly proportional to his degree of wisdom', but as far as the logical structure of the argument goes the comparatives and superlatives are irrelevant. 3 may be read simply as

$$(x)\,(Wx \to Dx)$$

(see above, pp.152–3), and 7a as a simple restatement of that premiss. 7b may be read either as 'Since they are most daring they are therefore most courageous', i.e.

$$(x)\,(Dx \to Cx),$$

or as 'Since they are most daring (and also wisest) they are therefore most courageous', i.e.

$$(x)\,(Dx \ \& \ Wx \to Cx).$$

The decision which interpretation to adopt depends in part on the interpretation of 350b6–7, where the MSS. have 'What do you say about (or 'What do you call') the courageous? Isn't it that they are the daring?', to which Protagoras replies, 'Yes, I stick to that.' The normal interpretation, in Greek as in English, of the expression 'Say that the *F*s are the *G*s' is that what is being asserted is that all and only *F*s are *G*s, i.e.

$$(x) (Fx \leftrightarrow Gx).$$

In that case Socrates, whether consciously or unconsciously, is illegitimately converting the one-way implication of premiss 1

$$(x) (Cx \rightarrow Dx)$$

into the equivalence

$$(x) (Cx \leftrightarrow Dx),$$

and Protagoras' reply, recalling his earlier acceptance of 1 (349e2–3), must be meant to indicate that he fails to spot the shift. Socrates must then be assumed to use this equivalence to derive the former reading of 7b,

$$(x) (Dx \rightarrow Cx),$$

which, with 7a, gives by syllogism

$$(x) (Wx \rightarrow Cx).$$

And since, as was seen above (p.151), steps 1 and 6 are sufficient to derive the converse implication

$$(x) (Cx \rightarrow Wx),$$

Socrates might now claim to have established the equivalence

$$(x) (Cx \leftrightarrow Wx).$$

This appears to be how Protagoras is represented as understanding the argument (350c6–351b2). He complains (c6–d1) that while his initial assent was to premiss 1

$$(x) (Cx \rightarrow Dx),$$

Socrates has illegitimately converted that into

$$(x) (Dx \rightarrow Cx),$$

which Protagoras has neither agreed to nor is prepared to concede. He does not mention the equivalence which, on the present interpretation, Socrates has used to facilitate the illegitimate conversion. Protagoras then gives (d3–e6) a parallel argument to illustrate what he takes to be the fallacy committed by Socrates. This argument runs as follows (reading '*S*' as '... is strong', '*W*' as '... is knowl-

156

edgeable' and 'A' as '. . . is capable'):

1a.	$(x)(Sx \to Ax)$	Corresponding to	1.	$(x)(Cx \to Dx)$
2a.	$(x)(Wx \to Ax)$	Corresponding to	3.	$(x)(Wx \to Dx)$
3a.	$(x)(Ax \to Sx)$	Corresponding to	7b.	$(x)(Dx \to Cx)$

(by illegitimate conversion of 1a and 1 respectively)

therefore

4a.	$(x)(Wx \leftrightarrow Sx)$	Corresponding to	8.	$(x)(Wx \leftrightarrow Cx)$.

This formulation is remarkable in two respects. Firstly, the conclusion manifestly does not follow, even leaving aside the fallacious derivation of 3a; rather 2a and 3a entail the one-way implication

$$(x)(Wx \to Sx) \qquad \text{Corresponding to} \qquad (x)(Wx \to Cx).$$

Secondly, Protagoras' reconstruction omits any mention of steps 2 and 4–6 of the original argument. A possible explanation of the first point is that Protagoras is unclear about the difference between the conditional and the biconditional, and consequently unclear as to what thesis it is that Socrates is maintaining. His confusion would be all the grosser in that his own ground for denying the identity of courage with wisdom was the thesis that some courageous men are not wise, i.e.

$$(\exists x)(Cx \ \& -Wx),$$

which is, of course, inconsistent with the biconditional

$$(x)(Wx \leftrightarrow Cx)$$

but not with the simple implication

$$(x)(Wx \to Cx).$$

In that case it is a further question how far his unclarity is shared by (a) Socrates and (b) Plato; i.e. does Plato deliberately represent one or more of his characters as subject to an unclarity from which he is himself free, or do his characters argue in an unclear fashion because their creator is himself unclear on the point on which he represents them as arguing? The hypothesis that at least Socrates shares Protagoras' unclarity would explain the crucial slip at 350b6–7; on that hypothesis Socrates turns premiss 1 into biconditional form by inadvertence and then uses the biconditional to make the fallacious conversion of 1. Protagoras spots the fallacious conversion, but not the confusion which led to it, a confusion which he then repeats in his own analysis of the argument. If, on the other hand, Socrates is supposed to be clear about the difference between the conditional and the biconditional, while Protagoras is unclear, Socrates argues sophistically at 350b6–7. In that case he would be guilty of a fraud so clumsy that it involves a direct contradiction with the immediately preceding step 6, and so transparent that Protagoras immediately detects it. As it seems incredible that Plato should wish to represent Socrates as arguing in such a morally and intellectually discreditable fashion, and in being detected in such a humiliating way, we must either accept the unclarity hypothesis as applying to both Socrates and Protagoras (?because it applies to Plato also), or look for some other explanation.

Against the unclarity hypothesis is the fact that at 350e6–351b2 Protagoras is quite clear that Socrates' identity thesis requires the truth of both halves of the biconditional, and hence will fail if one half is true and the other false. Hence if there is an adequate alternative to the unclarity hypothesis, it is to be preferred.

An alternative explanation is available, which also takes account of the other odd feature of Protagoras' analysis, viz. his ignoring of steps 2 and 4–6 of the original argument. It was seen above (p.151) that step 6, together with step 1, allows the derivation of

$$(x)\,(Cx \to Wx),$$

though this is not pointed out by Socrates. Steps 2, 4, and 5 are used in the derivation of 6, and lead to the conclusion only to the extent (as yet unclear) to which 6 leads to it. It is possible that Protagoras intends his analysis to represent not the whole of Socrates' argument, but merely that part of it that he considers faulty. In that case he accepts the implicit derivation of

$$(x)\,(Cx \to Wx),$$

thereby accepting the contradictory of the thesis which he had urged at 349d5–8, but fastens on the derivation of the converse implication as fallacious. On this view there is no need to suppose that Plato represents either Protagoras or Socrates as confused between implication and equivalence; both are clear that from 350b6 Socrates is not trying to prove the whole equivalence

$$(x)\,(Wx \leftrightarrow Cx),$$

but merely the second half of it

$$(x)\,(Wx \to Cx),$$

having implicitly proved the converse by the time he reaches 350b6.

On this interpretation it still remains to ask whether Protagoras is correct in his diagnosis of Socrates' fallacy. That interpretation is indeed the natural one if 350b6–7 is taken as an equivalence. But while that is the most natural way to read the Greek, there are in Plato some instances of the expression 'Say that the *F*s are the *G*s' (or 'Call the *F*s the *G*s') where it is at least unclear that the meaning is 'Say that all and only Fs are G' rather than simply 'Say that all Gs are F' or 'Say that all Fs are G'. Thus at *Gorg.* 491e when Callicles says 'It's the silly whom you call the self-controlled' (or 'By "the self-controlled" you mean "the silly"') he may mean no more than that all self-controlled people are silly, which is in fact what he goes on to urge. Again, at *Lach.* 195e Laches criticizes Nicias' suggested definition of courage as knowledge of things to be feared and things not to be feared on the ground that 'He is calling the courageous the seers', when in fact his criticism is that only seers could possess the required knowledge. Another instance is *Prot.* 342b where 'those whom Protagoras called "the Sophists"' may mean simply 'those whom Protagoras called sophists' (cf. n. on 333d5–6, p.132 above). (For other references see O'Brien *TAPA* 61, who, however, regards the evidence as conclusive in favour of the equivalence interpretation.) Thus it seems at least possible that the crucial sentences may mean no more than 'What do you say about the courageous? Isn't it that they are daring?', i.e. a simple restatement of premiss 1, which is how Protagoras evidently understands them. If that is so, then how does Socrates derive 7b? We should note that immediately before asserting 7 Socrates repeats step 6, i.e.

$$(x) (Dx \ \& \ -Wx \rightarrow -Cx) \ (350c1{-}2).$$

This, a redundant intrusion on the other interpretation, is explained if Socrates asserts 7b in the second of the two alternative senses mentioned above (p.155), i.e.

$$(x) (Dx \ \& \ Wx \rightarrow Cx),$$

and if he derives that proposition fallaciously from 6. He may then be seen as arguing that, since he has shown that it is the absence of knowledge which prevents daring from counting as courage, therefore the presence of knowledge must be sufficient to make daring into courage. Just so, if it is lack of oxygen in the atmosphere which prevents a lighted match from setting fire to wood shavings, the addition of oxygen will be sufficient, together with the ignition of the match, to cause the shavings to catch fire. The argument fails because step 6 does not allow Socrates to assert that knowledge is the only condition necessary, together with daring, if one is to be courageous, but merely that it is *a* necessary condition of being courageous.

There are, then, at least two possible accounts of the derivation of 7b, giving rise to four views of the whole argument. (i) 7b is read as

$$(x) (Dx \rightarrow Cx),$$

and is derived by the fallacious conversion of premiss 1, mediated by the fallacious assimilation of 1 to the biconditional at 350b6–7. This account generates two alternative accounts of the argument as a whole: (ia) 7b is used to derive the implication

$$(x)\,(Wx \to Cx)$$

which is confused with the required biconditional conclusion

$$(x)\,(Wx \leftrightarrow Cx);$$

(ib) 7b is used to derive the above implication on the understanding that the converse implication necessary for the derivation of the biconditional has already been established. (ii) 7b is read as

$$(x)\,(Dx\ \&\ Wx \to Cx),$$

which is fallaciously derived from 6. This account generates alternative accounts of the whole argument (iia) and (iib), corresponding to (ia) and (ib). In favour of either version of (i) may be cited the facts that Protagoras is made to give this explanation of the fallacy, and that it involves the most natural reading of the Greek of 350b6–7. Neither point is conclusive; it is well within the bounds of reasonable dramatic possibility that Plato should represent Protagoras as giving an *in*correct diagnosis of the fallacy, in order to expose his limitations as a critic of arguments, while we have seen that another account of 350b6–7 is at least possible. There are three strong arguments against (ia): 1 it ignores several steps of the argument, 2 it requires Protagoras to confuse implication and biconditional despite the fact that he is tolerably clear on the distinction at 350c–351b, and 3 it requires Socrates either to share that confusion or to argue dishonestly. These arguments seem to be decisive. Arguments 2 and 3 also tell strongly against (iia), with this difference, that whereas (ia) requires Protagoras and Socrates to confuse implication and biconditional twice (firstly between 349e1–3 and 350b6–7 and secondly at 350c4–5), (iia) requires the second confusion only. For these reasons the choice appears to rest between (ib) and (iib). The latter is favoured by considerations of economy, in that it does not require, as (ib) does, that we postulate at 350b6–7 confusion on the part of Protagoras and confusion or dishonesty on that of Socrates; further, (iib) gives a better explanation of the repetition of 6 immediately before 7. Against that must be set the fact that (iib) requires a somewhat conjectural, though possible, interpretation of 350b6–7. On the whole, I tentatively incline towards (iib). Since questions of this kind are ultimately questions about the intentions of the writer, we must accept that we are often not in a position to do more than judge that one conjectural account of his intentions is more plausible than another, or even that of two equally plausible accounts one is methodologically superior to another. This is far from the suggestion that all speculation about a writer's intentions is futile, since his writing of the work provides the same sort of indication of his intentions as does the behaviour of any agent. It is merely to emphasize the obvious fact that the evidence available about the intentions of long-dead authors is frequently so fragmentary that no conclusion can pretend to more than reasonable plausibility. *

350c6–351b2 *Protagoras objects to Socrates' argument and attempts to show a fallacy in it.*
On this section as a whole see above, pp.156–61.

351a3 'good natural condition and nurture'. The coupling of the two items (lit. 'nature and good nurture', repeated at b2) is significant. Protagoras is presumably maintaining his doctrine that physical and moral excellences require the right endowment to start with and the proper development of that endowment. See n. on 323d7, pp.89–90 above.

351b3–e11 *Socrates breaks off the discussion of wisdom and courage to introduce a thesis to the effect that pleasure is in itself something (? the supreme, ? the only) good. It is agreed to examine this thesis.*

The final section of the dialogue, to which this passage serves as introduction, poses many major problems of interpretation (see below). This passage itself presents three interconnected problems.
(a) How is the passage connected with what precedes it?
(b) How is it connected with what follows?
(c) Precisely what is the thesis which Socrates introduces?
(a) The abruptness of the shift from the previous argument is quite remarkable. There is no indication in the text that the discussion of wisdom and courage is being broken off (as there was at 332a2–4), nor any attempt to show a connection with the new direction of the argument. Instead Socrates launches without preliminary into an apparently new theme, the conditions necessary and sufficient for the achievement of a satisfactory life. The only verbal hint of any connection is provided by 'and' in the first sentence, but this connective functions, as in English, not to introduce any significant change in the direction of the thought, but to indicate a direct continuation with what immediately precedes.

* It is very hard to resist the conclusion that the present section was originally part of a more continuous treatment, in dialogue form, of the contribution of pleasure to the good life, and that its juxtaposition in our texts to the preceding discussion represents a later (and perhaps not necessarily final) stage in Plato's discussion of Protagoras. The hypothesis of an earlier version of the *Protagoras*, of which our actual dialogue is a possibly incomplete revision, cannot be further explored here. In order to show the connection which underlies the *prima facie* incoherence with what has preceded, it will be necessary to sketch in a preliminary and dogmatic fashion the course of the whole argument from 351b to 360e. That is to say, a satisfactory answer to question (a) proceeds via the answer to question (b).

(b) At 351e3–11 it is agreed to examine Socrates' thesis (on which see below) on the contribution of pleasure to a satisfactory life. But immediately (352b1–c7) Socrates shifts the discussion yet again, to the question of whether knowledge (sc. of what one should do) is always sufficient to determine conduct, or whether someone who knows what he should do may yet fail to act on his knowledge because he is overcome by pleasure, pain, fear or some similar impulse. Socrates and Protagoras themselves agree in accepting the former alternative (b1–d3), while the mass of ordinary people reject it and accept the latter (d4–e2). Socrates proposes to show where the ordinary man goes wrong, on the ground that this will throw light on the original question, viz. the relation of courage to the other virtues (e5–353b6). The connection emerges as follows. The ordinary man is first induced to acknowledge (353c1–354e2) that he regards anything whatever as good if and only if it is either predominantly pleasant in itself or a means to the attainment of something predominantly pleasant, and bad if and only if it is either predominantly unpleasant in itself or results in something predominantly unpleasant. Hence since the phenomenon of being overcome by pleasure consists in taking what one realizes to be the worse course of action, he must accept the redescription of that phenomenon as knowingly taking the course of action which one realizes will lead to less favourable consequences, assessed in terms of pleasure and distress (354e4–356a5). Socrates now argues (356a5–357e8) that the only possible explanation of a choice of less favourable consequences, measured in terms of pleasure and distress, is failure to estimate those consequences correctly. Hence it is impossible to make a wrong choice knowingly, i.e. the ordinary man must admit that given his hedonistic scheme of evaluation all wrong action is due to ignorance or mistake, and specifically to the lack of the proper technique for the estimation of the pleasant and unpleasant consequences of action. Socrates now applies this result to the question of courage. Protagoras and the other sophists are induced to agree, not merely that the ordinary man's assumptions oblige him to accept that all wrong action is attributable to ignorance, but that in fact all wrong action *is* so attributable, and specifically that cowardly action arises from mistaken estimation of the pleasurable and unpleasant consequences of action. Hence courage proves to be the same thing as wisdom concerning what is and is not to be feared, and Protagoras is obliged to abandon his thesis that a man who is altogether lacking in wisdom may yet be outstandingly courageous (358a1–360e5). It is not until this tortuous argument is fully worked out that we can see it as directly continuous with and as intended to make good the deficiencies of the first argument on wisdom and courage (349e–350c). That argument, we can now see, was abandoned because of the manifest inadequacy of the conception of wisdom which it embodies, i.e. technical expertise. The argument which succeeds it seeks to remedy this defect by substituting another conception of knowledge, viz. knowledge of what should be sought and what avoided, in this case analysed in terms of pleasure and distress. It therefore appears that the same development which was implicit in the structure of the *Laches* (see above, pp.153–4) is here made explicit.

If the above is correct, it explains how the argument from 352b1 (i.e. from Socrates' second shift of topic, see above p.162) continues the investigation of the relation of courage to wisdom begun at 349e. But it has still to be shown how the section at present under investigation (351b3–e11) itself fits into the argument as a whole. The most obvious assumption is that the argument from 352b1 makes use of whatever thesis about pleasure it is that Socrates seeks to establish in this section. This is confirmed by the fact that at 358a5–6 Socrates begins the transition from the argument with the ordinary man to the substantial proof of the identity of courage with wisdom by securing the agreement of the Sophists to the thesis asserted in this section, viz. 'The pleasant is good and the painful bad' (on the interpretation of that thesis see below, pp.164–70). Moreover, that very thesis is agreed immediately (358b6–c3) to lead directly to the conclusion that all wrong action results from mistake, a conclusion which has merely to be applied to the particular case of cowardly action to complete the entire argument. The structure of the whole passage is then as follows. At 351b–e Socrates enunciates a certain thesis on the relation of pleasure and goodness, which is challenged by Protagoras. Socrates then shows that acceptance of that thesis commits one to the doctrine that all wrong action comes about through some mistake on the part of the agent; this conclusion is reached by examination of the views of the ordinary man, who implicitly accepts the Socratic thesis about the value of pleasure while rejecting the doctrine about wrong action, a position which is shown to be inconsistent. Socrates then gains the assent of the sophists, including Protagoras, to his thesis about pleasure, and consequently to the doctrine which follows from it. Finally, that doctrine is applied to the disputed case of cowardly action, thereby showing the identity of courage with wisdom. For a different view see Manuwald *Phron* 75.

(c) In order to determine precisely what Socrates' thesis is, we must undertake a detailed examination of the passage.

351b4 'live well': equivalent to 'have a satisfactory, worthwhile life', without the specific implication of 'live a morally good life', as is clear from b4–7. Cf. Ar. *EN* I.4, 1095a19–20: 'They (i.e. philosophers and ordinary men alike) understand living well and doing well to be the same thing as having a worthwhile life' (= *to eudaimonein*, frequently if inexactly translated 'being happy').

351b7–c1 Socrates' conclusion follows immediately from the two preceding propositions, both of which Protagoras has so far accepted without question. Unqualified, the conclusion asserts that a life in which pleasure predominates is a good one, independently of any other value, and that a life in which unpleasantness predominates is a bad one, independently of any other value. The conclusion thus falls short of the strongest thesis of evaluative hedonism, viz. the thesis that pleasure is the only good thing and unpleasantness the only bad thing, since (a) it is not a universal thesis about goodness as such, but a thesis about what makes one's life as a whole good or bad, and (b) it allows that a life in which neither pleasure nor unpleasantness predominates may yet be good or bad for some other reason. It thus allows a criterion of value independent of pleasantness or unpleasantness, and provides no further criterion for judging the relative value of a life good *qua* pleasant and a life good for some other reason. But it does not allow a pleasant life to be judged worse than an unpleasant life by any independent criterion, such as moral worthiness. For a pleasant life is a good life, an unpleasant life a bad life, and while x may be good and yet worse than y, which is better, and p may be bad and yet better than q which is worse, it is axiomatic that nothing which is good can be worse than anything which is bad, provided that the evaluation uses the same standard. Hence if life A is a good life, being pleasant, and life B is a bad life, being unpleasant, A must be a better life than B, no matter how far B excels A on some other criterion. Thus someone who maintains the common-sense view that a life spent in the successful pursuit of (morally or otherwise) undesirable pleasures is not a good life must reject the conclusion. That is in fact the force of Protagoras' rejoinder.

351c1–2 Though the form of Protagoras' caveat is as translated, it must be understood as 'provided one takes pleasure in *nothing but* praiseworthy things'. Socrates' assessment of pleasure and unpleasantness has lacked moral implications (see above, p.164); a pleasant life is something good (*agathon*) in the sense of something worth having from the point of view of the person who has it, an unpleasant life is something bad (*kakon*) in the sense of something undesirable from that point of view. These are the ordinary implications of the terms; see e.g. *Meno* 77b–78b. Protagoras' caveat introduces a further dimension of assessment; he suggests that a life is a good one for the agent only provided that its pleasures are *kala*, i.e. praiseworthy, honourable, noble, as opposed to *aischra*, i.e. shameful, disgraceful, undignified, dishonourable. This pair of terms provides a range of assessment, ranging from the aesthetic via the area of social propriety to the more specifically moral, which is less closely tied to considerations of the advantage and disadvantage of the agent. Thus while there can be no question that an agent should, in his own interest, avoid what is *kakon*, there can be a genuine question as to whether he should avoid what is *aischron* (e.g. where he can gain some great advantage by an undetected fraud). At times Plato makes a clear distinction between the two pairs of terms, e.g. *Gorg.* 474c–d, where Polus maintains that while it is indeed more shameful (*aischion*) to wrong someone than to be wronged oneself, it is worse (*kakion*) to be wronged, and consequently one ought to do what is more shameful rather than suffer what is worse. In contrast, both Socrates and Callicles agree that the worst thing i.e. the most disadvantageous thing, to do is also the most shameful, but disagree on what is worst, Callicles insisting that a man harms himself by self-restraint and benefits himself by self-indulgence, Socrates maintaining the contrary. Similarly, at *Meno* 77b Socrates and Meno agree by implication that whatever is *kalon* is *agathon.* So here (c2–3) Socrates takes Protagoras to imply that some pleasures are bad, whereas someone who had a strong sense of the distinction would take him to imply that some pleasures are ignoble, leaving it as a further question whether such pleasures are bad. Consciousness of the distinction indicates a sense, apparent in the *Gorgias*, of the difference between and possible non-coincidence of socially imposed values on the one hand and values derived from the agent's desires and interests on the other. One may disregard the distinction either from lack of consciousness of the different kinds of value-judgement, or from the conviction that, while they are indeed different, they must in fact coincide; there is no evidence for the attribution of one attitude or the other to the characters in this dialogue. It is, however, safe to say that in putting forward this qualification Protagoras is to be seen as proposing a criterion of value which is not only independent of pleasantness or unpleasantness, but capable of outweighing pleasantness where the two criteria conflict.

351c2–3 'Surely you don't go alone with the majority'. Up to this point Socrates has not clearly committed himself to any view on the relation of pleasure to goodness. So far he has elicited from Protagoras acceptance of the theses that a life is (a) bad if it is unpleasant and (b) good if it is pleasant, without any indication of whether he too accepts either thesis. With this phrase, however, he makes it clear that he thinks that Protagoras and the majority are wrong to think that anything pleasant is bad and anything unpleasant is good. i.e. Socrates here commits himself to the view that everything pleasant is good and everything unpleasant bad.

351c4 'What I say is'. On this rendering Socrates here makes an explicit assertion of his own view, in the form of a rhetorical question. It is also possible to take the Greek as 'What I mean is' (see n. on 333d5–6, p.132 above). In that case Socrates is here giving his grounds for his assertion that Protagoras and the majority are wrong. In either case the rhetorical question which follows (c4–5) gives Socrates' own view.

'In so far as things are pleasant, are they not to that extent good?' The Greek is literally 'With reference to that in which they are pleasant, are they not in reference to that good?' That form of expression may be taken in one of two ways. Firstly, it may mean 'In the respect in which they are pleasant, they are in that respect good', i.e. their being pleasant is an aspect in which they display goodness. That formulation allows that pleasant things, even considered in isolation from their consequences (see below), may display badness in other respects, respects, furthermore, which may outweigh their goodness in respect of pleasure and thereby make the pleasant things bad over all. There is, therefore, no incompatibility between Socrates' own view, thus interpreted, and the view which he is engaged in denying, viz. that some pleasant things are bad. All that Socrates' opponents have to make clear is that those pleasant things which are bad are bad for some other reason than that they are pleasant (e.g. that they are dishonourable), a thesis which must surely have been taken for granted both by them and by Socrates. On this interpretation, then, Socrates must be seen as confused. This difficulty is obviated by the alternative rendering, which is adopted in the translation. On this view, what Socrates is saying is that to the extent to which anything is pleasant it is to that extent good; the actual Greek phrase indicating extent (*kath' hoson*) is used at c6 and again in Socrates' recapitulation of his position at e2. While the use of this phrase is not itself decisive, since it could be used in the sense given by the former interpretation, the latter view fits better with Socrates' argument. For on this view if x is over all pleasant, it must be over all good, no matter what other considerations (e.g. its being dishonourable) may be brought against it, and if x is pleasanter than y then x must be better than y. Hence on this rendering Socrates' view is incompatible with the thesis that something may be pleasant but yet bad, and we are consequently relieved of the necessity of attributing confusion to Socrates. This view is stronger than that produced by the conjunction of the two theses enunciated at b4–5 and 6–7. Given those two theses, it was yet possible that a life which contained neither pleasure nor pain in a predominant degree could be a better life than a life which was predominantly pleasant (see n. on b7–c1, pp.164–5 above). Here, on the other hand, Socrates is committed to the view that the pleasanter life is *ipso facto* the better life. Consequently, he already espouses at least the thesis that pleasure is the supreme good, in that nothing can outweigh it as a factor contributing to the over all goodness of a life.

It is uncertain whether he is to be seen as espousing the yet stronger thesis that pleasure is the only good. That depends on whether he is maintaining that the goodness of anything is determined *solely* by its pleasantness, or allowing that, while no other factor can outweigh pleasantness, other factors may contribute to over all goodness; the text is indeterminate. In either case his own position is substantially stronger than that attributed to him by Vlastos *Phoenix* 69, viz. the simple view that all pleasure is good and all pain evil. That view amounts to the former interpretation of Socrates' position, which, though not impossible, we have seen to fit the rest of the passage less readily than the interpretation here adopted.

351c5 'leaving their other consequences out of account'. This qualification is necessary, since Socrates does not deny that some pleasant activities and experiences are in fact bad (cf. 353c–354e), but merely maintains that such things are bad, not in themselves but in so far as they have bad (i.e. unpleasant) consequences. The latter are 'other' than the pleasure which is thought of as the immediate effect of the activity or experience; for the contrast between the effect which something has 'in itself' and the things which 'result from' it cf. the discussion of the value of justice in *Rep.* II, esp. 358b–d, 366e and 367b–e.

351d7–e1 The distinction is obscure. Plato may have in mind the fact that both feelings (whether reactions like excitement or bodily sensations) and the activities which give rise to them may be called pleasant, and may wish to make it clear that the ensuing discussion is independent of whether one analyses pleasure as an effect of activities (i.e. as something like a mental state) or as a feature of the activities themselves (in which case pleasure is assimilated to pleasantness). Alternatively he may intend to introduce an extention of the sense of 'pleasant' from its normal sense of 'characterized by pleasantness' to 'characterized by or productive of pleasantness', i.e. 'pleasant in itself or having pleasant consequences'. An extended sense is required if the later identification of 'the pleasant' with 'the good' (355b ff.) is to be taken literally.

351e1–3 Socrates' attempted elucidation of his position merely creates further problems. The wording of the first question suggests the stronger interpretation of his thesis suggested above, viz. 'To the extent to which things are pleasant, they are to that extent good', but the explanation in the next sentence suggests the weaker, viz. 'Being pleasant is an aspect in which things display goodness', since it is most natural to take the Greek in the sense 'Pleasure is (something) good.' It is, however, also possible to understand it as 'Pleasure is (the) good', an expression which may itself be taken in either of two ways, (a) 'Pleasure is the only thing which is (underivatively) good', or (b) 'Pleasure (= pleasantness) is the same thing as goodness.' While (a) is the more natural interpretation of the English sentence 'Pleasure is the good', the Greek may equally well be taken either way, and it seems in fact from e5–6 that Protagoras understands Socrates' position in sense (b) (see p.170 below).

It is likely that, if Plato does intend that Socrates' thesis be taken as 'Pleasure is the good', he makes no distinction between (a) and (b). A distinction is required only if either of two conditions is satisfied: (i) a distinction is intended between pleasure as a certain mental state and pleasantness as a characteristic of objects, viz. their production of that mental state, (ii) (b) is understood as ' "Pleasant" and "good" have the same meaning.' On (i) it seems likely that no distinction is intended (see n. on d7–e1 above and 355a–b, where the thesis that the good is nothing other than *pleasure* is held to license the treatment of the adjectives 'good' and *'pleasant'* as interchangeable). This assimilation is rendered more comprehensible by consideration of the expressions used to designate pleasure. While the term in 351e1–3 is indeed the noun *hēdonē*, that is treated as interchangeable with *to hēdu* (lit. 'the pleasant'; compare e1–3 with e3–6); that usage occurs elsewhere (e.g. *Gorg.* 495a–d) and conforms to the regular grammatical pattern in which an abstract noun is interchangeable with an expression formed by the definite article followed by the adjective corresponding to the noun (e.g. 'justice' and 'the just', cf. n. on 330c2–7, p.112 above) *To hēdu* is used to designate pleasure (e.g. *Ph.* 60c) as well as pleasantness or what is pleasant (e.g. *Hipp. Maj.* 298a ff.), and sometimes occurs in contexts which suggest no differentiation (e.g. 356a).

As regards (ii), the reading of (b) as a thesis about the meaning of the words 'pleasant' and 'good' requires a distinction between (a) and (b), for (a) is a substantial value judgement about what is worth pursuing. But if (b) is taken as 'Pleasantness is that quality in things which alone makes them worth pursuing', then it is itself evaluative, and amounts to 'Pleasure is the only thing worth pursuing.' Thus understood, it identifies the goodness of anything (i.e. that quality which by definition makes it desirable) with its pleasantness, but not via the synonymy of the terms 'good' and 'pleasant'. As is seen in the discussion of the unity of the virtues (see pp.103–8 above and 211–14 below), Plato's identification of attributes is at least sometimes to be interpreted as asserting identity of reference rather than identity of sense of the terms designating the attributes; since the former is a weaker thesis than the latter, economy suggests that we should interpret Plato as committed merely to the former, unless explicit evidence obliges us to construe him in terms of the latter. We find a similar connection of thought in *Rep.* VI, 505a–b, where, having said that it is necessary to examine the nature of goodness, Socrates points out that many people think that pleasure is the good. Clearly their thesis is not the analytic one that 'good' and 'pleasant' are synonymous terms, but rather the evaluative thesis that only pleasure is worth seeking for itself, whence it follows that it is pleasure which makes other things worth seeking. While Plato regards that answer (at least in the *Republic*) as mistaken, he does not suggest that it is the wrong kind of answer, as he should if the investigation of the nature of goodness were an inquiry into the meaning of the word 'good'.

It appears, then, that it is possible that Socrates here proposes a thesis stronger than either of the two suggested above, viz. the undifferentiated thesis that pleasure is the only (underivatively) good thing and that 'pleasant' and 'good' are different names for one and the same characteristic. From this it follows immediately, and would presumably be seen by Plato to follow, that all and only pleasant things are good. This passage, then, so far from settling the issue between the two alternatives discussed above, merely adds a third.

The formula 'Pleasure is the good' has the further defect of ambiguity between (a) 'The goodness of an action etc. is identical with its immediate pleasantness' and (b) 'The goodness of an action etc. is identical with its contributing to a life in which pleasure predominates.' It is clear that (b), not (a), is the view of the common man (see n. on 355a2–5, pp.178–9 below), but the argument against him confuses (a) and (b) (see n. on 355c1–8, pp.180–1 below). For evidence that (b) represents Socrates' own position, see n. on 360a2–3, pp.208–10 below. The thesis that pleasure is the good is attacked in the *Gorgias* (495a–500a). *Republic* VI (505b–c) and *Philebus* (13a–c, 20c–21d) in terms which indicate that (a) rather than (b) is Plato's target.

351e3–4 'as you always say': e.g. 343c6.

351e5–6 Protagoras' account of Socrates' thesis raises two questions: (a) How does he understand it? (b) Does he understand it correctly?

(a) The rendering given in the translation 'Pleasant and good are the same' is that accepted by all commentators; given this rendering Protagoras understands Socrates as committed to the strongest of the three theses mentioned above. This rendering requires that 'pleasant and good' be the subject and 'the same' the predicate of the subordinate clause following 'it appears that', whereas the Greek more naturally suggests the converse, i.e. 'It appears that the same thing is pleasant and good.' But firstly it is doubtful whether that reading gives a satisfactory sense, and secondly the reading adopted here is strongly suggested by comparison with *Gorg.* 495a, where the context shows that the same expression must be taken as 'Pleasant and good are the same.'

(b) It is possible that Plato represents Protagoras as misunderstanding Socrates, the latter's own position being one or other of the weaker theses. On the other hand, Socrates may himself be represented as committed to the strongest thesis. It is not possible from examination of this passage alone to remove all ambiguity from Socrates' position.

352a1–357e8 *Socrates states his thesis that if one knows what is the right thing to do one necessarily does it, and defends this thesis against the common man's objection*

*that people frequently know what to do but fail to do it
because they are overcome by pleasure or other appetitive
forces. He argues that the common man's hedonistic assumptions oblige him to admit that the man whom he describes
as overcome by such forces is in fact led astray by error in
his calculation of the consequences of his actions.*

352a1–c7 The medical analogy makes it clear that the question
of the relation between pleasure and goodness (corresponding to the
inspection of the face and hands) is subsidiary to the question of
the relation between courage and knowledge (corresponding to the
complete physical examination).

352a6–8 'your view about the pleasant and the good is as you
say'. The reference is to 351d4–8. It is unclear whether the view
expressed there is in fact inconsistent with Socrates' position. If
Socrates asserts merely that pleasure is something good, then there
is no inconsistency. But even if he asserts either of the two stronger
theses, viz. that pleasure is either the supreme or the only good
(see above), there need be no inconsistency, provided that by 'bad
pleasures' Protagoras means pleasures whose unpleasant consequences
outweigh their intrinsic pleasantness, and similarly for 'good pains'.
Inconsistency arises only if Protagoras maintains his position while
accepting either Socrates' prohibition on consideration of consequences (351c5; see pp.167–8 above) or the extension of the sense
of 'pleasant' mentioned above (p.168). While it is perhaps more
probable that he is to be seen as doing the former, the text gives
no explicit indication on the point.

352b1–c7 The following points should be noticed.
  (a) The problem posed by the confrontation of the views of
Socrates and of the common man is expressed purely in terms of
knowledge, viz. whether it is possible to act against one's knowledge
of what it is best to do. There is no indication at this stage that this
problem is seen as related to the more general problem of whether
it is possible to act against one's beliefs. The development of the
argument shows that Socrates also accepts the impossibility of acting
either against one's knowledge or against one's belief as to the best
course of action (see below, pp.202–4)
  (b) Socrates is not very explicit about the content of the knowledge in question. He speaks merely of knowing what is good and bad
(c4–5), and says nothing of how this knowledge is acquired, what
distinguishes it from mere belief or opinion, and whether he

envisages a systematic body of knowledge as opposed to a set of disconnected bits of knowledge. It must at least embrace the application of such general principles as 'Pleasure is good' to particular instances. This is confirmed by the use in the next sentence of the word 'intelligence' (*phronēsis*), as synonymous with 'knowledge', since the term is regularly employed, even before its canonization as a technical term by Aristotle, with the implications of prudence and good sense.

(c) The list of appetitive forces, which is obviously not intended to be exhaustive, could be readily extended, e.g. by citing laziness, shyness, or boastfulness. It is natural to see pleasure and pain as more basic than the others, in that the other emotions cited, and any others which may be supplied, can all be analysed as involving desires to achieve certain states and to avoid others, while the hedonistic picture of desire which is here accepted requires that all these particular desires be treated as forms of the basic desires to have pleasure and avoid pain. This no doubt accounts for the fact that in the development of the subsequent argument in its general form (up to 357e) we hear only of pleasure and pain, and that the ensuing treatment of cowardice (358d–360e) is treated as a direct application of the general principle which has been enunciated in terms of pleasure and pain. (N.B. 'Pain' is used here and subsequently to render *lupē*, whose sense is considerably wider than that of 'physical pain'. *Lupē* functions as the internal accusative of verbs equivalent to 'find unpleasant' or 'find disagreeable', and is naturally used in any context in which such verbs are appropriate. 'Pain' is used because in English it is conventionally opposed to 'pleasure', and because, like *lupē* but unlike 'unpleasantness', it has a natural plural.)

(d) 'They just look on knowledge as a slave who gets dragged about by all the rest': c1–2. Aristotle twice alludes to this sentence (*EN* VII.2, 1145b23–4; 3, 1147b15–17) with reference to Socrates' thesis that no one acts against knowledge. Aristotle gives no reasons for Socrates' having held this view, beyond the assertion that it would be 'terrible' or 'astonishing' (*deinon*) if knowledge could be dragged about and overcome by anything else; he thus reproduces not merely the vocabulary but also the dogmatic character of this passage.

352c8–d3 Since his profession was the imparting of wisdom and knowledge, one would expect Protagoras to agree enthusiastically that these are the most important and influential human attributes, but that falls far short of the thesis which Socrates is maintaining, viz. that if one possesses knowledge of what is good and bad one *invariably* acts on it. It is possible that Protagoras is represented as slipping between, or intentionally playing on, the two senses of *kratistos*, viz. 'strongest' or 'mightiest' and 'noblest'. There is no evidence that the historical Protagoras accepted the strong form of the Socratic thesis; see n. on 345d9–e4, p.147 above.

352d6–7 'many people who know what is best are not willing to do it, though it is in their power'. In this formulation of the common-sense view of what happens when one is overcome by pleasure etc., it is explicitly stated that neither condition is fulfilled which would disqualify the agent from being free and responsible. He both knows that he should do something other than what he in fact does (i.e. his action is not excusable on grounds of ignorance), and has it in his power to do the right thing (i.e. he is not compelled to do what he in fact does). Thus he acts *hekōn*. The common-sense view thus sees no incompatibility between the description of someone as having been overcome by some appetitive force and the judgement that he is responsible for having acted under the influence of that force. It thus accords both with traditional Greek morality, which held a man responsible for acting from his desires, even when they were prompted by some external force such as a god (see Lloyd-Jones, index s.v. 'Responsibility for action, human'), and with ordinary modern intuitions; we recognize that if *in general* we allow 'I couldn't help it, I was overcome by desire' as a valid excuse, then we can never hold anyone responsible for anything. (For an instance of that defence, where the implications for ordinary moral judgements are very clear, see Gorgias' *Encomium on Helen* (DK 82 B 11), paras. 15–20, discussed by Barnes ch. 23 (c).) At the same time we, like the Greeks, feel that there are *some* irresistible desires, and find serious moral and legal problems in the attempt to demarcate that restricted class. In the subsequent discussion Socrates accepts that the man who is 'overcome by pleasure' has it in his power to act rightly, and concentrates exclusively on the attempt to refute the view that he knows that he should do something other than what he does. Cf. n. on 345d4, p.146 above.

352d8–e1 'overcome by pleasure'. This and similar phrases occur with the noun in the singular here, at 353a3 and 355c3–4, and in the plural at 352e7–353a1, 353c2, 355a8–b1, 355b3 and 356a1. The variations between singular and plural convey no significant difference. As in the English 'pleasures' the plural *hēdonai* generally signifies things enjoyed, whereas the singular *hēdonē* signifies the mental state of enjoyment or of finding something in other ways agreeable, which, as was suggested above (pp.168–9), is not clearly distinguished from the pleasantness of the things which are enjoyed. In discussing someone's motivation, it is indifferent whether we describe him as seeking pleasure or as seeking pleasures, since to desire enjoyment is *ipso facto* to desire enjoyable activities and to desire enjoyable activities (because they are enjoyable) is *ipso facto* to desire enjoyment. Similarly, it is indifferent whether we speak of being overcome by pleasure or by pleasures; Plato's use of these phrases as interchangeable clearly reflects his awareness of this.

352e3–4 Here and at 353a7–8 Protagoras makes it abundantly clear that at least in intention he is no mere mouthpiece for currently accepted views. It is a further question whether Plato intends to represent him as such, despite his protestations.

353c1–354e2 This first section of the discussion of the purported phenomenon of 'being overcome by pleasure(s)' is devoted to making explicit the assumptions contained in the popular view. We must consider (a) what these assumptions are and (b) how far they are shared by Socrates.

(a) It is a commonplace of modern ethical theory to distinguish ethical, evaluative, or normative hedonism, i.e. the doctrine that pleasure and the absence of pain are the only things *worth seeking* for their own sakes, from psychological hedonism, i.e. the doctrine that pleasure and the absence of pain are the only things which *are in fact sought* for their own sakes; for this distinction, and for discussion of the relations between the different forms of hedonism see e.g. Sidgwick Bk 1, ch. 4, Broad pp.146–7, 180–92, 227–39. This distinction is not drawn or clearly presupposed in this passage. The main thesis on which Socrates insists is that the mass of mankind accept evaluative hedonism, i.e. anything which they regard as good they regard as such if and only if it promotes pleasure or the absence of pain, and anything which they regard as bad they regard as such if and only if it promotes pain or the absence of pleasure. That they regard something as good if it is pleasant and bad if it is painful is stated at 354c3–5, that they regard something as good only if it causes pleasure or the cessation of pain is stated at 354b5–c2, and that they regard something as bad only if it causes pain or the deprivation of pleasure is stated at 353e5–354a1. It is not, indeed, said in so many words that they make these evaluations about anything whatever; rather their evaluative views are reached by consideration of a series of examples. But it seems clear that these examples, which are paradigm cases of different kinds of good and bad things, are intended to stand for the entire classes. Hence we may safely conclude that in this passage Socrates attributes to the mass of mankind the central thesis of evaluative hedonism, viz. that anything is good if and only if it is pleasant, and bad if and only if it is unpleasant. (Here 'pleasant' is to be construed as 'causing pleasure or the absence of pain' and 'unpleasant' as 'causing pain or the absence of pleasure'.) Socrates also says (354c3–5) that they pursue pleasure as being good, and seek to avoid pain as being bad; we must take this to mean that they act in accordance with their evaluations as described above, i.e. they pursue pleasure and only pleasure, and seek to avoid pain and only pain. That is to say that their actions satisfy the theory of psychological hedonism, but not, of course, to say that they themselves hold that or any other general theory of motivation. In this passage, then, Socrates secures agreement to the assertions that most people (i) accept and (ii) act in conformity with evaluative hedonism, which is to say that psychological hedonism gives a true account of their actions. Neither here nor elsewhere in the dialogue is any distinction drawn between egoistic evaluative hedonism, i.e. the doctrine that any action or experience is good if and only if it is pleasant to the person who does or undergoes it, and bad if and only if it is unpleasant to him, and what might be termed pluralistic evaluative hedonism, i.e. the doctrine that something is good if and only if it promotes the pleasure of some number of persons (who may be specified in different ways according to different versions of the theory), and bad if and only if it causes pain to that number. The best-known version of this latter theory is universalistic evaluative hedonism or utilitarianism, according to which the class of those whose pleasure and pain must be taken into account is the class of all persons, or in some versions the class of all sentient beings (for details see Broad locc. citt.). Nothing in the text entitles us to say that Plato sees popular evaluations as based on utilitarianism in this sense; most of his examples suggest, if anything, egoistic hedonism. On the other hand, in citing examples such as the power and safety of the city Plato may be representing the common man as drawing in these contexts no distinction between his own pleasures and pains and those of his fellow citizens, but rather as making the natural assumption that all will have a more enjoyable life if the city is strong and wealthy and a more miserable one if it is defeated by its enemies.

(b) The emphasis with which Socrates insists that the evaluations in question are those of the common man would naturally lead one to suppose that he is implying a contrast between that view and his own, an interpretation which has been accepted by several commentators. (One might note in particular the continuous passage from 354a1 to e2, where all the evaluative verbs are in the second person plural (except 'are good' b6, where the context none the less requires 'in your opinion' to be supplied), and the thrice-repeated challenge (b7–c2, d1–3, d7–e2) to the common man to propose some standard of good and bad other than pleasure and pain. But against this we appear to have an explicit statement that Socrates associates himself with at least some of the common man's evaluations in his question at 353e5–354a1: 'Don't you think that, *as Protagoras and I maintain*, the only reason that these things (i.e. poverty and diseases) are bad is that they result in pain and deprive one of other pleasures?' If this sentence is read as translated here (also by Jowett[4] and Croiset), then Socrates says in his own person that two paradigm cases of bad things are bad for no other reason than they cause pain and loss of pleasure, which in context (see p.174 above) justifies us in associating Socrates' own view with that of the common man throughout the passage.

It is, however, also possible to take the sentence as 'Don't you think, as Protagoras and I maintain (sc. that you think), that the only reason . . .' This is how it is taken by Guthrie: 'So the only reason why these pleasures seem to you to be evil is, we suggest, that they result in pains and deprive us of future pleasures', and by Ostwald. While this rendering cannot be definitely excluded, it seems less attractive, since in his presentation of the imaginary dialogue with the many Socrates has so far represented himself as concerned to elicit their views by questions, and not as anticipating their replies in such a direct fashion. On either reading the sentence presents the difficulty that it asserts a unanimity between Socrates and Protagoras which is not justified by anything said previously. In view of the ambiguity of this crucial sentence it is best to conclude that this passage gives us insufficient information for a decision on how far the assumptions of the many are shared by Socrates.

353c7 'wrong'. This renders *ponēros* (also at c9). The word is used in this passage interchangeably with *kakos* 'bad', which replaces it at d5 and is used thereafter. *Ponēros* has a range of implications from 'base, ignoble' (cf. *aischros*) to 'harmful' (cf. *kakos*). It is possibly the former nuance which determines its application in c7 to undesirable (i.e. discreditable) conduct such as getting drunk. But since the point of the argument is precisely that such conduct is undesirable in so far as it is harmful (by causing pain and lack of pleasure), the shift from *ponēros* to *kakos* is natural and unproblematic.

353e3 'pains': not specifically bodily pains, but more generally 'distress'. Cf. n. on *lupē*, p.172 above; as *ania* (the word used here) and its cognates are interchangeable with *lupē* and its cognates (see particularly 354e−356c, with n. p.178 below), both are rendered by 'pain'. *Ania* is cognate to the participle rendered 'in misery' at 351b5. The rendering 'pains' is chosen for the sake of the plural, which preserves the parallelism with 'pleasures'.

354b7 'Result' renders *telos*, lit. 'end' or 'completion' (so in d2 and 8). The things in question are judged good because they result in (*apoteleutai eis* b6) pleasures and avoidance of pains, and the common man looks to that result and no other in judging their value. Jowett[4] renders 'end', 'end or standard', and 'standard' in these three places, followed by Ostwald except in the first, where Ostwald has 'standard'; Croiset renders 'criterium' at d2. But while Plato certainly regards the result as providing the standard by which the common man judges, it is clearly mistaken to make him *say* 'standard' when what he actually says is 'result'.

354c3−6 The Greek presents the same ambiguity as 351e2−3 (cf. pp.168−9 above). It may be read either (a) 'So you pursue pleasure as *something* good, and seek to avoid pain as something evil. ... So it's this that you consider to be something evil, viz. pain ...', or (b) 'So you pursue pleasure as *the* good, and seek to avoid pain as evil. ... So it's this that you consider evil to be, viz. pain ...' As in the earlier case, the former is the more natural reading of the words in isolation from their context. But given the emphasis of the preceding sentences that nothing is good or bad for any reason other than that it causes pleasure or pain, it is impossible to take the sentences other than in sense (b), as a summary of the strong evaluative hedonism to which the common man is committed. This is put beyond any doubt by 355a1−2 where the common man is said explicitly not to be able to give any account of *the* good other than pleasure or of evil (= the bad) other than pain. ('Evil' is used synonymously with 'bad' to render *kakos*; it is preferred chiefly because it has a use as a substantive, enabling it to function as the polar opposite of 'the good' instead of the highly unnatural phrase 'the bad'. Further, the substantive 'evil' may mean either 'badness' or 'that which is alone or supremely bad', thus reproducing the duality of sense which pervades the Greek (see next note).

354c5−e2 The argumentative structure of these sentences presents some problems. The initial 'so' in c5 suggests that the main clause is inferred from what has preceded; i.e. 'You *pursue* pleasure as the good . . . so you *regard* it as the good . . .' In that case the subordinate clause 'since you even call . . .' gives an additional reason for so regarding it. Alternatively the 'so' looks forward to the subordinate clause, a construction which, if less natural, seems not impossible. In neither case does the argument begun in the subordinate clause and completed at d4–e2 appear particularly strong. Socrates argues that pain must be the only bad thing and pleasure the only good thing because pain is the only thing which can make pleasure itself bad and pleasure the only thing which can make pain itself good; the reason for these latter assertions is that the common man is unable to suggest what else could make pleasure bad and pain good. But this argument does not exclude the possibility that, while it is pain that makes pleasure itself bad and pleasure that makes pain itself good, it is some thing(s) other than pain and pleasure which make(s) some other thing(s) good or bad. Plato perhaps assumes that the common man will be unable to meet his challenge anywhere, but in that case it is not clear that the particular instances of pleasure itself and pain itself add anything to the argument, as Plato appears to think. The argument would indeed be stronger if Socrates were merely represented as arguing that pleasure is something good and pain something bad, but, as was seen above (see previous note), the surrounding context excludes that possibility. As before, it is likely that in this argument Plato makes no distinction between 'Pleasure is the only good thing' and 'Pleasure is the same thing as goodness' and between 'Pain is the only bad thing' and 'Pain is the same thing as badness (evil)'; see n. on 351e1–3, pp.168–9 above.

354e3–357e8 In this section the assumptions elicited in the last section are used to show that, in the view of the common man, the description of someone as doing wrong because overcome by pleasure involves an absurdity.

355a1–2 See n. on 354c3–6, p.177 above.

355a2 'Pain' renders *ania*, though the previous argument was all in terms of *lupē*. 'Pains' in the next line renders *lupai*. The adjective rendered 'painful', which is substituted for 'good', is *aniaros*, but Plato switches back to *lupē* and *lupēros* at 356a and uses the terms interchangeably in 356b.

355a2–5 These lines give the most precise statement of the hedonistic position of the common man. While in continuous discussion it is convenient to summarize that position as 'Pleasure is the only good' or 'Pleasure is the supreme good', the previous discussion (e.g. 353e5—354a1) has made it clear that 'pleasure' is to be understood as an abbreviation for 'the predominance of pleasure over pain'. Moreover, any instance of that predominance is good only on the condition that it does not lead to some further situation in which pain predominates over pleasure in such a degree as to outweigh the predominance of pleasure in the first situation; e.g. a drinking-party which is in itself predominantly pleasant is something good only on the condition that it does not produce a hangover whose unpleasantness outweighs the pleasantness of the party (353c—d). Strictly speaking, therefore, the only thing which is absolutely, i.e. unconditionally, good is the predominance of pleasure over pain in one's life as a whole. (N.B. Plato's actual expression 'a pleasant life without pains' states too strong a condition, for even on hedonistic grounds a life which contained some pains might be more desirable than a life with none, provided that the pains were necessary for the production of greater pleasures; thus a hedonist might deliberately induce pangs of thirst, if the pleasure of satisfying them were much more exquisite than enjoyments not preceded by discomfort.) Similarly, while it is convenient to say of some particular action, experience, etc. that it is good if and only if it is pleasant, this is to be understood as an abbreviation for the more precise formulation given here, viz. that it is good if and only if it contributes towards a life in which pleasure predominates over pain. The expression 'Are you content to say' does not then imply that the common man has retreated from his original hedonistic position to a weaker one; rather its force lies in the contrast with 'You are at liberty to withdraw', i.e. 'You can still change your mind, if you think any other position better. Or are you content with your actual position, viz. . . . ?'

355b3—c1   These lines contain the core of the argument, the mutual substitution of the pairs of terms 'pleasant' and 'good' and 'unpleasant' and 'bad', on the ground that it has already been agreed that each of these pairs consists of two names for the same thing. As before, economy of interpretation indicates that this identity should be understood, not as identity of sense between the members of each pair, but as identity of reference, the reference of these adjectival terms being understood as the attribute which, in Mill's terminology (*System of Logic* I.ii.5) they connote. The use of this argument is further confirmation of the interpretation of the common man's position as involving the undifferentiated assertion of the theses (a) 'Pleasure is the only good thing' and (b) 'Pleasure is the same thing as goodness' (see n. on 354c5—e2, pp.177—8 above).

355c1—8 The substitution is now put to work, leading to the following description of the man who is overcome by pleasure: he does what he knows to be bad because he is overcome by the good. This use of the substitution presents a number of problematic features.

(i) In a2—5 it has been explicitly recognized that the goodness of any action, situation, etc. is to be identified, not with its pleasantness, but with its contribution to a life in which pleasure predominates (see pp.178—9 above). Hence it is natural to interpret the substitution as involving extended senses of 'pleasant' and 'unpleasant', viz. 'pleasant' = 'contributing to a life in which pleasure predominates over pain' and 'unpleasant' = 'contributing to a life in which pain predominates over pleasure' (cf. n. on 351d7—e1, p.168 above; the formula suggested there as an extended sense of 'pleasant' may perhaps be regarded as a first approximation to the more precise one given here). But given those senses the argument collapses; for the weak man can no longer be described as being overcome by *pleasure*, and hence by the good, since what he is overcome by (viz. short-term pleasure with painful consequences) is not pleasure in the extended sense of the term which has been identified with goodness. Nor does the argument fare better if 'pleasant' and 'unpleasant' keep their ordinary senses. For then the weak man is indeed overcome by (short-term) pleasure. But neither the common man who is arguing with Socrates, nor the weak man himself (who is presumed to share the same hedonistic assumptions) has agreed that short-term pleasure is the same thing as goodness, nor short-term unpleasantness the same thing as badness. Hence on either view the substitution is invalid, in that it depends on ignoring the distinction central to any sensible hedonistic theory, viz. the distinction between on the one hand what is immediately pleasant or painful and on the other what contributes to a life which is, taken as a whole, pleasant or painful.

(ii) The substitution is invalid for a further, independent, reason. It is an instance of the general principle of the indiscernibility of identicals, i.e. the principle that if x is one and the same thing as y, whatever is true of x is also true of y. But it is well-established that there are certain contexts under which that principle does not hold, among which are intentional contexts, i.e. contexts where either x or y is described as the object of some such mental attitude as belief or desire (cf. e.g. Quine 'Reference and Modality'). Thus if John believes that Cicero denounced Catiline, though Tully is the same person as Cicero, it does not follow that John believes that Tully denounced Catiline, since John may be ignorant of the identity, and hence not be prepared to accept the statement 'Tully denounced Catiline'. Similarly, if John wants to drink what is in the glass, thinking it to be whisky, but what is in the glass is in fact a deadly poison, it does not follow that John wants to drink deadly poison. The context of substitution of 'good' for 'pleasant' is an intentional context, since 'overcome by pleasure' has to be expanded into 'overcome by the desire for pleasure'. Hence, even if (leaving objection (i) above out of account) it is accepted that pleasure is identical with the good without qualification, from the fact that someone does what is bad through being overcome by *the desire for* pleasure it does not follow that he does it through being overcome by the desire for the good, since he may not believe that pleasure is identical with the good. It might be replied that, as was recognized above (p.180) the hedonistic assumptions of the common man are assumed to be shared by *all* common men, and hence by the man who is overcome by pleasure. Hence, if he accepts that pleasure is the good, and is overcome by desire for pleasure, it must follow that he is overcome by desire for the good. Unfortunately, it does not follow; for in the sentence 'A acts wrongly through being overcome by the desire for x' the expression 'x' specifies some aspect of the thing wanted which accounts for its being wanted and hence accounts for the action to which that desire leads. Some other description 'y' of the thing wanted, even if true and accepted by the agent at the time of acting as true of one and the same thing as 'x' is true of, may fail to explain the action, and hence may give to the sentence 'A acts wrongly through being overcome by the desire for y' a different truth-value from that of the original sentence. Thus even if 'John got drunk through being carried away by his passion for whisky' is true, 'John got drunk through being carried away by his passion for something which rots his liver' may be, at least on one reading of that sentence, false, even though at the time in question John accepted that the description 'something which rots your liver' is true of whisky. The sentence is false on that reading which implies that John's recognition of the whisky as something which rots his liver was itself instrumental in bringing about his getting drunk. In general, it cannot be assumed that, when an action is explained by an agent's having had a conception of an object under one description, and having aimed for it under that description, a further true explanation-sentence will be formed by the substitution in the original explanation-sentence of any other true description of the same object, irrespective of whether that description was accepted as true by the agent at the time of acting. (For the main point of this paragraph I am indebted to Mr. M. J. Woods.)

355d1–3 There has been considerable controversy over the precise nature of the absurdity alleged here and at 355a5—c1. Among the views which have been proposed are the following:

(i) The explanation here enunciated is seen as 'a kind of self-contradiction' (Vlastos in Ostwald).

(ii) The explanation is absurd in that it is transformed by means of the analysis of the expression 'being overcome by pleasure' into an explicit contradiction, viz. 'Though people know that certain things are bad they nonetheless do them through ignorance of the fact that they are bad' (Gallop *Phron* 64).

(iii) The explanation is absurd in that it commits the common man to a direct contradiction with the thesis of psychological hedonism enunciated by Socrates at 356a8—c1 and accepted by the common man at c3 (Santas *PR* 66).

(iv) The explanation is absurd, not *qua* self-contradictory, but *qua* entailing e2—3, which is to be seen as manifestly unacceptable (Vlastos *Phoenix* 69).

Interpretation (iii) may be dealt with briefly. For reasons for rejecting the view that 356a8—c3 contains an assertion of psychological hedonism, and hence for rejecting this interpretation, see pp.189—90 below.

The vagueness of the notion of 'a kind of self-contradiction' makes it hard to be clear whether (i) is actually a distinct alternative from (ii), since an implicit contradiction which is made explicit by further analysis is certainly a kind of self-contradiction. Another possibility (suggested by a remark of Vlastos's in *Phoenix* 69, p.81) is that the view in question is intended to be seen not as strictly self-contradictory (i.e. of the form '*P* and not-*P*') but as self-refuting, i.e. such that its being asserted is a sufficient condition of its being false, or commits the speaker to its falsehood; examples of such utterances abound in recent philosophical literature, e.g. 'It's raining but I don't believe that it is', 'I do not exist' (for further discussion see Passmore ch. 4). But since Plato has no terminology which allows him to distinguish self-refutation or other vaguer notions of absurdity from strict self-contradiction, we should be justified in taking him to have the former in mind only if the actual argument which he employs can be seen to depend on self-refutation as distinct from self-contradiction. There is, however, nothing whatever in the context to suggest that Plato thinks that anyone who states the view under discussion *thereby* shows it to be false, or commits himself to its falsehood; contrast *Soph.* 252b—c, where the self-refuting character of the thesis that no terms can be combined in speech is emphasized by a picturesque metaphor. In his criticism of Vlastos's earlier discussion, Gallop understands (i) as the thesis that the view in question is presented as *self-evidently* absurd, i.e. as such that it can be seen to be absurd without further argument. If that is a correct account of (i) (and in his later discussion Vlastos makes no objection to it), then Gallop's objection appears justified, since the context strongly suggests that the absurdity of the view in question is not *merely* asserted, as something obvious, but is intended to be shown by some argument. For one thing, the 'ill-mannered questioner' is represented as following up his initial assertion of the absurdity of the view by an argument leading to the analysis of the concept of 'being overcome' (d3–e3), an analysis which is itself a necessary stage in the final account of being overcome as a kind of intellectual error; it is hard to see why Plato should make the 'ill-mannered questioner' do so if he means him to be seen as already having delivered the knockout blow with his first punch. In so far, then, as (i) can be distinguished from (ii), it is to be rejected; the view in question is represented neither as self-refuting nor as *purely* self-evidently absurd, but its absurdity is argued for. (Precisely what the argument is will be discussed below.) I have emphasized *'merely'* and *'purely'* because, while Plato does indeed argue for the absurdity of the view, it does not follow that he does not *also* regard it as obviously absurd, and indeed the introduction of the 'ill-mannered questioner' suggests that this is in fact Plato's view. The questioner exclaims mockingly about the manifest absurdity of the thesis that one could do bad things through being overcome by good things (for how could the good by itself cause one to do anything bad?), and then sets about demonstrating the incoherence which underlies this *prima facie* absurdity.

In this connection it should be pointed out that, irrespective of the merits of Vlastos's interpretation (iv) (see below), his argument for adopting it in preference to his earlier interpretation (i) depends on an obvious error. He argues that the view in question cannot be represented by Plato as self-contradictory, because it is expressed as 'A man, knowing that certain things are bad and that he ought not to do them, does them, defeated by goods', and *not* 'A man, knowing etc. . . . defeated by *good*.' The latter, Vlastos argues, would be self-refuting, but Plato deliberately avoids this formulation in favour of the former, since only the former can be derived from the earlier statements of Socrates' opponents (a6–b3) that 'A man, knowing that evils are evils, nevertheless does them . . . because he is beguiled and seduced by *pleasures*' and that 'A man, knowing the goods, does not want to do them *because of the pleasures of the moment*, by which he is defeated' (Vlastos's rendering and emphasis). According to Vlastos, while it is in fact self-contradictory (or self-refuting; he makes no clear distinction between the two concepts) to say that someone does bad things from his desire for good as such, it is not self-contradictory to say that he does bad things from his desire for certain particular good things. Plato's presentation of the argument shows him to be aware of this distinction.

It was, however, already seen (see n. on 352d8—e1, pp.173—4 above), that Socrates' opponents, in stating the possibility of being overcome by pleasure, use the noun in the singular or the plural indifferently. Hence Vlastos is wrong to fasten upon formulations which employ the plural 'pleasures' as alone expressing their position. Moreover, it cannot be suggested that the indifference between singular and plural is confined to the earlier statement of their position at 352e ff., for it is a feature of the very passage which Vlastos is discussing (355a—d). The common man's view is indeed expressed with 'pleasures' in the sentences quoted by Vlastos from 355a—b. But the transformation of that view by substitution which follows immediately uses the terms 'pleasure' and 'good' in the singular: 'We can no longer say "(Overcome) by pleasure", for it has got another name 'good' instead of 'pleasure', and so when he says "Overcome by what?" we shall answer, if you please, "Overcome by the good".' This formulation, using the term 'the good', is then paraphrased by the 'ill-mannered questioner' as 'that somebody should do bad things, though he knows they are bad, because he is overcome by the good things'. Hence if this paraphrase is to be a true rendering of the view of the common man, it is necessary that there should be *no* difference between 'overcome by the good' and 'overcome by the good things', just as there was no difference between 'overcome by pleasure' and 'overcome by pleasures'. Otherwise, the 'ill-mannered questioner' (i.e. Plato with the gloves off) is not merely ill-mannered, but downright dishonest. It is a further weakness of Vlastos's interpretation that the assertion that someone knowingly does bad things from a desire for good is in fact no more self-contradictory or self-refuting than the assertion that someone knowingly does bad things from a desire for some particular good things; indeed, as the sense of the former assertion is not clear (for precisely what is the sense of 'a desire for good'?) one possible elucidation of it is to regard it precisely as equivalent to the latter, which is no doubt how Plato himself regards it, just as he clearly regards a desire for pleasure as identical with a desire for pleasures. Hence not merely would it be inadmissible for Plato to rest his argument on the distinction, as Vlastos claims he does, but in fact no such distinction exists.

On interpretation (iv), the demonstration of the absurdity of the common man's view is complete at e2—3, where it is shown to

lead to the view that some people knowingly choose fewer good
things at the cost of greater evils. The main attraction of this view
is that the 'ill-mannered questioner' takes no further part in the
discussion from this point. Hence it is not unreasonable to suppose
that Plato regards the argument begun by the questioner at d1 as
finished at e3, as is indicated by 'So much for that' at e4. Against
this, the interpretation is open to serious objections. It depends on
the assumption that the theses 'A man knowingly does what is bad
because he is overcome by the good' and 'A man knowingly does
what is less pleasant because he is overcome by pleasure' are separate
theses refuted by independent arguments, the former by an argument
running from d1 to e3, the latter by an argument running from e4
to 356c3. But the above sentences are clearly presented by Plato,
not as separate theses, but as alternative versions of a single thesis,
which may be expressed either way in view of the supposed identity
of pleasure with the good. The sentence 'So much for that' marks,
not the conclusion of an independent argument, but a stage in a
single argument which is not complete until 357e8. For at 355e2–3
the 'ill-mannered questioner' does *not* say, as Vlastos maintains,
that what the common man means by being overcome is *knowingly*
choosing fewer good things at the cost of greater evils. He says
simply that what the common man means by being overcome is
taking (i.e. choosing, see n. on e2–3, pp.186–7 below) fewer good
things at the cost of greater evils. And, so far from its being an
acknowledged absurdity that anyone should so choose, an absurdity
so blatant that Socrates does not have to pause for a single sentence
to point it out, the subsequent argument (to 357e) requires that
people *do* choose in precisely that way. For that argument is devoted
to the demonstration that the explanation of the fact *that* they do so
choose can be nothing other than intellectual error; see esp. 357d3–5:
'You have agreed that *those who go wrong in their choice of
pleasures and pains*—which is to say, of good and bad things—go
wrong from lack of knowledge.' And going wrong in one's choice of
pleasures and pains (i.e. good and bad things) is nothing other than
choosing fewer good things at the cost of greater evils. The absurdity
does indeed seem to arise when that sort of error is described as
committed knowingly.

Of the interpretations discussed, then, (ii) should be accepted as
broadly correct. Gallop is right in his central contention that the
argument for the incoherence of the common view is not complete
until 357e. It is, however, true that Plato's main interest in arguing
against the common view is in establishing his thesis that wrong
choice of pleasures and pains cannot occur otherwise than through
error, and that having done so he does not trouble to make explicit

the contradiction in the common view to which he calls attention
at 355d1–3.

355d3 'the good things': i.e. the pleasures accruing from what he
does.

355d3–4 'worth the bad': lit. 'worthy to conquer the bad', but
the rendering given is preferable (a) in avoiding the potentially
confusing moral overtones of 'worthy' and 'unworthy', and (b) in
catching the commercial connotations of the Greek, which continue
down to e3.

355d4 'in your view': lit. 'in you'. For the reasons for adopting
this rendering see Vlastos *Phoenix* 69, p.80, n. 28.

355d6 'acted wrongly'. The verb (*examartanein*) is equally at home
in contexts where it is equivalent to 'make a mistake' and in more
specifically moral contexts.

355d6–e1 (i) Plato is presumably thinking of unequal aggregates
of good and bad things, which might be made up in two ways (a) of
equal numbers of units, the units of one aggregate being larger than
those of the other ('larger and smaller'), (b) of different numbers of
units, the units of both aggregates being of the same size ('more and
fewer'). This distinction does not play any part in the argument.
(ii) 'Not commensurate with' translates *anaxia*, which is synonymous with *ouk axia*, rendered 'not worth' above. 'Not worth' is
impossible here, for Plato refers to two contrasting situations,
(a) where the disadvantages of a course of action outweigh the
advantages, (b) where the advantages outweigh the disadvantages.
But the English sentences 'The bad things are not worth the good'
and 'The good things are not worth the bad' both describe situation
(a), being paraphrasable respectively as 'It's not worth putting up
with the bad in order to get the good' and 'It's not worth having the
good if it brings so much bad with it.'

355e2–3 'mean'. Cf. n. on 333d5–6, p.132 above.
'Taking fewer good things at the cost of greater evils': lit.
'taking greater evils as the price for fewer good things'. The Greek
anti, like the English 'for' may govern either element in a commercial exchange, i.e. the thing bought or the price paid. Thus we have
two constructions: (i) *X* sold *Y* (*Y* bought from *X*) a loaf for (*anti*)
two obols, (ii) *Y* paid *X* (*X* received from *Y*) two obols for (*anti*) the
loaf. In the present context the disadvantage is thought of as the

price one pays for the advantage. The most natural English phrase 'at the cost of' has to govern the price paid, hence the Greek order has to be reversed (cf. Stocks *CQ* 13).

It does not seem that any significance attaches to the shift from 'fewer good things' to 'greater evils'. The phraseology of d8–e1 suggests that if Plato had been attempting to be precise he ought to have said 'fewer and/or smaller good things' and 'more and/or greater evils' (see n. above). This passage does not attempt such a degree of precision, since the looser expression adequately conveys the essential meaning.

'Taking' is to be understood as choosing by acting, as distinct both from receiving independently of one's choice and of performing an internal act of choice which does not necessarily lead to action. It cannot be the former since, as Santas points out (*PR* 66, p.16), it is adduced as an explanation of the phenomenon of receiving fewer goods at the cost of greater evils, and so cannot be identical with it. It cannot be the latter because (a) the verb (*lambanein*) has the implication 'receive' and (b) in 356b3–c1 'take' and 'do' clearly refer to the same action.

356a2–3 'except that one should be more and the other less' lit. 'except excess and deficiency with respect to one another'

356a3–5 This sentence lists three ways in which an aggregate of pleasures or pains may be larger or smaller than another. The first two are those mentioned in d6–e1 (see p.186 above), while the third apparently introduces something new. The Greek phrase is 'more and less', where 'more' and 'less' are adverbs, not adjectives. Hence they must be understood as modifying the appropriate verbs, i.e. the phrase must be read as an abbreviation of 'one is more or less pleased and more or less distressed'. In default of any precise definitions it is not clear what the difference is between having more or fewer pleasures and being more or less pleased. One can, of course, *draw* distinctions such as that between having more or fewer episodes of pleasure and enjoying oneself more or less during each episode (which is what is intended by the translation), but that rendering is adopted rather on the assumption that Plato must have meant something of the kind than in the confidence that that is his precise meaning. On the notions of units of pleasure and pain and of aggregates of such units see pp.197–9 below.

356a5–7 The force of the imaginary objection may be understood in either of two ways:
(i) The objector is suggesting, consistently with the view of

187

Bentham (*Principles of Morals and Legislation*, ch. 4), that Socrates should add propinquity and distance in time to his list of conditions determining the value of pleasures and pains. On Bentham's view a nearer pleasure (i.e. one which is expected to occur sooner) is *ipso facto* more valuable than one more remote, presumably because there is less chance of something's intervening to prevent the occurrence of the former (i.e. propinquity appears not independent of certainty as a criterion of value). The situation under consideration has so far been described as that in which one chooses short-term pleasures while aware that they are in the long run less valuable. On this view the objector is challenging that description by adducing a reason for supposing the short-term pleasures to be more valuable than Socrates has so far acknowledged. But if the force of the challenge is that the agent in fact thinks that the short-term pleasures really are more valuable than the long-term alternatives, in so far as they are nearer, then the objector is abandoning the fundamental position of the common man, viz. that people really do take the alternative which they are aware is less valuable. If, on the other hand, the objector means merely that the difference in value between the alternatives is less than Socrates has so far allowed, he is suggesting at most a minor modification in Socrates' position.

(ii) The objector is concerned, not to challenge or to modify the hitherto agreed description of the situation, but to give an explanation, overlooked by Socrates, of why it is that we often choose things which we know or believe to be less valuable than available alternatives. In so doing, he draws attention to a psychological fact of some importance, viz. the fact that we are frequently more concerned about, and influenced by what is near, both in space and time, than by what is more distant, even though we may know that it is the more distant thing which will have the greater effect on our happiness and misery in the long run. Thus even some of those who are clearest about the dangers of cigarette smoking continue to smoke, because the present pleasure matters more than the prospect of future disease. Such people may indeed hold the pursuit of short-term pleasure justified by the uncertainty of the future evils, but they need not. Nor is it necessarily the case that their attitude is 'I think the pleasure worth the risk now, though I am sure that I shall think differently later'; for even at the time of pursuing the short-term pleasure they may accept that it is not worth it (i.e. not rationally justified), but yet for the time being want the pleasure more than they want their long-term happiness. Rational calculation of one's own interests requires that one abstract oneself from one's present situation in space and time and give equal weight to one's desires, feelings, etc. at future times; this principle underlies all forms of forward-looking activity, from investing to secure one's retirement to going to the dentist for a check-up (see Nagel, part II). But this requirement of rationality runs counter to the psychological attachment to the present and immediate which we have just mentioned, and which manifests itself in many different forms: we feel less ashamed of the misdeeds of many years ago than those of yesterday, and less upset by reports of horrors in distant lands than e.g. by an accident which we actually witness, while we accept with equanimity the inevitability of death at an unspecified and presumably distant time, but feel stark terror should the prospect become immediate. When looked at in the context of these various manifestations of this psychological principle, action against one's better judgement appears a less isolated and consequently less paradoxical phenomenon.

356a7–8 Socrates' reply is disappointing. It can be understood as totally trivial, in that any respect in which pleasure and pain differ from one another is describable as 'simply pleasure and pain'. But Socrates should probably rather be understood as insisting that immediate and distant pleasures and pains differ only in those respects which he had previously listed. If the first account of the objection is accepted, Socrates simply rejects it, without any reasons given. If the second, the point of his reply is to insist that the psychological principle of attachment to the present is itself to be explained as an effect of mistaken assessment of the amount etc. of future pleasures according to the dimensions he had already mentioned. While that is a defensible position, Socrates merely asserts it without argument.

356a8–c3 It is disputed whether Socrates here describes the operation of weighing up pleasures and pains and choosing greater pleasure or less pain as one which *should* be carried out or as one which *must*, as a matter of psychological necessity, be carried out. The argument has been thought to require the latter, on the ground that, while Socrates has to show somewhere that, as a matter of fact, no one knowingly chooses a lesser preponderance of pleasure when he could have a greater, it does not seem that he either has shown this so far or that he shows it during the rest of the argument (to 357e8). Moreover, a recommendation to make correct choice of pleasures and pains seems to have little point in the argument, since none of the parties disputes that everyone *should* do as Socrates says; what they disagree about is whether it is possible to do otherwise. Accordingly, since the English expressions 'have to take' and 'have to do' can as readily indicate what one cannot but do as what one should do, some commentators (e.g. Gallop and Santas) understand these expressions and thus the passage as a whole in the former sense. But while the English expressions have that ambiguity, the Greek words which they render (*lēptea, prakteon, praktea*, lit. 'to-be-taken, to-be-done') generally have the force of 'should'. While the verbal adjective ending in *-teos* can also indicate what has to be done, this is in the sense of what one is obliged to do, either to achieve some purpose (e.g. Arist. *Lys.* 411 'I have to sail to Salamis') or in obedience to some rule (e.g. Xen. *Lac. Pol.* ix.5, a man judged guilty of cowardice has to stand aside in the street etc.). See Goodwin pp.378–9. I have not discovered any clear instance of the use of this construction to signify a universal psychological necessity, where it is literally impossible for the agent to act otherwise. Moreover, in all the Platonic uses of the adjectives *lēpteos* and *prakteos* recorded by Ast, the context is one where a course of action is recommended. Consistently with this, the first sentence of the present passage (a8–b3), with its comparison to someone *good at* weighing and its employment of the imperative 'say' suggests that Socrates is setting out a procedure to be followed. It appears, then, that it is somewhat less plausible to take Socrates here to be asserting the impossibility of knowingly choosing the lesser aggregate of pleasure. Rather, we should understand the function of the passage to be the application of the *evaluatively* hedonistic assumptions of the common man to the notion of an aggregate of pleasures. Socrates does not in fact recommend a way of choosing, which would indeed be pointless; rather, he induces the common man to accept his account of how one chooses *correctly*, in order to pave the way for his account, which follows at once, of how incorrect choices come to be made. If that is correct, then the following section must after all contain the argument which seeks to show that incorrect choice cannot come about otherwise than through a deficiency of knowledge (see below).

356b2–3   For the reasons for adopting the rendering given here, in preference to the alternative 'add up all the pleasant things and all the unpleasant, and put them in the scale, the near and the distant alike', see Gallop, *Phron* 64, p.126, n.8.

356c4–357e8   Socrates argues from a number of examples that correct choice of quantities requires a technique of measurement, from which it follows that correct choice of quantities of pleasure and pain requires such a technique. From this he infers that failure to make a correct choice can have no explanation other than lack of such a technique.

In this passage I discuss
(a) Socrates' general principle,
(b) his argument,
(c) Some particular points of interpretation,
(d) the concept of a technique of measuring pleasures and pains.

(a) Socrates begins from the fact of ordinary observation that things look, sound, etc. quantitatively different under different conditions of observation, e.g. things in the distance look smaller than the same things seen at close quarters. He draws the unexceptionable conclusion that, if it is important to give a correct answer to the question 'Is x bigger etc. than y?', ordinary observation of whether x looks bigger must be superseded by a technique of measurement which provides answers independent of variations in the observation conditions. Socrates' emphasis on saving one's life is deliberate; he does not say that one can never correctly judge whether x is bigger than y without measuring. What he does say is that, if one's life depended on *regularly* making correct judgements and choices based on them (note the plurals in d1—2 'taking steps to get large quantities and avoid small ones'), one would not be able to rely on observation of how things look etc., but would require a technique of measurement. That is plainly true.

The contrast in d4 between the art of measurement and the power of appearance is the nearest thing in the dialogue to a direct reference to Protagorean subjectivism. Socrates is chiefly concerned to insist on the distinction between 'x looks bigger than y' and 'x is bigger than y'. He points out (d4—7) that we may in different conditions make equally well-grounded judgements 'x looks bigger than y' and 'x does not look bigger than y', and that the impasse has to be resolved by recourse to measurement, which 'shows us the truth' (d8—e1), i.e. shows whether x is in fact bigger. The central tenet of Protagorean subjectivism, by contrast, is the elimination of the distinction between 'x looks F to A', and 'x is F (to or for A)'. Thus there is nothing which can be said beyond the judgements 'x looks bigger than y to A at time t' and 'x does not look bigger than y to A at time $t+1$', and consequently the question of whether x really is bigger than y cannot be asked.

(b) At 357b1—4 Socrates gains (through Protagoras) the agreement of the common man that if anyone regularly makes correct choices of pleasures and pains he employs the appropriate sort of knowledge. He then (357d3—7) treats that as identical with the thesis that anyone who fails to make correct choices does not employ the appropriate knowledge. For immediately after winning the common man's agreement to the former, on the basis of his survey of various kinds of quantities (356c4—357b4), he gives a brief résumé of his original disagreement with the common man over the occurrence of weakness of will (357c1–d1), and then claims (d3–7) that the common man has now agreed that those who go wrong in their choice of pleasures and pains do so through lack of knowledge. The agreement must be supposed to be that of b1–4. But what was there agreed was that if one is to be regularly right in one's choice of pleasures and pains, one must employ the appropriate knowledge. From that it does not follow that if one is not regularly right in one's choice one does not employ the appropriate knowledge, still less that if on any single occasion one is not right in one's choice, one did not on that occasion employ the appropriate knowledge. But the conclusion which Socrates requires is the latter, since only that is sufficient to show that no one *ever* makes a wrong choice knowingly, which is what Socrates maintains.

The argument thus fails on two counts. (i) It ignores the distinction between being regularly right and being right on every occasion which Socrates' exposition requires (see above). (ii) It commits the fallacy of denying the antecedent, i.e. of inferring

$$-P \to -Q$$

from $P \to Q$.

(In fact Plato treats the two as identical, see above.) The fallacy is obvious, even in the present instance, since even if consistently correct choice requires the employment of a technique, it does not follow that incorrect choice, whether on a number of occasions or a single occasion, implies failure to employ a technique, since it may equally well consist in failure to act on the result which is reached by correct employment of the technique. Of course, failure to act on the result could itself be defined as failure to employ the technique correctly, but in that case Socrates' thesis would reduce to the triviality that no case of incorrect action occurs otherwise than in a situation where one acts incorrectly. Socrates is attempting to show that only one *explanation* of incorrect action is possible, viz. failure to employ correctly a technique of measurement; the proposed definitional move would deprive that concept of any explanatory force. As it is, his argument fails to show that the alternative explanation posited by his opponents, viz. that one may act incorrectly because one is overcome by the desire for immediate pleasure, involves any absurdity.

(c) **Particular points of interpretation**

356c5–6   This takes up the imaginary objection at a5–7 (see n. pp.187–9 above). Socrates assumes that the man who is overcome by the desire for immediate pleasures is overcome because he overestimates certain features of those pleasures, just as one tends to overestimate the size of objects near at hand by comparison with objects at a distance. In this context we should avoid confusing two propositions, (a) An object seen at close quarters looks bigger than an object of similar size seen at some considerable distance, and (b) When required to estimate the relative sizes of objects seen at different distances, one tends to overestimate the size of those seen at close quarters and/or underestimate the size of those seen at a substantial distance. (a) states a fact of optics, whereas (b) neither follows from (a), nor is it obvious that it is true. What (a) states is, roughly, that the distant object occupies a smaller expanse of the total visual field than the nearer, and consequently presents a visual appearance similar to that presented by an object substantially smaller than the nearer one when seen at roughly the same distance as the latter; but it does not follow that because a distant object looks smaller in that sense that we tend to judge that it *is* smaller, which is what (b) asserts. In fact, since we are familiar with the phenomenon from childhood, we compensate for the effect of distance in making estimations of actual size, and while it is doubtless the case that we frequently undercompensate, it seems equally plausible that we sometimes overcompensate and sometimes get things about right. It appears that Plato does not observe this distinction, since his description (especially d4—e2) implies that variation in apparent size determined by distance is a source of confusion and of conflict in judgement, which is the case only if (a) and (b) are not distinguished.

Given Socrates' assumption, it is reasonable to infer the need for a technique of accurate estimation of near and distant pleasures and pains. But, as was pointed out, it need not be the case that one prefers the immediate pleasure because one overestimates any feature of it, or underestimates any feature of the more distant; the immediate pleasure may be more attractive, not in virtue of any supposed preponderance in features such as duration or intensity, but simply because it is nearer in time (see n. on 356a5—7, pp.187—9 above). In that case no over- or underestimation occurs, and consequently the agent does not require to perfect any technique of estimation. What he does require is the ability to abstract himself from his actual temporal situation, so as to give his future desires and interests equal weight or importance with his present desires and interests. This does indeed have *some* analogy with the adoption of a technique of measurement of observable quantities. Thus in the latter case the agent may say 'x looks bigger than y from here, while y looks bigger than x from there; so I had better measure them and compare their sizes.' In the case of pleasures and pains the analogous reasoning is 'x matters more than y now, but y will matter more than x later; so I had better weigh up the contribution of x and y to my happiness as a whole rather than looking at them exclusively from any particular point in time.' In each case the agent must abstract himself from his present location, in the former with respect to place and in the latter with respect to time; but the analogy extends no further, since the comparison in the latter case does not involve the application of any quantitative scale (see below, pp.195–9). Hence the assimilation of the two situations is importantly misleading.

356d2–3 'taking steps to get large quantities and avoid small ones': lit. 'doing and taking large quantities and avoiding and not doing small ones'. It seems likely that 'and' has the force, as frequently in Greek, of 'i.e.', so that 'doing and taking' and 'avoiding and not doing' mean respectively 'taking by doing' and 'avoiding by not doing'. Similarly, 'actions and choices' at d6–7 is probably to be taken as 'actions by which we choose' (see n. on 355e2–3, pp.186–7 above). Paraphrase is necessary, since 'doing large quantities' is impossible English.

356e6–8 'either each kind against itself or one against the other': i.e. the choice may be between two odd or two even numbers ('each kind against itself') or between one odd and one even ('one against the other'). This rendering of the difficult phrase (lit. 'either itself with respect to itself or the one with respect to the other'), which must be correct, is suggested by Guthrie.

357a2 'larger and smaller quantities': lit. 'excess and deficiency'. Cf. n. on 356a2–3, p.187 above.

357a7–b1 'more or less, larger or smaller'. Cf. n. on 355d6–e1, p.186 above.

357b2–3 'to determine which are more, or less, or equal to one another': lit. 'an examination of excess and deficiency and equality relative to one another'.

357b4 'an art which embodies exact knowledge': lit. 'an art (*technē*) and a knowledge (*epistēmē*)'. Besides the use which is precisely parallel to the English 'knowledge', *epistēmē* is sometimes (as here) used to mean 'department of knowledge', e.g. arithmetic; in that use it can occur in the plural.

357b5–6 Since we already know that the art in question is the art of measuring pleasures and pains, Socrates must mean that the specification of the art will give details of how pleasures and pains are measured, e.g. what the unit of measurement is. This undertaking is not kept anywhere in Plato's works.

(d) The concept of a technique of measuring pleasures and pains is suggested by certain aspects of the ordinary, untheoretical ways in which we talk about our actions. We find it natural to talk of weighing up the consequences of some proposed action, whether in terms of pleasure and pain or in other terms, of balancing the pleasure which a given action will cause A against the distress which it will cause B, of wondering whether it will be worse to hurt a few people very much or a larger number less intensely, and so on. These idioms indicate an intuitive acceptance of the notion of quantities of pleasure and pain, which can be added up, balanced against each other, etc. These intuitive notions, however, lack precision; consequently, anyone who is attracted by the idea of giving precise answers to practical and moral questions is likely to look for some method of quantifying pleasures and pains, and thereby establishing precisely how much one pleasure exceeds another, how many pains or units of pain are equal to a given pleasure etc. Such an advance would be parallel to that achieved when quantitative measurement of length, weight, etc. supersedes the primitive assessment of the look, feel, etc. of things. The passages already discussed make it clear that Plato was influenced by this line of thought.

Techniques such as weighing, counting, and linear measurement have two main features: they are (a) quantitative and (b) intersubjective, i.e. they give results which are accessible to all those who have mastered the technique in question, independent both of the particular conditions of observation and of the attitudes, preferences etc. of the particular person making the judgement. Ideally, therefore, the desired technique of measuring pleasures and pains should share both features. It should, therefore, give numerically precise and universally accessible answers to such questions as

(i) How pleasant (painful) is x?

(ii) By how much is x pleasanter (more painful) than y? Since Plato's interest, like that of most hedonistic theorists, is concentrated on the development of a technique for guiding action, he is most interested in the comparative question (ii), which in any case presupposes the possession of the answer to (i).

The action-guiding function of the proposed technique suggests an immediate difficulty. The techniques on which it is modelled, weighing, measuring, etc., all involve operations carried out on actual objects. But since the proposed technique is a technique of deliberation, it is concerned, not with actual objects, but with prospective or hypothetical objects, i.e. various possible actions and the consequences which would ensue if these possible actions were actually performed. Such objects cannot literally be put in a scale, measured, etc. Hence, whatever sort of comparison is involved, it must be a very different sort from that suggested by the simple model of weighing and measuring, operations which involve the direct physical juxtaposition of objects either with one another or with a standard object such as a balance or measuring-rod. For the same reason, it is not comparable even with more complicated techniques by which objects not directly observable are observed by means of their effects, e.g. observations of electrons by means of a cloud chamber. For in the latter cases, though the object itself is unobservable, its effect (e.g. the trail in the cloud chamber) is actually present and available for observation; but in the measurement of pleasures and pains, neither the actions which are to be assessed nor their consequences are available for inspection at the time when deliberation takes place. The assessment of actions in terms of pleasures and pains does not, in fact, demand a technique of observation in any ordinary sense. Rather, it requires something much more complicated, involving hypotheses of the likely effects of possible actions, and some sort of imaginative comparison of the various effects thus envisaged, both aspects of the process in turn relying on memory of similar effects and similar comparisons in the past. While these considerations do not of themselves show that there can be no technique of assessing pleasures and pains, they indicate that the description of such a technique as one of measurement, with its implied assimilation to such simple techniques as linear measurement, is highly misleading.

Nonetheless, even allowing for the differences brought out above, the treatment of the assessment of pleasures and pains as a kind of measurement might be defended if it could be shown that it shares the cardinal features of inter-subjectivity and quantitative precision.

Inter-subjectivity. An inter-subjective judgement is one whose truth can be determined independently of the observation-conditions under which it is made and of the beliefs, attitudes, etc. of the individual making it. It is immediately apparent that judgements such as 'x is pleasant' and 'x is pleasanter than y' cannot be inter-subjective, since they fail to satisfy the second independence-condition. For either such judgements are themselves simply expressions of the preferences of the person making them, being equivalent to 'I find x pleasant (enjoy x)', 'I find x pleasanter (enjoy x more) than y', etc., or they assert that most people, or most members of some specific group, agree in finding x pleasant, preferring x to y on grounds of pleasantness etc. Moreover, in the latter case it is implied that the person making the assertion shares the general attitude or preference; 'x is pleasanter than y but I personally don't find it so' seems just as odd as e.g. 'Ice floats on water but I don't believe that it does' (see n. on 355d1–3, p.182 above). It is this personal commitment of the utterer which prevents us from counting 'x is pleasant' as inter-subjectively true in the same way as e.g. 'Honey is sweet' or 'Grass is green.' For while the truth of judgements of the type represented by the latter two examples is not independent of what seems to be the case to the normal observer under normal conditions (assuming those to be capable of specification without circularity), it is independent of what seems to be the case to the person making the particular judgement. Hence there is no self-refutation or other oddity in 'Honey is sweet but it doesn't taste sweet to me', or 'Grass is green but it doesn't look it to me'. It is, indeed, possible that linguistic habits might so change as to assimilate judgements about what is pleasant and unpleasant to judgements about sensory qualities such as colour and taste; in that case the truth of 'x is pleasant' would be determined entirely by the judgement of some standard observer, or of the majority (though the problem of specifying the standard observer would be even more formidable, or rather insuperable). But the effect of such a change would be to make the assessment of pleasures and pains useless as a technique of deliberation. For from the fact that A is, in the judgement of the standard observer or of the majority (and therefore *is* inter-subjectively) pleasanter than B it does not follow that it will in fact be found pleasanter by the agent or by those who will experience it, since they might happen to be non-standard observers, or have minority tastes. Hence, given that what the agent is aiming at is the maximization of actual pleasure, whether his own or that of others as well, he must be guided not by the judgement of the 'standard' observer or the majority, but by his own judgement and by what he takes to be the judgement of those who will be affected by his action. Hence the technique of deliberation by assessment of pleasures and pains will give different results according to the different attitudes, tastes etc. of those who apply it and of those who are likely to be affected by the actions of the former. i.e. it fails to satisfy the condition of inter-subjectivity.

Quantitative precision. In view of the above conclusion, it is to be expected that there can be no numerically specifiable unit of measurement of pleasures and pains, since the ability to describe an object in quantitatively precise terms implies that the description is inter-subjectively true. This is confirmed by our linguistic habits.

While we are quite happy to say that we enjoyed something more than we normally do, or less than someone else did, the question 'How much more or less?' can elicit such answers as 'Very much more' or 'Just a little less', but not answers such as 'Seventeen times more' or 'Less by one and a half units'. In this respect pleasure and pain resemble other attitudes and character-traits such as interest, boredom, embarrassment, shyness, depressiveness, clumsiness, and vivacity; all of these may be manifested in varying degrees, as evinced by observable behaviour and subjective reports, but none admits of quantitative measurement in terms of units which can be added together. Our present concepts allow us neither to apply quantitative measurement to the pleasures and pains of each individual, nor *a fortiori* to make use of it in inter-personal comparison. Hence the kind of sum beloved of Benthamites, according to which an action which causes 8 units of pleasure to A and -4 units of pleasure (i.e. 4 units of pain) to B, totalling 4 units, is to be preferred to one causing 12 units of pleasure to A but -5 each to B and C, thereby totalling 2 units, is without literal significance, and is merely a spurious dressing-up of the familiar process by which we decide that a situation where one person gets a fair amount of pleasure and another is hurt to a certain extent is preferable to that in which the first individual gets considerably more pleasure while two persons are each hurt rather more than the person hurt in the first case.

It might be objected that this inability to measure pleasures and pains is merely contingent on technological backwardness. Thus future physiological investigation may reveal different amounts of pleasure and pain to be systematically correlated with measurable physical quantities, say numbers of cells excited in a certain area of the brain. It is theoretically possible that whenever someone reported an increase in enjoyment an increase was observed in the number of cells excited, and a decrease in the number whenever he reported a decrease in enjoyment. In that case we should indeed be able to *give* a sense to such a statement as 'John is enjoying this party four and a half times more than the previous one.' The sense would be that John is enjoying the party considerably more, and that his greater level of enjoyment is accompanied by an increase of 350 per cent in the number of brain cells excited. But firstly this kind of indirect quantitative measurement of pleasure and pain does not permit of direct inter-personal comparison of the Benthamite variety. From the fact that A has precisely twice as many cells excited as B it does not follow that A is experiencing twice as much pleasure as B. In so far as it is possible to make any comparison, it must depend as before on what A and B say about what they are feeling and on the way in which they manifest their feelings in their behaviour. If those criteria indicate that A is markedly more enthusiastic about the activity or experience than B, then that information is not made in any way more precise by the additional information that A has precisely twice more cells excited than B. And if, on the other hand, they show that both are equally enthusiastic, then the physiological information merely shows an interesting difference between the physical make-up of the two, and nothing whatever about their relative 'levels' of pleasure. Secondly, this 'quantitative' assessment of pleasure and pain is, obviously, no more inter-subjective than the ordinary assessment on which it is dependent. For just as, using our present concepts, A can find x pleasanter than y and B find y pleasanter than x, and neither be mistaken, so, using the proposed quantitative language, A may find that x is pleasanter than y by 183 units (i.e. x fires 183 more cells than y), while B finds that y is pleasanter than x by 47 units, and there too neither is mistaken. Using this language we have indeed a description of a phenomenon which is both quantitatively precise and therefore (see above, p.197) inter-subjectively true. That description is the description of the physiological accompaniments (leaving aside questions of cause and effect) of enjoyment; it is neither a description of enjoyment itself, conceived as the agent's absorption in, enthusiasm about the activity, nor a description of the pleasantness or enjoyability of the activity. While a theoretically possible change in the concept of enjoyment would allow us to count that description as a description of enjoyment itself, it would still be *theoretically* impossible to construct from such descriptions an inter-subjectively true description of the total pleasantness or painfulness of an object. And since the concept of a technique of quantitative measurement of pleasures and pains to serve as a scientific guide for choice requires that such descriptions be possible, it can be seen to be incapable of realization. (For further discussion see Brandt in Edwards ed. with bibliography under the heading 'Measurement of Pleasure'.)

The course of the whole argument from 352a1 may now be summarized briefly. The ordinary man holds that pleasure is the only good (evaluative hedonism) and acts on that evaluation (i.e. psychological hedonism is true of him). Socrates argues that it is a necessary condition of his being successful in his aim of achieving the maximum of pleasure that he should possess knowledge of the consequences of his actions in terms of pleasure and pain, that knowledge being acquired by the application of a technique of measuring pleasures and pains. He then infers fallaciously that the possession of that knowledge is a sufficient condition of his taking the appropriate steps to achieve the maximum of pleasure, i.e. that, given the ordinary man's assumptions, it is not possible for him to act against his knowledge of what is the course of action which will bring him the maximum of pleasure. The following should be noted.

(i) Although Socrates originally introduced the thesis that it is impossible to act against knowledge independently of the assumptions of the common man (352c–d), as something which he and Protagoras accept but which the common man denies, he has not yet given any independent arguments in its support, but has merely attempted to show that the common man's denial of the thesis is inconsistent with his own assumptions. This procedure would amount to a positive argument in support of the thesis only if it is assumed either that the common man's assumptions are true, or that there can be no reason for disputing the thesis other than that adduced by the common man. It is as yet unclear whether Socrates is represented as making either assumption, or alternatively as having been so far engaged merely in removing an objection to a thesis for which he has yet to give his positive argument.

(ii) Up to this point the discussion has concentrated exclusively on the question of whether it is possible to act against *knowledge*, and has not dealt with the wider question of whether it is possible to act against one's beliefs (see n. on 352b1–c7, p.171 above). Socrates insists (esp. 357a5–b5) that 'the thing that saves our lives' in the choice of pleasures and pains is knowledge, i.e. it is the possession of knowledge which is a necessary condition of correct choice, from which he infers the impossibility of incorrect choice provided that one possesses knowledge. The thesis that knowledge is a necessary condition of correct choice is stronger than that finally accepted in the *Meno*, where it is agreed (97b) that true opinion is in no way inferior as a guide to action than knowledge (*phronēsis*, equiv. to *epistēmē*). If that modification were incorporated in the common man's position here, presumably Socrates would draw his conclusion as before, but in the revised form that it is impossible to make incorrect choice provided that one possesses knowledge or true belief about the pleasures and pains which will result from one's actions. The fundamental explanation of the phenomenon would remain the same, viz. error or mistake (*amathia*), but the connotation of 'error' would have been widened from 'lack of knowledge' (357d3–4) to the more ordinary sense 'lack of knowledge or true opinion' (as at 358c4–5; cf. *Euthyd.* 286d, *Symp.* 202a). It is possible that in the *Protagoras* Plato draws no distinction between knowledge and true opinion: see pp.202–3 below.

358a1–360e5 *Socrates applies the conclusion of the foregoing discussion to the disputed case of courage and* *cowardice, obliging Protagoras to assent to his thesis that the coward too goes wrong through error. Hence Protagoras is obliged to withdraw his contention that it is possible to be courageous while lacking in knowledge.*

358a1–5 The discussion with the common man is now explicitly concluded, and from this point on Socrates may be taken to argue *in propria persona*. He secures the explicit assent of the sophists to what he has said in the foregoing discussion. This must embrace whatever Socrates has said *in propria persona* up to this point, including his assertions as to what the common man will agree to. It is, however, unclear whether it extends to the content of those admissions themselves, e.g. that correct estimation of the pleasures and pains resulting from one's actions is both a necessary and sufficient condition of correct action. If Socrates is represented as forcing on the common man acceptance of a thesis which he himself maintains as true, then the sophists here accept the common man's admissions as true. If, on the other hand, Socrates has been solely concerned with the consequences of the common man's assumptions, irrespective of his own views, then the sophists need not be committed to the truth of the common man's admissions. It was seen above (pp.175–6) that the text so far is inconclusive on whether Socrates is represented as sharing the common man's assumptions. For further evidence on this point, see n. on 360a2–3, pp.208–10 below.

358a5–6 Socrates here secures agreement to his own original thesis of 351b–e (see pp.164–70 above).

358a6–b3 See n. on 337a1–c4, pp.136–40 above. Socrates here implies, and Prodicus accepts, that the terms are synonymous or virtually so. This is in fact the case, the main distinctions being that the word rendered 'enjoyable' (*charton*, cognate with *chara* 'joy') is very rare in prose, while that rendered 'delightful' (*terpnon*), though not so rare, is yet less common in prose than 'pleasant' (*hēdu*). It is, however, likely that the historical Prodicus intended some difference of sense between these terms (see pp.138–9 above).

358b3–6 Socrates here secures without discussion agreement on the point on which Protagoras challenged him at 351c1–2 (see n., pp.165–6 above). There Protagoras was prepared to accept that a pleasant life is good only subject to the qualification that the pleasures in question are praiseworthy. If, as here, it is accepted that everything which promotes a pleasant and painless life is *ipso facto* praiseworthy, then the objection lapses. It is hard to see what can have produced Protagoras' change of mind other than the intervening argument, where the common man was made to accept that pleasure is the only good. That in turn suggests that Protagoras regards the admissions of the common man as among the things which Socrates had shown in the foregoing argument to be true (see n. on a1–5 above), i.e. that Protagoras does not distinguish between Socrates' own views and those which he elicites from the common man. The question then arises whether Plato represents him as *correctly* assimilating the two, or as being confused in so doing. On that see further below, pp.208–10.

The MSS. read 'Aren't all actions praiseworthy and beneficial which lead . . .'; modern editors and commentators agree in removing 'and beneficial', which is an intrusion into the argument 'Whatever promotes a pleasant life is praiseworthy, and whatever is praiseworthy is good and beneficial.' The point of this argument is presumably to make explicit that, given the assumption (a5–6) that a pleasant life is good, whatever leads to it is itself instrumentally good. As before (see n. on 356d2–3, p.194 above) 'and' is probably explanatory, requiring 'good and beneficial' to be taken as 'good *in the sense of* beneficial'.

358b6–c3 The proposition that no one does other than what he thinks is instrumentally best is represented as following from the original assumption 'What is pleasant is good.' Since no further arguments are given for it, it would be natural to see it merely as a restatement of the conclusion of the argument with the common man, viz. that if one knows that a certain action produces more pleasure than the alternatives one necessarily does it, clarified by the more explicit treatment of the instrumentally good at b3–6, so as to read 'If one knows that a certain action is instrumental in bringing about more pleasure than the alternatives, one necessarily does it.' But the present formulation introduces the important addition 'No one who either knows *or believes* that something else is better than what he is doing, and can do it, subsequently does the other . . .' As was pointed out (pp.171 and 200 above), the previous argument has said nothing whatever about the impossibility or otherwise of acting against one's belief about, as distinct from one's knowledge of, the best thing to do. Hence if Plato intends here merely to represent the sophists as accepting something which has already been agreed by the common man, he is seriously mistaken. The mistake is readily explicable if (a) Plato has true belief exclusively in mind and (b) when writing the *Protagoras* he had not yet arrived at a clear distinction between true belief and knowledge. Both hypothesis are plausible; (b) is not excluded by 356d–357a, where the contrast is not between knowledge and true belief, but between scientific knowledge and confusion produced by uncritical reliance on perceptual data.

358c2 'giving in to oneself': lit. 'being inferior (*hēttōn*) to oneself'. The expression is clearly used as equivalent to the related expressions 'be overcome (*hēttasthai*) by pleasure(s)' and 'be weaker (*hēttōn*) than pleasure(s)'. 'Controlling oneself' renders the opposite expression, lit. 'being superior to oneself'. See Adam and Adam's note, pp.189–90.

358c4–5 Cf. p.200 above.

358c6–d4 This assumption is in fact independent of the preceding argument; it may, however, not be seen as such by Plato (see above). Given the predominantly self-interested connotations of 'good' and 'bad' (cf. n. on 351c1–2, pp.165–6 above), it amounts to the assertion that no one freely pursues what is or is taken by him to be disadvantageous to himself in preference to what is or is taken by him to be more advantageous (c6–d2) or less disadvantageous (d2–4). This assertion, which is made in different words at *Meno* 78a, *Gorg.* 468c and (by Socrates) at Xen. *Mem.* III.ix.4, is one of the central tenets of Platonic psychology and ethics. As Santas shows (*PR* 64), it is from this proposition, together with the theses that every action is directed towards the attainment of some good and that morally bad action is always disadvantageous to the agent, that Plato derives the well-known Socratic thesis that no one ever freely does what is morally wrong (345d–e). The most complete working-out of that derivation is in the argument with Polus in the *Gorgias*, 466a–481b. See Taylor *Mind* 80.

That Plato subsequently modified his view on the Socratic thesis, at least to the extent of recognizing that desire can lead someone to act against his *belief* as to what he should do, is clear e.g. from the story of Leontius at *Rep.* IV, 439e–440b (cf. *Laws* IX, 863a–e), while *Laws* III, 689a–b and IX, 875a–d suggest that he may even have admitted that desire can similarly overrule knowledge. *Laws* IX, 860c–863e shows that Plato continued to maintain the Socratic thesis that no one does wrong of his own free will, while acknowledging the possibility of action against one's better judgement (cf. *Laws* V, 734b). This position is consistent, provided that action against one's better judgement is treated as a case of action under (psychological) compulsion, which is how it is described at *Laws* 863b (cf. Hare *Freedom and Reason* ch. 5, with discussion by Taylor *Mind* 65, and Santas *PR* 66). An alternative strategy is that of redefining action against one's better judgement as itself a sort of ignorance, which is apparently what Plato does at *Laws* 689a–b;

this move is facilitated by the fact that terms such as *amathia* convey no clear distinction between 'mistake', 'ignorance', and 'folly' (see n. on 349d7–8, p.150 above). See Walsh ch. 3, O'Brien, *Soc. Paradoxes* ch. 6, Saunders *Hermes* 68, Penner in Vlastos ed. *Plato.*

While the assertion made at c6–d4 has great plausibility as a truth about human nature, it seems on further examination unsatisfactory on two counts. Firstly, the assertion that everyone invariably pursues what he takes to be his own greatest interest is open to counter-examples provided by those who sacrifice their own interest for the good of others. That attack may be met by the stipulation that in such circumstances the agent regards doing what he takes to be the right thing (e.g. throwing himself on a grenade to save the lives of his comrades) as itself his greatest interest. But the effect of that move is simply to assimilate the concept of the agent's greatest interest to that of what the agent regards as the best thing or the most desirable thing to do; hence the original thesis is transformed into the quite distinct thesis that everyone invariably does what he thinks it best or most desirable to do. But this latter thesis is simply a denial of the occurrence of action against the agent's better judgement, not the statement of a theory which would explain why that phenomenon cannot occur. Secondly, even if the above objection is waived and the assumption of self-interest granted, people act against their better judgement in matters affecting only their own interest just as much as in other matters, as is apparent from the cases of people who smoke, drink, etc. to excess in the knowledge that it is bad for their health. Laziness, self-indulgence, procrastination, etc. are obstacles as much to the pursuit of one's own interest as to the pursuit of moral righteousness or the good of others (cf. Davidson in Feinberg ed. pp.101–2). We are led to overlook this fact by our acceptance of the inherently plausible assumptions (a) that everyone makes his own interest his predominant goal and (b) that if anyone wants x more than y he will, assuming knowledge of all relevant facts, choose x in preference to y; both assumptions are broadly but not universally true. Given the further analytic assumption that 'x is A's predominant goal' entails 'A wants x more than he wants anything else', it follows that A must always choose his own interest in preference to anything else, i.e. action against one's better self-interested judgement is impossible. One source of error is the additional assumption; for while there is a sense in which 'x is A's predominant goal' does entail 'A wants x more than he wants anything else', that sense is that A wants x more than he wants the attainment of any other long-term goal. But it does not follow that on every occasion *A* wants the attainment of his long-term goal *x* more than he wants anything else whatever, including short-term satisfactions, since action against one's better judgement occurs precisely when one wants (for the moment) some short-term satisfaction more than one wants the attainment of one's long-term goal. (For further discussion see Mortimore ed. and Charlton.)

'Freely': see n. on 345d4, p.146 above. The word is picked up by 'forced' in d2; the sequence of thought is 'No one *freely* chooses evils (sc. at all), and even if one is *forced* to a choice of evils (and is therefore unable to act freely) one will still choose the lesser evil.'

'In preference to': the Greek is *anti*, rendered 'at the cost of' on its occurrence in similar context at 355e2—3 (see pp.186—7 above). The word may have either sense. But while the previous context required that it convey the notion of taking evils as the price one pays for advantages, here the idea conveyed is that one goes for the evils rather than the advantages, i.e. one does not go for the advantages at all. If the present passage were read in terms of exchange the meaning would in any case have to be different from that of the earlier passage; whereas there the evils which one got were seen as the price for the advantages which one also got, one would now have to render 'to go for what you think to be bad at the cost of what is good', i.e. the price of pursuing the evils is giving up the pursuit of advantages, not getting fewer advantages as in the earlier passage. This rendering seems less natural than that adopted in the translation.

358c7—d7 For the shift from 'bad' to 'evil' (both rendering *kakos*) see p.177 above.

358d5—e2 Cf. n. on a6—b3, p.201 above. Once again Greek usage supports Socrates; the two terms are regularly used without any indication of distinction of sense and are frequently coupled in a formulaic phrase (cf. 'alarm and despondency'). While Ammonius, a fifth-century A.D. commentator on Aristotle, distinguished 'apprehension' (*deos*) as 'anticipation of evil' from 'fear' (*phobos*) as 'immediate excitement' (see LSJ s.v. *deos*), this distinction is not borne out by the actual usage of the terms. There is no evidence as to whether Ammonius' distinction derived originally from Prodicus.

The definition 'expectation of evil' (given also at *Lach.* 198b, cf. *Laws* I, 646e) is defective in that it omits the connotation of painful excitement or disturbance which is essential to the emotion of fear; a man who expects something bad to happen but remains perfectly composed, without even feeling any disturbance of his thoughts, is not afraid. On the other hand, 'expectation of evil' will do as an account of the motive from which someone acts when he is described as acting from or for fear of something, e.g. someone who buys gold bars for fear of inflation. While such a person may actually feel the emotion of fear while or before he acts, the explanation of his action does not say so. What it does say is that, since he expects that something undesirable may happen, in this case a fall in the value of his assets, he takes steps to avoid or minimize it. The concept of the expectation of evil is indeed central to the concept of fear, since it is that which is common to the emotion of fear (which may or may not function as a motive for action) and to the motive (which may or may not be accompanied by the emotion). But since the substantive 'fear' normally stands, outside such phrases as 'for fear of', as the name of the emotion and not of the motive, it is misleading to treat 'expectation of evil' as itself a complete definition of the term. (Ammonius' distinction may be seen as suggesting the distinction between fear as an emotion (*phobos*) and fear as a motive (*deos*).)

358e2−359a1 Socrates argues that, given the above definition of fear and the proposition (agreed at 358c3) that no one freely chooses what he thinks to be bad, it follows that no one goes for (i.e. chooses) what he fears, when he has the option of going for what he doesn't fear. He is correct to point out that, given those premisses, the situation of the man who is prepared to do something which causes him fear, e.g. to risk his life in battle, must be that of a man choosing the lesser of two evils. While he would prefer not to have to fight at all, he would rather do that than endure the consequences of defeat. In that situation he does not have the option of 'going for what he doesn't fear', and there is also a sense in which, being *obliged* to choose between evils, he does not choose of his own free will (d2−4). The sense is precisely that he does not of his own free will choose some evil when he could have avoided choosing any evil at all. It does not, of course, follow that, given that he must choose *either* the lesser evil or the greater, he does not choose freely *between the two* when he chooses the lesser.

The above provides additional grounds for emphasizing the distinction between fear as an emotion and fear as a motive. For it is not necessarily the case that the man who is prepared to undergo something which inspires him with the emotion of fear does so in order to avoid something which also inspires him with that emotion, but more intensely. e.g. someone may be very frightened at the thought of going to the dentist, but be prepared to do so in order to avoid having trouble with his teeth in later life. He must regard the prospect of tooth decay in the future as something undesirable, but it need not be the case that it inspires him with the emotion of fear. Yet, in so far as he acts because he regards it as undesirable, we can say that he has his teeth seen to for fear of tooth decay in later life. That is to say, even granted that no one freely chooses the greater of two evils, it is false that someone who chooses something which he fears does not have the option of choosing something which he does not fear; for the thing that he recognizes as the greater evil may yet be something which he does not *fear*, i.e. which does not inspire him with the emotion of fear. But if 'fear' refers to the motive rather than the emotion, then it is true that the man who chooses between evils must choose between things which he fears, i.e. between things which he regards as undesirable and is therefore motivated to avoid.

'Of his own free will' (e6) renders *hekōn*, being interchangeable with 'freely', as at 345d4–8.

359a4 'right at the beginning': 329d–330b.

359a7 'later': 349d.

359b7–c1 'So I asked him . . .': 349e.

359c5–6 'things they are confident about'. The Greek is *tharralea*, the neuter plural of the adjective rendered 'daring' at 349e–351b and at 359b8. It is formed from *tharros*, 'boldness, daring, confidence' (see footnote, p.153), and may be applied either to the person who possesses that disposition, or as here to the things about which he is daring or confident.

'Courageous men (go) for fearful things'. This might be taken either as (a) 'Courageous men are prepared to endure things which frighten most people *but not them*' or (b) 'Courageous men are prepared to endure things which frighten most people *including them*', i.e. courageous men conquer their fear while cowards don't. In the former case Aristotle would count them as courageous, in the latter merely as 'men who control their fear' (*enkrateis phobou*) (*EN* I.13, 1102b13–28; II.3, 1104b7–8; III.6, 1115a33–5). The fact that Socrates goes on to *argue* that courageous men do not go for things that they regard as fearful (d5–6) suggests that (b) is the sense in which it is 'generally said'.

359d2–6 Strictly speaking, both Protagoras and Socrates are mistaken in taking 358e2–359a1 as an assertion that no one knowingly goes for what he thinks of as something to be feared.

What was asserted there was that no one knowingly goes for what he fears *when he has the opportunity of going for something which he does not fear*, i.e. except as a choice of evils. Another way of putting the same point would be that no one knowingly goes for anything other than what he thinks of as the least fearful of the available alternatives. On a charitable interpretation, the present statements of Protagoras and Socrates may be taken in that sense.

The force of the explanatory comment 'since ... error' is presumably to remind the hearer of the removal of the main objection to the thesis that no one knowingly chooses what he thinks to be bad, from which, together with the definition of fear, it follows that no one knowingly chooses what he thinks of as something to be feared.

In this argument Socrates shifts from 'No one goes for what he fears' (*dedoiken*; 358e3)' to 'No-one goes for what he regards as fearful' (*deina hēgeitai*; 359d5) without any suggestion that these expressions might not be equivalent. This further reflects the absence of the distinction between fear as an emotion and fear as a motive; in terms of the latter the expressions are indeed equivalent, but in terms of the emotion, even if it is true that no one goes for what he fears (i.e. for what inspires him with the emotion), it does not follow that no one goes for what he regards as fearful, since he may regard some things as such without feeling fear of them (see above, pp.206–7). Conversely, a man who knows that he has some irrational fears may feel the emotion of fear about things which he does not regard as fearful.

359d7–e3 Even granted Socrates' assumptions there is no inconsistency between 'Courageous men and cowards go for the same things' (viz. whatever inspires them with confidence) and 'Courageous men and cowards go for opposite things' (e.g. the former go into battle, the latter run away). While going into battle and running away are indeed opposite in the sense of incompatible, they both fall under the same description 'action which inspires the agent with confidence'. Cf. 'Everyone wants the same thing' (viz. to be happy) and 'Everyone wants something different' (some want wealth, others spiritual fulfilment, etc.).

359e5–7 The reference is to 358b5–6.

360a2–3 Here Socrates gains by implication the sophists' assent to the proposition that everything good is pleasant (i.e. that only pleasant things are good), on the ground that it has already been agreed to be true. 'Pleasant' has to be understood in the extended sense of 'contributing to a life in which pleasure predominates'. Going to war is, obviously, far from immediately pleasant, while the common man's agreement, which is here relied on, assumed the extended sense. (See notes on 351d7–e1, p.168, 351e1–3, last para., p.170, 353c1–354e2, p.175 and, especially, 355a2–5, pp.178–9.) In fact this proposition was agreed in the sense of being implicitly accepted by the common man at 354b–c, but it has not been agreed anywhere else (though it is possible that it may have been part of the position which Socrates originally maintained (see n. on 351e1–3, pp.168–70 above)). The sophists, however, clearly regard it as one of the propositions to which they are committed by their agreement at 358a3–5 that what *Socrates* says is true, i.e. like Protagoras at 358b3–6 (see pp.201–2 above) the sophists make no distinction between what Socrates himself maintains and what the common man was induced to accept. And since Socrates is here arguing in his own person it would be dishonest on his part to allow the sophists to accept his inference if he were aware that the proposition had not been previously agreed at all, but merely accepted by an imaginary opponent on the basis of assumptions which he (Socrates) himself rejects.

In any case this particular inference is not necessary for Socrates' argument, since the conclusion for which he is aiming, viz. that cowardly action results from error about the best course of action, follows directly from what was established at 358e, viz. that no one goes for anything other than what he takes to be the least fearful of the available alternatives (see pp.206–7 above). That in turn follows from the thesis 'No one freely chooses what he thinks bad' enunciated at 358c6–d3, and the definition of fear as expectation of evil accepted at d5–e1; the whole argument is quite independent of the thesis that whatever is good is pleasant. That thesis appears to be reintroduced merely to add emphasis to the paradoxical description of the coward's supposed choice; it plays no further part in the argument. It seems implausible that Socrates should be represented as arguing with conscious dishonesty on such a subsidiary point.

This passage is therefore the strongest evidence that Socrates is represented by Plato as sharing the assumptions of the common man and the conclusions which he (Socrates) derives from those assumptions, rather than merely forcing the common man to accept the implications of assumptions which he (Socrates) rejects. Socrates then asserts in his own person that all and only pleasant things i.e. all and only things which contribute to a life in which pleasure predominates, are good, probably because he himself maintains the thesis that pleasure is identical with the good (on the interpretation of which see pp.164–70 above).

      Lack of space prevents discussion of the relation between
* Socrates' position in this dialogue and Plato's treatment of pleasure
in other dialogues. In so far as there is divergence between Socrates'
position here and elsewhere (and such differences as exist are
sometimes exaggerated by commentators) a possible explanatory
hypothesis is that the Socrates of the *Protagoras* approximates more
closely to the historical Socrates than the Socrates of other dialogues
(cf. pp.123–4 above). Treatments of this topic include Grote II,
pp.87–9, Adam and Adam pp.xxix–xxxiii, A.E. Taylor pp.260–1,
Hackforth *CQ* 28, Dodds *Gorgias* pp.21–2, Sullivan *Phron* 61,
Crombie I, pp.225–69, Raven pp.44–9, Gulley *Philosophy of
Socrates* pp.110–8, Vlastos *Phoenix* 69.

360a8–b2   On the courageous man's honourable fear see Ar. *EN*
III. 6–7.

360b2–3   Socrates here treats *kalon* and *aischron* as contradictories, not as polar opposites, as he did at 332c and 346c–d (see
notes, pp.127–8 and 147 above). The former relation is better suited
to the antithesis 'praiseworthy, creditable–discreditable', the latter
to the antitheses 'beautiful–ugly' and 'fine, noble–base, shameful'.

360b4–5   On madmen and the foolhardy see 350b–c and 351a–b,
where the two classes are not differentiated.
    Plato's doctrine and terminology enable him to assimilate the
case of the coward to that of the madman and the foolhardy man,
since both are explained as the preference of the worse to the better
course, through mistaken estimation of the consequences. The
coward avoids danger which he ought to face, the madman and the
foolhardy man face danger which they ought to avoid. Plato describes
the former as fearing the danger and having confidence in flight, the
latter as having confidence in the danger (? and fearing flight); in
each case the confidence and the fear are disgraceful. Plato appears
to assume that the foolhardy man too shows disgraceful fear in his
action, which is problematic; perhaps he is thinking of someone who
attempts impossible feats for fear of losing face by refusing. But some
cases of foolhardiness and madness do not seem to involve any fear,
unless one makes the arbitrary stipulation that the foolhardy man is
to be described as fearing to take the sensible course, no matter
what his actual reason for rejecting it may be.

360b6–7   To be precise Socrates should specify that disgraceful
fear, as well as disgraceful confidence, arises from no other cause
than ignorance and error. For his argument requires him to identify

the cause of cowardly conduct as error, in order that he can prove by transitivity of identity that cowardice, which is by definition the cause of cowardly conduct (c1–2) is nothing other than error (c5–7). And the full specification of cowardly conduct includes disgraceful fear as well as disgraceful confidence. But since, given Plato's curious terminology, these two aspects necessarily coexist in every cowardly act (see preceding note), the meaning is not distorted if only one is actually mentioned. While, therefore, it is possible that the words 'fear and' (*phobountai kai*) have been accidentally omitted from the MSS. before 'confidence' (*tharrousin*), as a result of the verbal repetition from the preceding sentence, it is not necessary to assume this, since the looseness in the text as it stands is not intolerable.

360c1–2   While the proposition here accepted is clearly seen as true by definition, the relationship between cowardice as a state of character and cowardly conduct is none the less a causal one. Implicit in the argument is the definition of the state of character as 'whatever state of the person accounts for his behaving in a cowardly fashion', behaving in that fashion being in turn implicitly defined as avoiding danger which one ought to face. Consideration of the supposed facts of human nature having revealed that that state is the state of being in error about the consequences of one's actions, the latter state is said (c6–7) actually to be cowardice. This argument would be impossible if cowardice were thought of simply as the disposition or tendency to perform cowardly acts, as suggested e.g. by Ryle. For to say of someone that he has that tendency is merely to say that he is the sort of person who frequently or generally acts in a cowardly way; hence the tendency itself is not any state or feature of him which could be identified with any independently specified state or feature, such as the state of being in error about the consequences of one's actions. This argument therefore provides strong evidence that in the *Protagoras* Plato treats the virtues and vices as motive-forces rather than tendencies (see p.110 above).

360c7–d5   The argument reaches the conclusion that courage is identical with knowledge (or its equivalent, wisdom, see p.152 above) of what is to be feared and what is not to be feared. The conclusion is not formally agreed, since Protagoras refuses (d6) to indicate assent or dissent, but that is immaterial.

Socrates gives merely the premisses and conclusion, leaving the steps of the argument to be supplied. The reconstruction which comes nearest to formal correctness appears to be the following.

Let A = courage, B = cowardice, C = knowledge, D = error. Then

360c7–d1	1. A is the opposite of B.
360d1–2	2. C is the opposite of D.
360d3	3. $B = D$
	($\therefore$ 4. A is the opposite of D) (by 1, 3, and the principle of the indiscernibility of identicals (see p.180 above)).
	(5. Each thing has only one opposite.)
360d4–5	$\therefore$ 6. $A = C$ (by 2, 4, and 5).

On the additional (understood) premiss 5, and on the form of the argument, see pp.122 and 127–9 above. The present argument corresponds to the second of the two patterns exemplified on pp.128–9, i.e. the truth of the conclusion does not depend solely on the meaning of the terms composing it.

360d8–e5 Though Protagoras' main thesis has already been refuted, Socrates insists on an explicit retraction of the assertion in which Protagoras stated the grounds for holding his main thesis (349d, 359a–b; cf. n. on 349d5–8, p.149 above). This is presumably in accordance with the rules of the dialectical game; the verbal retraction has the air of a formal acknowledgement of defeat.

360e6–361d6 *Socrates summarizes the course of the argument.*

360e6–361a3 The thesis that it is impossible, for any subject x and predicate F, to answer the question 'Is x F?' until one can answer the question 'What is x?' is familiar Socratic doctrine; cf. *Meno* 71b, *Rep.* I, 354b–c. This thesis enshrines the truth that the ability to determine whether an attribute qualifies a subject presupposes the ability to identify the subject, to know, in some sense, what it is that one is talking about. Socrates, however, equates being able to identify what one is talking about with being able to give a definition or other verbal specification of what one is talking about, which is an unacceptably rigorous requirement, since one may be able to supply the necessary level of identification by other means, e.g. by pointing out standard examples. Thus I may know whether money is in short supply, or the carburettor is clogged, without being able to define 'money' or 'carburettor', provided that I can physically point to or otherwise indicate the individual or the kind of thing in question. (For further discussion see Geach *Monist* 66, Santas *JHP* 72.)

In this sentence Socrates might appear to imply the even less

212

plausible thesis that the ability to give a definition or specification answering the question 'What is x?' is sufficient to enable one to answer the question 'Is x F?' for any predicate F. But it is fairly clear from b3–7 that what Socrates has in mind is not that universal thesis, but rather the specific thesis that the ability to answer the question 'Is excellence identical with knowledge?' (i.e. 'Is it the possession of some sort of knowledge which makes a man a good or outstanding man?') is sufficient to enable one to answer the question 'Is excellence something which can be taught?' (i.e. 'Can the qualities which make a man a good or outstanding man be imparted by teaching?'). It is sufficient since, in Socrates's view (expressed in that sentence) all and only knowledge is capable of being taught; cf. *Meno* 86e–89c, esp. 87c.

361a5–b3 The appearance of contradiction is illusory, since Socrates is now operating with a conception of excellence quite different from that which underlay his original claim that excellence cannot be taught. The grounds for that claim, viz. the alleged facts that the Athenians acknowledge no experts in political affairs and that outstanding men fail to hand on their excellence to their sons, were if anything grounds for the belief that excellence as popularly conceived neither is nor presupposes any scientific technique, and hence cannot be transmitted by teaching. But in the discussions with the common man and subsequently with the sophists Socrates has shown to his own satisfaction that it is a necessary and sufficient condition of making the right choice of actions, and hence of being a good man, that one should employ a scientific technique of assessment of the consequences of one's actions, specifically a technique of measuring pleasures and pains. On this view what makes a man a good man precisely is the employment of that technique, from which it follows that the qualities which make a man a good man are such as to be capable of acquisition by a process of teaching, i.e. excellence is something which can be taught.

The identity of the specific virtues with knowledge has been argued only for the cases of soundness of mind (332a–333b) and courage (349e–351b and 351b–360e); justice has been related with knowledge only indirectly via the uncompleted attempt at an identification with soundness of mind (and hence with knowledge) at 333b–334a, and holiness has been related only with justice (330c–331b). It seems likely, however, that Plato regards the argument establishing the identification of courage with knowledge as applicable to each particular virtue. For that argument was itself the application to the particular case of courage (358a–360e) of the general principle that right choice of action depends on nothing other than correct assessment of pleasures and pains (351b–357e); and that general principle, if true, is necessarily applicable to the other specific virtues in a similar way.

The slogan 'All things are knowledge' (*panta chrēmata estin epistēmē*) with which Socrates sums up his position is surely intended to recall, and to signify Plato's rejection of Protagoras' famous dictum 'Man is the measure of all things' (*pantōn chrēmatōn metron estin anthrōpos*).

361b3–7 See n. on 360e6–361a3, pp.212–3 above.

361b7–c2 As in Socrates' case (see above), there is in fact no inconsistency in Protagoras' position throughout the dialogue. That position consists of two main theses: (a) it is possible to teach someone how to be a good man, in a broad sense of 'teach' which includes conditioning in social mores as well as instruction in specific techniques such as rhetoric, (b) the settled states of character which produce the conduct specified as appropriate to the various particular virtues (e.g. just or courageous actions) are not identical with one another. There is no inconsistency between these two theses. In attempting to uphold (b) Protagoras is committed to denying that every kind of virtuous conduct arises from the application of a single universal knowledge, whether that be knowledge of the consequences of one's actions or some other kind of knowledge. But the denial of that thesis does not commit Protagoras to abandoning thesis (a); for he can still maintain that, in his broad sense of 'teach', it is possible to teach someone to be a good man, even though it is not the case that good action invariably springs from the application of some unitary knowledge describable as 'knowledge of how to be a good man'. Similarly, making due allowance for natural abilities (as Protagoras did, cf. notes on 323d7, pp.89–90 and on 351a3, p.161 above), it is possible to teach someone how to be good at cricket, even though it is not the case that skill in batting, bowling, and fielding arises wholly from the application of a single exact science of how to be a good cricketer. Plato's insistence that learning how to be a good man must consist in the acquisition of just such an exact and unitary science leads him to impute to Protagoras inconsistency where none in fact exists.

361c2–6 See n. on 349d2–5, pp.148–9 above.

361d1–2 The reference is to 321b6–c7.

361d3–5 Cf. e.g. *Apol.* 36c, *Gorg.* 500c, *Rep.* I, 344e and 352d.

361d7–362a4 *The farewells.*

361d7–e6 Socrates' silence in response to this encomium is positively deafening. Plato may mean to suggest that Protagoras is being insincere, or (perhaps more plausibly) that because Protagoras is *not* insincere, Socrates, being unable to make a reply which will be both sincere and polite, makes no attempt to return Protagoras' compliments.

362a1–3 The reference is to 335c–d.

ADDITIONAL NOTES

A. Translation

p. 18
326e6 'worthless' translates *phaulos*, rendered 'poor' at 327b—c and 'bad' at 328c. English idiom uses different epithets to different-iate technical evaluation ('a poor player' rather than 'a bad player') from general (including moral) evaluation (where 'bad' and 'worth-less' are appropriate, but 'poor' inappropriate). Greek idiom does not mark this differentiation.

p. 26
333d5 'And by acting sensibly you mean thinking well' replaces 'And by being sensible you mean showing good sense'. The Greek is *to de sōphronein legeis eu phronein*. 'Act sensibly' was used to render *sōphronein* in 332a—333b, and it is clearly desirable to mark the continuity of vocabulary. Further, as Code and Dybikowski point out (*CJPhil* 80, p.324) 'good sense' is given on p.122 as a rendering of *sōphrosunē* and 'show good sense' on p.123 as a rendering of *sōphronein*, which makes it undesirable to use it here to render another expression, whose relation with *sōphronein*, is under discussion. The admittedly unnatural use in this context of 'thinking well' reproduces the Greek closely and has the advantage of pointing up the implication in d5—6 from 'thinking well' (*eu phronein*) to 'planning well' (*eu bouleuesthai*).

p. 45
351e4—5 'And if the question seems to the point' replaces 'And if your thesis seems reasonable'. Stokes points out (pp.363—5) that Plato's use of the expression *pros logon* does not support the transla-tion 'reasonable', but rather 'to the point, to the purpose' (cf. 343d1, 344a4—5). Further, what is thus described is a *skemma*, literally 'a thing examined, investigated', which takes up Protagoras' 'let's investigate it'. Socrates has asked a question, viz. whether pleasure itself is not good, and Protagoras has said that they should investigate it; the immediate referent of 'it', i.e. the thing to be investigated, is that question. The *upshot* of the question's being to the point is indeed that Socrates and Protagoras will both accept the thesis that pleasure and the good are the same thing, but it is a clear case of

overtranslation to make Plato *say* that that thesis is the thing under examination.

351e10–11 'it's you who are in charge of the discussion' replaces 'it's you who are introducing the thesis'. In the light of the change made above 'thesis' now appears too tendentious a rendering of the non-commital *logos*. Further, the verb *katarchein* is not well rendered by 'introduce'. It has connotations of beginning and of leading, being frequently used of the leading performer in a religious rite (as in 'the priest led the prayers'). As 'led' has been used to translate *hēgemoneuein* in the preceding sentence, 'be in charge of' seems the best available equivalent.

p. 47
353b4 'the way that I think best suited to make the matter clear' replaces 'the way that I think will best reach a conclusion'. Nothing in the Greek corresponds to 'conclusion', whether in the sense of a proposition deduced from premisses or in the sense of 'termination'.

p. 48
354e3 'you asked me' replaces 'they asked us'. From the beginning of this speech Socrates is speaking, not to Protagoras, as the first edition incorrectly implied, but to the imaginary interlocutors.

p. 54
359e1 'in this way, at any rate' replaces 'therefore'. See Stokes p. 424.

360b1 'Now' replaces 'So', See Stokes p. 430. 'Now' renders *oukoun*, as at b4. See Denniston pp. 434–5.

p. 57
362a4 'That was the end of the conversation, and we left' replaces 'With that we left'. In a review of Goldberg, Francis Sparshott (*AP* 85) remarks *obiter* (p. 86) that my original rendering 'demonstrat[es] to the world that he has no interest in what Plato actually wrote'. What Plato actually wrote was a Greek sentence, and one constraint on an adequate translation of that sentence is that it should be idiomatic. A word-for-word rendering 'Having said and listened to these things we left' manifestly fails to satisfy that constraint, and at the time I believed that what I wrote was the best available rendering in idiomatic English of what Plato wrote. I no longer believe that. The natural referent of 'that' in 'with that we left' is the last utterance of the persons leaving, or the immediate conversational context

of that utterance, whereas the referent of Plato's *taut'* ('these things') is the whole conversation. The new rendering captures that reference.

B. Commentary

p. 66
312a2–7 Add:
Daybreak at a2–3 symbolizes the start of the process of Hippocrates' enlightenment. See Klär *AGP* 69, p. 255.

p. 67
312e1 'about what he teaches you': lit. 'about what he makes you knowledgeable in'.

p. 68
315b9 Add:
Here and at 315c8 Socrates speaks with the words of Odysseus, describing his visit to the underworld, where he sees the ghosts (Greek *skiai*, lit. 'shadows') of the dead. A similar allusion occurs at *Meno* 100a, where Socrates says that an outstanding citizen (*politikos*) who was capable of making others outstanding would be like Tiresias, whom Homer describes (*Od*. X. 494–5) as 'the only one alive of those in Hades, while they flit about as shadows'. The resemblance is not coincidental. At *Gorg*. 521d Socrates claims to be the only genuine *politikos*, since he alone cares for the real (i.e. the moral) good of his fellow citizens. Shadows are a mere image or semblance of reality (*Rep*. 509e, *Soph*. 265b–c), and the sophist is a maker of misleading images, in particular of counterfeits of genuine instances of knowledge (*Soph*. 232–6, 264–8). The representation of the sophists as ghosts indicates immediately that they are mere shadows compared to Socrates, who is 'the real thing as regards excellence' (*Meno* loc. cit.), and derivatively that their purported expertise is mere semblance. The fullest working out, via the imagery of shadows, of Plato's complex symbolism of deception and enlightenment occurs in the image of the cave in *Rep*. VII, 514a–532e. See Klär op. cit.

p. 71
318e1–2 'school studies' translates *technai*, lit. 'arts, crafts'.

p. 72
319a3–7 '... every adult male citizen ... executive functions.' Add:
Alford *CW* 88 shows that, on plausible assumptions about the size

of the population, every Athenian citizen might expect to hold office once in his lifetime.

p. 83

At the end of the first paragraph (after '. . . much reduced sense') add:

This tension in Protagoras' defence is emphasized by Coby ch. 2. See also Goldberg ch. 1.

p. 84

322b1 The interpretation of the Greek adverb rendered 'in scattered units' (lit. 'scatteredly') maintained in this note is disputed by Kerferd *SM* p.140. See the discussion between Nicholson and Kerferd, *Polis* 82. Code and Dybikowski op. cit. object to the *translation* 'in scattered units', without however expressing a view on the substantive issue of whether the units in question are groups or individuals (pp.315−16). Their claim that this translation illegitimately supports the 'objectivist' interpretation of Protagoras' speech maintained above (pp.100−3) seems to me baseless.

p. 96

323c8−324d1 Delete the final sentence and substitute the following:

For a fuller discussion see Saunders in Kerferd ed.: he argues, plausibly, that Plato here reproduces the views of the historical Protagoras. On Plato's general treatment of punishment see also Mackenzie part III (pp.188−91 deal with the *Protagoras*).

p. 97

326a4 'see to it that the children are well behaved': lit. 'take care of <their> soundness of mind (*sōphrosunē*)'. For an explanation of this rendering see n. on 322a7, pp.122−4.

326b1−6 Add:

The process of psychological conditioning is emphasized by the choice of vocabulary: rhythm and melody make the children's characters more graceful (lit. 'more rhythmical') and better adjusted. The word rendered 'better adjusted' (*euarmostoteroi*) can also mean 'more melodious', since the noun *harmonia* from which it is formed has a range of senses including 'adjustment' and 'melody'.

p. 102

'Protagoras would not have had a public . . . were true.'

Code and Dybikowski op. cit. claim (p.316) that this objection 'is easily answered by the relativist since he can reassure his pupils that their beliefs are true (for them)'. It is not clear why a suspicious pupil should count that as reassurance. Having been promised that as a result of Protagoras' teaching he will believe that he is successful, he naturally asks whether that belief will be true, i.e. will he really be successful? How is he *reassured* if he is told that that belief will be true for him (but not necessarily for anyone else)? A pupil who retains a belief in objective truth will be reassured by nothing less than the assurance that his belief will be true, not true for him, but just true. Perhaps Code and Dybikowski think that Protagoras might 'reassure' a doubter by converting him to Protagorean relativism, and thereby inducing him to abandon the belief in objective truth altogether. I take it that it will be agreed that there is no hint of that undertaking in this dialogue.

p. 107
Various critics, including Janet Sisson in her review in *CR* 78, have found fault with my exposition at this point. The following is offered in an attempt at clarification.

'He would, moreover . . . accounts for *B*.' Delete and substitute the following.

He would, moreover, be justified in so doing, since sentences containing 'in virtue of' or 'because' generate contexts where substitutivity may fail. An example will make this clear. Suppose that a single set of physical and psychological attributes, including hand-eye co-ordination, balance, stamina, motivation etc. (let us label this state '*E*') is necessary and sufficient to account for excellent performance at various games, e.g. tennis and squash. In virtue of the causal power to produce outstanding performance at tennis, *E* may be designated as 'excellence with respect to tennis', and in virtue of the distinct causal power to produce outstanding performance at squash *E* may be designated as 'excellence with respect to squash'. In those circumstances the following are all true:

1. John performs outstandingly at tennis because he possesses *E*,
2. John performs outstandingly at tennis because he possesses excellence with respect to tennis.
3. John performs outstandingly at squash because he possesses *E*,
4. John performs outstandingly at squash because he possesses excellence with respect to squash.

The truth of 1–4 does not, however, oblige one to accept either

5. John performs outstandingly at squash because he possesses excellence with respect to tennis, or

6. John performs outstandingly at tennis because he possesses excellence with respect to squash.

For the purpose of this argument it is unnecessary to determine whether 5 and 6 are false, or whether, though true, they are unacceptable because of their misleading pragmatic implications (viz. that John's excellence *vis-à-vis* tennis *explains* his outstanding performance at squash, and vice versa). The latter, weaker, thesis is sufficient rejoinder to Vlastos.

p. 108
329d1 Add:
For an illuminating defence of the thesis that the names of the virtues are non-synonymous specifications of a single state see Ferejohn *JHP* 82. A similar view is defended by Woodruff in Shiner and King-Farlow eds. See also Irwin ch. 4 and Hartman *Apeiron* 84.

Vlastos has vigorously contested this thesis in additional material in the 2nd edition of *PS*. The following are in reply to his main points.

(i) In 'Socrates on "The Parts of Virtue" ', op. cit., pp.418–23, Vlastos argues that in *Laches* and *Meno* Socrates accepts that courage, piety, etc. are parts of total virtue, which is incompatible with the strong version of the unity of virtue which I have maintained. Hence that version cannot be Socratic, i.e. Platonic doctrine.

There seems to me little doubt that the traditional conception of the virtues saw them as separable members of a set of attributes, each attribute making its distinctive contribution (*dynamis*) to total excellence. That is the conception of the parts of virtue which Protagoras maintains and Socrates tries to refute. In the *Laches* Socrates and Nicias are represented as accepting that conception and reaching the conclusion that it is incompatible with the proposed definition of courage as knowledge of good and evil, from which Socrates concludes that 'we have not discovered what courage is' (199e). But since that definition was not merely introduced as one which Socrates had himself suggested (194d) but is explicitly defended by Plato's Socrates at *Prot.* 360d and by Xenophon's at *Mem.* IV.vi.10–11, it is likely that the reader is intended to recognize it as the Socratic view and to draw the conclusion that it is the separation of the virtues rather than the account of courage which is to be rejected.

The situation in the *Meno* is more complex, in that there we find Socrates both arguing, as in the *Protagoras*, that excellence is a single cognitive state and using the terminology of parts of virtue, without any suggestion that there is even any tension between the two. A possible explanation is that the parts of virtue terminology expresses Meno's view, not that of Socrates, and is utilized by Socrates *ad hominem* (so Irwin pp.304–5). Against this, there is no indication in the text that Socrates has any reservations about the use of this terminology (so Vlastos, op. cit., p. 421). Another explanation, which I prefer (see Taylor *Phron* 82, p.116) is that Socrates is implicitly shifting the sense of the parts of virtue terminology to express a doctrine demanded by the cognitive theory, viz. that the names of the individual virtues pick out the same cognitive state under different aspects. It might be objected that this suggestion is entirely *ad hoc*, designed merely to explain away the inconsistency between my account of the unity thesis and what Socrates says in the *Meno*. But Socrates in the *Meno* is firmly committed to the cognitive theory, which implies the strong version of the unity thesis, and interpretative charity demands that he be seen as maximally consistent.

Incidentally, Vlastos is clearly mistaken in maintaining that Socrates' treatment of the distinction between shape in general and specific shapes such as roundness shows that he 'thinks that justice is to virtue as is the round to figure and white to color" (p. 421). Socrates knows that the specific shapes are incompatible with one another (*enantia* 74d), and takes it for granted that the specific virtues are not incompatible (78d). It is significant that he nowhere says that e.g. round is part of shape or white part of colour; yet those locutions (which sound as absurd in Greek as they do in English) ought to be what he should find it natural to say, if it is true that he thinks that justice (a part of virtue) is to virtue as is the round to figure or white to colour. The point of the distinction between the round and shape is to insist that what is being sought is an account of excellence in general, which will apply to any specific excellence, just as the account of shape will apply to any specific shape. That claim carries no commitment to the falsehood that the relation of any specific excellence to excellence in general is the same as that between any specific shape and shape in general.

(ii) Vlastos rejects the suggestion that the names of the specific virtues are non-synonymous names of the same cognitive state on the ground that 'For Plato *Form-naming* words get their sense through their reference' (p.433: his italics). He concedes to Irwin (p.304) that Plato provides examples of the same individual bearing two non-synonymous names, but maintains, by the principle just quoted, that the same general character cannot be thus named. But he gives no evidence whatever to support this principle. He cites *Euth.* 5d3–4 and *Meno* 72c7 to show that every non-equivocal term *F* names a unique character; but that is uncontroversial. It is standard

Platonic doctrine that every general term names one character and not many, but what is at issue here is whether several terms name the same character. He also claims that these passages show that the terms in question derive their sense from the character which they name; but what both say is that the various Fs all have a single character, to which the *Meno* passage adds that it is to that character that one must look in answering the question 'What is F?' The discussion above (p.107) has shown that it is question-begging to insist that the question 'What is F?' is a request for a specification of the sense of the expression 'F'. In reply to Irwin's observation (p.304) that *Prot.* 357b and *Phil.* 60a treat 'pleasant' and 'good' as two names for the same thing, Vlastos claims that Socrates' treating these terms as intersubstitutable in the former context 'is sterling evidence that he does think that for this theory they would be synonymous' (p.433), but he does not explain why that is so. Standardly, intersubstitutability implies identity of reference but does not imply synonymy, and Vlastos therefore needs to provide evidence why Socrates' use of intersubstitutability should be taken as evidence of Socrates' belief that the intersubstitutable terms are synonymous.

All parties to the debate agree that Plato has no explicit linguistic theory containing the concepts of sense and reference, and *a fortiori* that he makes no explicit distinction between those concepts. What is at issue is whether Plato's statement that the names of the virtues are names of the same thing is best understood as committing him to co-reference but not to synonymy (*in the modern sense*, i.e. identity of content or of mode of presentation), or as committing him to the latter as well as the former. It would clearly be irrelevant to claim, as Vlastos may perhaps intend, that Plato's conception of meaning is such that the reference of a general term just is its meaning, since given that conception of meaning identity of meaning is compatible with absence of synonymy, and it is the latter concept which is here at issue.

In fact Vlastos's two main arguments against the unity of virtue thesis do not distinguish clearly between synonymy and co-reference. At *PS* pp.227–8 he gives separate arguments against the attribution to Socrates in the *Protagoras* of the thesis (i) that the five specific virtues are the same virtue and (ii) that their names are synonyms. At pp.105–6 above I point out that the argument against the attribution of (i) depends on the assumption that (i) would itself commit Socrates to treating the names of the virtues as synonyms, an assumption which I there argue to be false. Ironically, the argument against the attribution of (ii), purporting to show that the names of the virtues cannot be synonymous, is in fact directed against the weaker thesis that they cannot be co-referential. (Since synonymy entails co-reference, the refutation of the latter would refute the former.) Vlastos claims to demonstrate the failure of co-reference by showing that 'courage' cannot be substituted for 'piety' in 'Piety is that *eidos* in virtue of which all pious actions are pious' (*Euth*. 6d), and that 'justice' cannot be substituted for 'piety' in 'Piety is that part of justice which has to do with service to the gods' (*Euth*. 12e). On the former example see the preceding note; on the latter see Taylor *Phron* 82 pp.116–18.

p. 110
330a4 Delete 'I therefore disagree with Vlastos' assertion ... "gives".'

Vlastos points out (*PS* p.434) that the deleted sentences ascribed to him a view which he did not in fact hold.

p. 111
330a8–b2 'Is it the same with the parts of excellence, that none is like any other, either in itself or in its power? Surely it must be, if it corresponds to our example.'

Code and Dybikowski op. cit. say (p.318) that I interpret this as meaning that the parts of virtue are not alike in all respects, i.e. that they are not numerically identical, and further (p.319) that I infer this interpretation from my interpretation of the parts of gold model, which (on my construal) says that the parts of Virtue are alike in all respects. My note on 3306–7 makes it clear that while Protagoras is indeed committed, *by his adoption of the parts of the face analogy*, at least to the thesis that the parts of Virtue are not alike in all respects, and perhaps also to the stronger thesis that it is not the case that they have most or a substantial number of their significant characteristics in common, since the parts of the face are *clearly* not alike in all respects, and *arguably* do not have most or a substantial number of their significant characteristics in common, his commitment to those theses is altogether independent of the parts of gold analogy. Code and Dybikowski are therefore in error to conclude (p.319), on the strength of the claim that my construal of the gold analogy is wrong (a claim which I do not here discuss), that 'nothing in the text requires that Socrates show some pair of Virtues to be alike in *all* respects if he is to refute [the thesis that no part of Virtue is like any other part]'. What Socrates has to refute is what Protagoras asserts and what Protagoras asserts is at least that no pair of virtues is alike in all respects.

p. 148
346d8–e2 Add:
For a stimulating account of the discussion of the poem, arguing

that much of Socrates' account of Simonides is intended to convey covert criticism of Protagoras, see Coby ch. 4. See also Scodel *AP* 86 and Trapp in Whitby, Hardie, and Whitby eds.

347c3–e7   Add:

Frede *RM* 85–6 takes this as a reference to Plato's *Symposium*, a hypothesis which she supports by the observation that, apart from Aristophanes, all the characters of the *Symposium* are present in the *Protagoras*, though only Socrates and Alcibiades speak. In order to reconcile this hypothesis with her assumed early dating of the *Protagoras* she posits a revision of the original discussion of the poem in the light of the doctrine of *Symp.* 207e that knowledge (contrary to *Meno* 97d) is not necessarily a stable possession.

For another view of the significance of the overlap of dramatis personae between *Protagoras* and *Symposium* see Goldberg pp.328–43 (criticized by me in *CR* 85, p.68). Kahn *OSAP* 88 cites this feature of the dialogue in connection with his proposal to date the *Protagoras* later than the *Gorgias*, and therefore closer to the *Symposium* than is normally assumed.

While all these suggested explanations strike me as implausible, I acknowledge that I am unable to offer one of my own.

p. 161
349e1–350c5   Add:

For an account of the argument favouring interpretation (ia) see Klosko *AGP* 79. Weiss *AP* 85 is closer to the account given above. See also Devereux *Apeiron* 75.

p. 162
Delete 'It is very hard . . . explored here.'

I have been convinced that the abruptness of the transition at this point, though striking, is not so extreme as to warrant the hypothesis expressed in the deleted sentence (which is at odds with the highly finished character of the dialogue as a whole, and for which I have not found any corroboration).

p. 192
After 'involves any absurdity' add:

For an opposed view see Klosko *Phoenix* 80. He asserts (p.319) that the 'ignorance-theorem' (that choosing incorrectly entails the absence of knowledge) follows non-fallaciously from psychological hedonism, but concedes (p.317) that the derivation is not in the text.

p. 210
360a2–3 Delete the final paragraph and substitute:

Commentators are divided on the question of whether Socrates is represented as seriously espousing hedonism. The thesis maintained here. that he is so represented, is defended by Grote II, pp.87–9, Adam and Adam pp.xxix–xxxiii, Hackforth *CQ* 28, Vlastos in Ostwald p.xl (note), Dodds *Gorgias* pp.21–2, Crombie I, pp.232–45 (with reservations). Irwin ch. 4, Nussbaum ch. 4, and Cronquist *Prudentia* 80. Various versions of the thesis that Socrates' espousal of hedonism is non-serious are maintained by A. E. Taylor pp.260–1, Sullivan *Phron* 61, Raven pp.44–9, Gulley *Philosophy of Socrates* pp.110–18, Vlastos *Phoenix* 69, Manuwald *Phron* 75, Kahn in Werkmeister ed., Dyson *JHS* 76, Duncan *Phron* 78, Zeyl *Phron* 80, Stokes pp.358–439, and Kahn *OSAP* 88 and *Methexis* 88.

For a full discussion of the relation between Socrates' position in this dialogue and Plato's treatment of pleasure in other dialogues, omitted here for reasons of space, see Gosling and Taylor chs. 3–4. There is an earlier discussion in Crombie I, pp.225–69.

SELECT BIBLIOGRAPHY

EDITIONS WITH GREEK TEXT

Adam, J., and Adam, A. M., *Platonis Protagoras*, 2nd. edn., Cambridge, 1905.

Croiset, A., *Platon, Protagoras* (with French translation, vol. III, part I of complete Budé edn. of Plato), Paris, 1923.

Lamb, W. R. M., *Plato, Laches, Protagoras, Meno, Euthydemus* (with English translation (Loeb)), London and Cambridge, Mass., 1924.

TRANSLATIONS

Guthrie, W. K. C., *Plato, Protagoras and Meno*, Harmondsworth (Penguin Classics), 1956. Reprinted in E. Hamilton and H. Cairns eds., *The Collected Dialogues of Plato*, New York, 1961.

Hubbard, B. A. F., and Karnofsky, E. S., *Plato's Protagoras: A Socratic Commentary*, London, 1982.

Jowett, B., *The Dialogues of Plato*, 4th. (revised) edn., Oxford, 1953. Vol. I contains the *Protagoras*. Cited as 'Jowett[4]'.

Vlastos, Gregory, ed., *Plato, Protagoras: Jowett's Translation Revised by Martin Ostwald*, Indianapolis and New York, 1956. Cited as 'Ostwald'.

WORKS ON THE *PROTAGORAS*

Adkins, A. W. H., "Αρετή, Τέχνη, Democracy and Sophists: *Protagoras* 316b–328d', *JHS* xciii (1973), 3–12.

Alford, C. Ford, 'A Note on the Institutional Context of Plato's *Protagoras*', *CW* lxxxi (1988), 167–76.

Coby, Patrick, *Socrates and the Sophistic Enlightenment*, Lewisburg, London and Toronto, 1987.

Code, Alan, and Dybikowski, James C., 'Critical Notice of Taylor *Plato: "Protagoras"* ', *CJPhil* x (1980), 311–25.

Cronquist, John, 'The Point of the Hedonism in Plato's *Protagoras*', *Prudentia* xii (1980), 63–81.

Devereux, Daniel T., 'Protagoras on Courage and Knowledge: *Protagoras* 351 A–B', *Apeiron* ix (1975), 37–9.

Donlan, Walter, 'Simonides Fr. 4D and P. Oxy. 2432' *TAPA* c (1969), 71–95.

Döring, Klaus, 'Die politische Theorie des Protagoras', in G. B. Kerferd ed., *The Sophists and Their Legacy* (*Hermes* Einzelschriften 44), Wiesbaden 1981, 109–15.

Duncan, Roger, 'Courage in Plato's Protagoras', *Phron* xxiii (1978), 216–28.

Dyson, M., 'Knowledge and Hedonism in Plato's *Protagoras*', *JHS* xcvi (1976), 32–45.

Festugière, A. J., 'Sur un passage difficile du "Protagoras"', *BCH* lxx (1946), 179–86. Reprinted in Festugière, *Etudes de philosophie grecque*, Paris, 1971.

Frede, Dorothea, 'The Impossibility of Perfection: Socrates' Criticism of Simonides' Poem in the Protagoras', *RM* xxxix (1985–6), 713–53.

Gallop, David, 'Justice and Holiness in Protagoras 330–331', *Phron* vi (1961), 86–93.

—— 'The Socratic Paradox in the Protagoras', *Phron* ix (1964), 117–29.

Goldberg, Larry, *A Commentary on Plato's* Protagoras, New York, Bern and Frankfurt-on-Main, 1982.

Gulley, Norman, 'Socrates' Thesis at *Protagoras* 358b–c', *Phoenix* xxv (1971), 118–23.

Hackforth, R., 'Hedonism in Plato's *Protagoras*', *CQ* xxii (1928), 39–42.

Hartman, Margaret, 'How the Inadequate Models for Virtue in the *Protagoras* Illuminate Socrates' View of the Unity of the Virtues', *Apeiron* xviii (1984), 110–17.

Kahn, Charles H., 'On the Relative Date of the *Gorgias* and the *Protagoras*', *OSAP* vi (1988), 69–102.

—— 'Plato and Socrates in the *Protagoras*', *Methexis*, Revista Argentina de Filosofía Antigua i (1988), 33–52.

Kerferd, G. B., 'Protagoras' Doctrine of Justice and Virtue in the '*Protagoras*' of Plato', *JHS* lxxiii (1953), 42–5.

Klär, Ingo, 'Die Schatten im Höhlengleichnis und die Sophisten im Homerischen Hades', *AGP* li (1969), 225–59.

Klosko, George, 'Towards a Consistent Interpretation of the *Protagoras*', *AGP* lxi (1979), 125–42.

—— 'On the Analysis of *Protagoras* 351b–360e', *Phoenix* xxxiv (1980), 307–22.

Levi, A., 'The Ethical and Social Thought of Protagoras', *Mind* NS xliv (1940), 284–302.

Loenen, D., *Protagoras and the Greek Community*, Amsterdam, n.d.

McKirahan, Richard D., 'Socrates and Protagoras on ΣΩΦΡΟΣΤΝΗ and Justice', *Apeiron* xviii (1984), 19–25.

—— 'Socrates and Protagoras on Holiness and Justice (*Protagoras* 330c–332a)', *Phoenix* xxxix (1985), 342–54.

Manuwald, Bernd, 'Lust und Tapferkeit: Zum gedanklichen Verhältnis zweier Abschnitte in Platons "Protagoras" ', *Phron* xx (1975), 22–50.

Moser, S., and Kustas, G. L., 'A Comment on the "Relativism" of the *Protagoras*', *Phoenix* xx (1966), 111–15.

Nicholson, Peter P., 'Protagoras and the Justification of Athenian Democracy', *Polis* iii.2 (1980–1), 14–24.

—— and Kerferd, G. B., 'Protagoras on Pre-Political Man: an Exchange', *Polis*, iv.2 (1982), 19–25.

O'Brien, M. J., 'The "Fallacy" in *Protagoras* 349d–350c', *TAPA* xcii (1961), 408–17.

Parry, Hugh, 'An Interpretation of Simonides 4 (Diehl)', *TAPA* xcvi (1965), 297–320.

Penner, Terry, 'The Unity of Virtue', *PR* lxxxii (1973), 35–68.

Richardson, Henry S., 'Measurement, Pleasure and Practical Science in Plato's *Protagoras*', *JHP* xxviii (1990), 7–32.

Santas, Gerasimos, 'Plato's *Protagoras* and Explanations of Weakness', *PR* lxxv (1966), 3–33. Reprinted in G. Vlastos ed., *The Philosophy of Socrates*, Garden City, NY, 1971 and in G. Mortimore ed., *Weakness of Will*, London, 1971.

Saunders, Trevor J., 'Protagoras and Plato on Punishment', in G. B. Kerferd ed., *The Sophists and Their Legacy*, 129–41.

Savan, David, 'Self-Predication in Protagoras 330–31', *Phron* ix (1964), 130–5.

Scodel, Ruth, 'Literary Interpretation in Plato's *Protagoras*', *AP* vi (1986), 25–37.

Stocks, J. L., 'The Argument of Plato, *Protagoras*, 351b–356b', *CQ* vii (1913), 100–4.

Sullivan, J. P., 'The Hedonism of Plato's *Protagoras*', *Phron* vi (1961), 10–28.

Trapp, Michael, 'Protagoras and the Great Tradition', in M. Whitby, P. Hardie, and M. Whitby eds., *Homo Viator: Classical Essays for John Bramble*, Bristol etc., 1987, 41–8.

Turner, E. G., 'Athenians Learn to Write: Plato, *Protagoras*, 326d', *BICS* xii (1965), 65–7.

Vlastos, Gregory, 'Socrates on Acrasia', *Phoenix* xxiii (1969), 71–88.

—— 'The Unity of the Virtues in the *Protagoras*', *RM* xxv (1971–2), 415–58. Reprinted with emendations in *PS*.

Wakefield, Jerome, 'Why Justice and Holiness are Similar: Protagoras 330–331', *Phron* xxxii (1987), 267–76.

Weiss, Roslyn, 'Courage, Confidence and Wisdom in the *Protagoras*', *AP* v (1985), 11–24.

—— 'The Hedonic Calculus in the *Protagoras* and the *Phaedo*', *JHP* xxvii (1989), 511–29. (Discussed by Gosling and Taylor and Weiss *JHP* xxviii (1990), 115–18.)

Zeyl, Donald J., 'Socrates and Hedonism: Protagoras 351b–358d', *Phron* xxv (1980), 250–69. Reprinted in J. P. Anton and A. Preus eds., *Essays in Ancient Greek Philosophy III*, Albany, NY, 1989.

OTHER WORKS

Ackrill, J. L., 'Plato and the Copula: *Sophist* 251–59', *JHS* lxxvii (1957), 1–6. Reprinted in R. E. Allen ed., *Studies in Plato's Metaphysics*, London, 1965, and in G. Vlastos ed., *Plato*, Garden City, NY, 1971, vol. I.

Acton, H. B., ed., *The Philosophy of Punishment*, London, 1969.

Adkins, A. W. H., *Merit and Responsibility*, Oxford, 1960.

Allen, R. E., *Plato's 'Euthyphro' and the Earlier Theory of Forms*, London and New York, 1970.

SELECT BIBLIOGRAPHY

Ast, Fridrich, *Lexicon Platonicum*, Leipzig, 1835–6. Reprinted Bonn, 1956.

Austin, J. L., 'A Plea for Excuses', *PAS* lvii (1956–7), 1–30. Reprinted in Austin, *Philosophical Papers*, ed. J. O. Urmson and G. J. Warnock, Oxford, 1961, and in D. A. Gustafson ed., *Essays in Philosophical Psychology*, London, 1967.

Bambrough, Renford, 'Plato's Political Analogies', in P. Laslett ed., *Philosophy, Politics and Society, First Series*, Oxford, 1956, 98–115. Reprinted in Bambrough ed., *Plato, Popper and Politics*, Cambridge and New York, 1967, and in G. Vlastos edn., *Plato*, vol. II.

Barnes, Jonathan, *The Presocratic Philosophers*, 2nd ed., London and New York, 1982.

Brandwood, Leonard, *A Word Index to Plato*, Leeds, 1976.

Brandt, Richard B., 'Hedonism', in P. Edwards ed., *The Encyclopedia of Philosophy*, London and New York, 1967, vol. III, 432–5.

Broad, C. D., *Five Types of Ethical Theory*, London, 1930.

Capizzi, Antonio, *Protagora*, Florence, 1955.

Charlton, William, *Weakness of Will*, Oxford, 1988.

Cole, A. T., 'The Apology of Protagoras', *YCS* xix (1966), 101–18.

—— 'The Relativism of Protagoras', *YCS* xxii (1972), 19–45.

Crombie, I. M., *An Examination of Plato's Doctrines*, London and New York, vol. I, 1962, vol. II, 1963.

Davidson, Donald, 'How is Weakness of the Will Possible?', in J. Feinberg, ed., *Moral Concepts*, London, 1969, 93–113. Reprinted in Davidson, *Essays on Actions and Events*, Oxford, 1980.

Davies, J. K., *Athenian Propertied Families 600–300 B.C.*, Oxford, 1971.

Denniston, J. D., *The Greek Particles*, 2nd edn., Oxford, 1954.

Devereux, Daniel T., 'Pauline Predication in Plato', *Apeiron* xi (1977), 1–4.

Dodds, E. R., *Plato, Gorgias*, Oxford, 1959.

—— *The Ancient Concept of Progress*, Oxford, 1973.

Dover, K. J., 'The Date of Plato's *Symposium*', *Phron* x (1965), 2–20.

—— *Aristophanes, Clouds*, Oxford, 1968. Introduction section v reprinted in G. Vlastos ed., *The Philosophy of Socrates*.

—— 'The Freedom of the Intellectual in Greek Society', *Talanta* vii (1976), 24–54.

—— *Greek Homosexuality*, London, 1978.

Ferejohn, Michael T., 'The Unity of Virtue and the Objects of Socratic Enquiry', *JHP* xx (1982), 1–21.

—— 'Socratic Thought-Experiments and the Unity of Virtue Paradox', *Phron* xxix (1984), 105–22.

Geach, P. T., 'Plato's Euthyphro: An Analysis and Commentary', *Monist* 1(1966), 383–402. Reprinted in Geach, *Logic Matters*, Oxford, 1972.

Goodwin, W. W., *Syntax of the Moods and Tenses of the Greek Verb*, London and New York, 1889.

Gosling, J. C. B., *Plato*, London and Boston, 1973.

—— and Taylor, C. C. W., *The Greeks on Pleasure*, Oxford, 1982.

Grote, George, *Plato and the Other Companions of Sokrates*, London, 1865.

Gulley, Norman, *The Philosophy of Socrates*, London, 1968.

Guthrie, W. K. C., *A History of Greek Philosophy*, Cambridge, 1962–81. Vol. III, part I, published separately as *The Sophists*, Cambridge, 1971.

Hare, R. M., *The Language of Morals*, Oxford, 1952.

—— *Freedom and Reason*, Oxford, 1963. Chapter 5 reprinted in G. Mortimore ed., *Weakness of Will*.

Hart, H. L. A., *Punishment and Responsibility*, Oxford, 1968.

How, W. W., and Wells, J., *A Commentary on Herodotus*, Oxford, 1928.

Irwin, Terence, *Plato's Moral Theory*, Oxford, 1977.

Kahn, Charles H., 'Plato on the Unity of the Virtues', in W. H. Werkmeister ed., *Facets of Plato's Philosophy* (*Phron* Suppl. Vol. II), Assen, 1976, 21–39.

—— 'The Origins of Social Contract Theory in the Fifth Century B.C.', in G. B. Kerferd ed., *The Sophists and Their Legacy*, 92–108.

Kenny, A. J. P., Mental Health in Plato's *Republic*', *PBA* lv (1969), 229–53. Reprinted in Kenny, *The Anatomy of the Soul*, Oxford, 1973.

Kerferd, G. B., 'Plato's Account of the Relativism of Protagoras', *DUJ* xlii (NS xi) (1949–50), 20–6.

—— 'Protagoras of Abdera', in P. Edwards ed., *The Encyclopedia of Philosophy*, London and New York, 1967, vol. VI, 505–7.

—— ed., *The Sophists and Their Legacy* (*Hermes* Einzelschriften 44), Wiesbaden, 1981.

Kirwan, Christopher, 'Glaucon's Challenge', *Phron* x (1965), 162–73.

Ledger, G. R., *Re-counting Plato*, Oxford, 1989.

Lloyd-Jones, Hugh, *The Justice of Zeus*, Berkeley, Los Angeles, and London, 1971.

Lovejoy, Arthur O., and Boas, George, *Primitivism and Related Ideas in Antiquity*, Baltimore, 1935.

McDowell, John, *Plato, Theaetetus*, Oxford, 1973.

Mackenzie, Mary Margaret, *Plato on Punishment*, Berkeley, Los Angeles, and London, 1981.

Morrison, J. S., 'The Place of Protagoras in Athenian Public Life', *CQ* xxv (1941), 1–16.

Mortimore, Geoffrey, ed., *Weakness of Will*, London, 1971.

Nagel, Thomas, *The Possibility of Altruism*, Oxford, 1970.

Nill, Michael, *Morality and Self-Interest in Protagoras, Antiphon and Democritus*, Leiden, 1985.

North, Helen, *Sophrosyne*, Ithaca, NY, 1966.

Nussbaum, Martha C., *The Fragility of Goodness*, Cambridge, 1986.

O'Brien, M. J., 'The Unity of the *Laches*', *YCS* xviii (1963), 131–47. Reprinted in J. P. Anton and G. L. Kustas eds., *Essays in Ancient Greek Philosophy*, Albany, NY, 1972.

—— *The Socratic Paradoxes and the Greek Mind*, Chapel Hill, NC, 1967.

Owen, G. E. L., 'Plato on Not-Being', in G. Vlastos ed., *Plato*, vol. I, 223–67. Reprinted in Owen, *Logic, Science, and Dialectic: Collected Papers in Greek Philosophy*, ed. M. Nussbaum, Ithaca, NY, and London, 1986.

Passmore, John, *Philosophical Reasoning*, London, 1961.

Patton, Thomas E., and Ziff, Paul, 'On Vendler's Grammar of "Good" ', *PR* lxxiii (1964), 528–37.

Penner, Terry, 'Thought and Desire in Plato', in G. Vlastos ed., *Plato*, vol. I, 96–118.

Peterson, Sandra, 'A Reasonable Self-Predication Premise for the Third Man Argument', *PR* lxxxii (1973), 551–70.

Quine, W. V. O., 'Reference and Modality', in Quine, *From a Logical Point of View*, 2nd edn., Cambridge, Mass., 1961, 139–59.

—— *Word and Object*, Cambridge, Mass., New York, and London, 1960.

Rankin, H. D., *Sophists, Socratics and Cynics*, London, Canberra, and Totowa, NJ, 1983.

Raven, J. E., *Plato's Thought in the Making*, Cambridge, 1965.

Robinson, Richard, *Plato's Earlier Dialectic*, 2nd edn., Oxford, 1953. Chapters 2, 3, and 5 reprinted in G. Vlastos ed., *The Philosophy of Socrates*.

Ross, Sir David, *Plato's Theory of Ideas*, 2nd edn., Oxford, 1953.

Ryle, Gilbert, *The Concept of Mind*, London, 1949.

—— 'Dialectic in the Academy', in R. Bambrough ed., *New Essays on Plato and Aristotle*, London, 1965, 39–68. Reprinted with revisions in Ryle, *Plato's Progress*, Cambridge, 1966.

Santas, Gerasimos, 'The Socratic Paradoxes', *PR* lxxiii (1964), 147–64. Reprinted in A. Sesonske and N. Fleming eds., *Plato's Meno: Text and Criticism*, Belmont, Calif., 1965 and in Santas, *Socrates*, London, Boston, and Henley, 1979, ch. 6.

—— 'Socrates at Work on Virtue and Knowledge in Plato's *Laches*', *RM* xxii (1968–9), 433–60. Reprinted in G. Vlastos ed., *The Philosophy of Socrates*.

—— 'The Socratic Fallacy', *JHP* x (1972), 127–41.

—— 'Socrates at Work on Virtue and Knowledge in Plato's *Charmides*', in *EA*, 105–32.

Saunders, Trevor J., 'The Socratic Paradox in Plato's Laws', *Hermes* xcvi (1968), 421–34.

Sidgwick, Henry, *The Methods of Ethics*, 7th edn., London, 1907.

Sprague, Rosamond Kent, 'An Unfinished Argument in Plato's *Protagoras*', *Apeiron* i.2 (1967), 1–4.

—— 'Dissoi Logoi or Dialexeis', *Mind* NS lxxvii (1968), 157–67. Reprinted in Sprague ed., *The Older Sophists*, Columbia, SC, 1972.

Stokes, Michael C., *Plato's Socratic Conversations*, London, 1986.

Taylor, A. E., *Plato, The Man and His Work*, London, 1926.

234

Taylor, C. C. W., Critical notice of R. M. Hare, *Freedom and Reason*, *Mind* NS lxxiv (1965), 280–98. Reprinted in G. Wallace and A. D. M. Walker eds., *The Definition of Morality*, London, 1970.

—— 'Plato, Hare and Davidson on Akrasia', *Mind* NS lxxxix (1980), 499–518.

—— 'The End of the Euthyphro', *Phron* xxvii (1982), 109–18.

Urmson, J. O., 'J. L. Austin', *JPhil* lxii (1965), 499–508.

—— 'Aristotle on Pleasure', in J. M. E. Moravcsik ed., *Aristotle*, Garden City, NY, 1967, 323–33.

—— *The Emotive Theory of Ethics*, London, 1968.

Vendler, Zeno, 'The Grammar of Goodness', *PR* lxxii (1963), 446–65.

Vlastos, Gregory, 'The Third Man Argument in the *Parmenides*', *PR* lxiii (1954), 319–49. Reprinted in R. E. Allen ed., *Studies in Plato's Metaphysics*.

—— 'Degrees of Reality in Plato', in R. Bambrough ed., *New Essays on Plato and Aristotle*, 1–19. Reprinted in *PS*.

—— ed., *Plato*, Garden City, NY, 1971.

—— ed., *The Philosophy of Socrates*, Garden City, NY, 1971.

—— 'A Note on "Pauline Predications" in Plato', *Phron* xix (1974), 95–101. Reprinted in *PS*.

—— 'Socrates on the Parts of Virtue', in *PS*, 418–23.

von Wright, Georg Henrik, *The Varieties of Goodness*, London and New York, 1963.

Walsh, James J., *Aristotle's Conception of Moral Weakness*, New York and London, 1963. Chapter 1 reprinted in G. Vlastos ed., *The Philosophy of Socrates*.

Woodruff, Paul, 'Socrates on the Parts of Virtue', in C. A. Shiner and J. King-Farlow eds., *New Essays on Plato and the Pre-Socratics* (*CJPhil* Suppl. Vol. II), 1976, 101–16.

Ziff, Paul, *Semantic Analysis*, Ithaca, NY, 1960.

INDEXES

Passages of ancient works cited in the Commentary (excluding the *Protagoras*)

GENERAL INDEX

Figures in bold type refer to the Translation.

Abdera: **309c**; 61, 68.
Achilles: **340a**.
Ackrill, J.L.: 111.
action against one's better judgement
(weakness of will): **352b–e,**
355a–357e, 358b–d; 171–4, 178–92,
199–200, 202–5.
Acton, H.B.: 96.
Adam, J. and Adam, A.M.: 68, 97,
115, 134, 136, 138, 142, 144, 146,
148, 203, 210, 226.
Adeimantus son of Cepis: **315e**; 69.
Adeimantus son of Leucolophides:
315e; 69.
Adkins, A.W.H.: 72, 74, 90.
against one's will (= *akōn*): **345d–**
346e.
Agathocles: **316e**; 70.
Agathon: **315e**; 69.
Alcibiades: **309a–c, 316a, 317d–e,**
320a, 336b–e, 347b, 348b–c; 62,
63, 64–5, 69, 75, 136, 225.
Alexander: 139.
Alford, C.F.: 218.
Allen, R.E.: 104.
Ammonius: 205–6.
Andron: **315c**; 69.
Antimoerus: **315a**; 68.
animal boldness, passsion (= *thumos*):
351a–b, 352b.
Antiphon: 141.
Antisthenes: 139–40.
Anytus: xx.
Apollo: **343b.**
Ariphron: **320a**; 75.
Aristophanes: 58, 61, 69, 225.
Aristotle: 58, 59, 84, 89, 90, 95, 108,
122, 133, 137, 138–40, 172, 205, 207.
art, craft, skill, subject, technique
(= *technē*): **316d–317c, 318e,**
319a–320c, 322a–323c, 327a–328a,
351a, 356d–357d; 75–6, 194–5, 218.

Ast, F.: 190.
Athena: **321d–e**; 84.
Athenians: **319b–d, 322d–323a, 324c–d,**
72–4, 98–100, 213.
Athens: **311c**; 61, 62, 68, 72, 97, 101,
136.
Austin, J.L.: 138.

bad (= *kakos, ponēros, phaulos*):
312c *(kakos)*, **313a–314b**
(ponēros), **326e** *(phaulos)*, **327b**
(phaulos), **328c** *(phaulos)*, **332c**
(kakos), **334a–c** *(ponēros, kakos)*,
341b–e *(kakos)*, **344c–345c** *(kakos)*,
345d–347a *(kakos, ponēros)*, **351b–e**
(kakos), **352a–357e** *(kakos, ponēros)*,
358a–360e *(kakos)*; 127–8, 133–4,
142, 145, 147, 164–7, 174–6, 177–8,
179–81, 181–6, 186–7, 205–8, 209,
216.
Bambrough, R.: 83.
Barnes, J.: 79, 173.
beautiful, fine-looking, handsome; also
praiseworthy, fine, fair (= *kalos*):
309a–c (handsome, fine-looking,
fine), **315e** (fine, fine-looking), **316a**
(handsome), **323d** (fair), **325d**
(praiseworthy), **332c** (beautiful),
346c–d (fair), **349a** (fine), **351c**
(praiseworthy), **358b** (praiseworthy),
359e–360b (praiseworthy); 64–5,
127–8, 134, 147, 165–6, 201–2, 210.
beneficial, useful (= *ōphelimos*):
332a, 334a–c, 358b; 124, 132–5,
202.
Bentham, J.: 188.
Bias: see Seven Sages
Bowie, E.L.: v.
Brandt, R.B.: 199
Brandwood, L.: xx.
Broad, C.D.: 174–5.
Burnet, J.: 136.

241

INDEX

knowledge (= *epistēmē*): **344c–345b, 350a–351a, 351b–d, 357a–e, 361b–c;** xi, 150–4, 162–4, 170–3, 191–2, 194, 200, 202–3, 211–14.

Laches: 159
laws (= *nomoi*, also conventions): **326d–e, 327c–d;** 95.
Ledger, G.R.: xx.
Lesbos: **341c;** 142, 143, 147.
Levi, A: 101.
like (= *hoion*): **330a–331d;** 109–11, 113–4, 120–21.
Lloyd-Jones, H.: 173.
Loenen, P.: 101, 141.
Lovejoy, A.O. and Boas, G.: 78.
lust, sexual desire (= *erōs*): **352b;** 64–5, 146.
Lycophron: 95.

McDowell, J.: 102.
Mackenzie, M.M.: 219.
McKirahan, R.D.: 120, 132.
Manuwald, B.: 164, 226.
Marathon: 136.
meaning, and reference: 103–8, 111–12, 168–70, 222–4.
——, sameness of (synonymy): 104–8, 128–30, 223–4.
measurement (= *metrētikē* (sc. *technē*)): **356c–357d;** 190–9.
Mende: **315a;** 68.
Meno: 165.
Mill, J.S.: 179.
moral sense, universality of: 86–7, 87–9.
Morrison, J.S.: 64.
Mortimore, G.: 205.
Moser, S. and Kustas, G.L.: 101.
Musaeus: 316d.
Myrrinus: **315c;** 69.
Myson: see Seven Sages.
Mytilene: 142.

Nagel, T.: 189.
nature (= *phusis*): **323c–d, 337c–d, 351a–b, 358d;** 89, 161.
——, opp. convention: **337c–d;** 112, 140–41.

Nicholson, P.P.: 101, 219.
Nicias: 159.
Nill, M.: 103.
North, H.: 123.
Nussbaum, M.C.: 226.

O'Brien, M.J.: 90, 154, 159, 204.
Olympic Games: 135
opposite (= *enantion*): **331d, 332a–333b, 360c–d;** 121, 122, 124–31, 147, 212.
Orpheus: **315b, 316d.**
Orthagoras: **318c;** 71.
Ostwald, M.: 176, 177.
Owen, G.E.L.: 111.

pain, distress (= *lupē* and *ania*), painful, unpleasant (*lupēros* and *aniaros*): **351b–e, 352a–357e;** 172, 174–81, 213–14.
Paralus: **315a, 328c.**
Parry, H.: 148.
Passmore, J.: 182.
Patton, T.E. and Ziff, P.: 135.
Pauline predication: 118–20, 155.
Pausanias: **315d;** 69.
Peloponnesian War: 64, 68, 78–9.
Penner, T.: 107, 109, 110, 120, 130, 204.
Pericles: **315a, 319a–320a, 329a;** 68, 75.
Peterson, S.: 119.
Phaedrus: **315c;** 68, 69.
Pheidias: **311c–e;** 65.
Pheidippides: 135–6.
Pherecrates: **327d;** 97–8.
Philippides: **315a;** 68.
Phrynondas: see Eurybatus.
Pindar: 58.
Pittacus: **339e–347a;** 142–4, 147.
Plato: xiv–xx, 58, 61, 64, 84, 87, 89, 95, 96, 101, 103–8, 111, 112, 113, 116, 118, 122, 124, 125, 126–7, 128–30, 131, 133–5, 137–9, 140–1, 144, 145, 147, 148, 158, 160, 162, 165, 168–70, 174, 177, 178, 179, 182–6, 187, 192, 193, 195, 202, 203, 209–10, 211, 213–15, 216–17, 218, 219, 221–3, 225, 226.

244

INDEX

pleasure (*hēdonē* and *to hēdu*),
pleasant (= *hēdus*): **337c, 351b–e,
352a–357e, 358a–360e**; 62, 137–9,
162–4, 164–200, 201–3, 208–10,
213–14.

——, 'pleasant', extended sense of:
168, 170, 171, 175, 178–9, 180,
208–9.

Plutarch: 59, 68.

poetry, criticism of: **338e–348a**; xiii,
141, 147–8.

Polus: 165.

Polycleitus: **311c, 328c**; 65, 78.

Polycrates: 64.

power (= *dunamis*): **330a–b, 331d,
333a**; 104, 109–11, 117–18, 131.

praiseworthy, fine, fair (= *kalos*)
see beautiful, fine-looking, handsome.

Prodicus: **314c, 315c–316a, 317c–e,
336d, 337a–c, 339e–341e, 342a,
357e, 358a–b, 358d–e, 359a**; 62,
63, 136–40, 142, 201, 205.

Prometheus: **320d–322a, 361d**; 76–81.

Protagoras: *passim*

Protagorean subjectivism: 61, 83–4,
100–3, 133–4, 191, 214.

punishment: **323c–324d, 325a–d,
326d–e**; 90–6, 219.

Pythocleides: **316e**; 70.

Quine, W.V.O.: 107, 180.

Rankin, H.D.: 63, 141.

Raven, J.E.: 210, 226.

result (= *telos*): **354b–d**; 177.

Robinson, R.: 67, 112, 121.

Ross, Sir David: 112.

Ryle, G.: 135, 211.

Santas, G.: 104, 120, 124, 154, 182,
187, 190, 203, 212.

Saunders, T.J.: v, 204, 219.

Savan, D.: 117–18.

Scamander: **340a.**

Scodel, R.: 225.

Scopas: **339a**; 142.

self-predication: 112–13, 116–17,
118–19.

self-refutation: 182–4.

Selymbria: **316e**; 69.

Seven Dwarfs: 152.

Seven Sages: **343a**; 144.

shameful, disgraceful, foul (= *aischros*)
see ugly.

Sidgwick, H.: 174.

Simoeis: **340a.**

Simonides: **316d, 339a–347a**; xiii,
141–8, 225.

Sisson, J.: 220.

Socrates: *passim.*

Solon: see Seven Sages.

sophists: **311e–314c, 314d, 316c–
317c, 318d–319a, 342b, 348e–
349a, 357e**; xi, xiii, xvii, 65–8, 103,
144, 218.

sophists' fees: **310d–311e, 313b,
328b–c, 349a, 357e.**

soul (= *psuchē*): **313a–314c, 326b,
351b**; 66, 68, 97, 103–5.

soundness of mind, good sense
(= *sōphrosunē*), sound in mind,
sensible (*sōphrōn*): **323a, 323b, 325a,
326a, 329c, 330b, 332a–333b, 333b–e,
349b, 361b**; 80–2, 85–6, 103, 105,
121–31, (esp. 122–4), 131–2, 141,
147, 148–9, 213, 216, 219.

Sparshott, F.: 217.

Sparta: **342a–343b**; 62, 136, 144.

Sprague, R.K.: 63, 79, 132.

Stahl, J.M.: 67.

Stocks, J.L.: 187.

Stokes, M.C.: vii, xiv–xv, xviii, 216,
217, 226.

Sullivan, J.P.: 210, 226.

Taras: **316d**; 69.

Taylor, A.E.: 100–1, 210, 226.

Taylor, C.C.W.: xvi, xix, 203, 222, 224,
226.

Thales: see Seven Sages

Theognis: 59, 145.

Thermopylae: 154.

Thessaly: 142.

Thrasymachus: xix.

Thucydides: 59.

Tiresias: 218.

Trapp, M.: 225.

Printed in the United Kingdom
by Lightning Source UK Ltd.
99107UKS00002B/11-30